actice

of **Training**

THE
Theory & Practice
of Training

5th edition

Roger Buckley
& Jim Caple

KOGAN
PAGE

London and Sterling, VA

First edition published in 1990
Fifth edition 2004

120 Pentonville Road
London N1 9JN
UK
www.kogan-page.co.uk

22883 Quicksilver Drive
Sterling VA 20166-2012
USA

ISBN 0 7494 4156 9

British Library Cataloguing in Publication Data

A CIP record for this book is available from the British Library.

Library of Congress Cataloging-in-Publication data

Buckley, Roger, 1936-
   Theory and practice of training / Roger Buckley and Jim Caple--5th ed.
       p. cm.
    ISBN 0-7494-4156-9
    1. Employees--Training of. 2. Organizational change--Management. 3. Performance--Evaluation. I. Caple, Jim, 1941-II. Title.
HF5549.5.T7B757 2004
658.3'124--dc22

                                        2003027392

Typeset by JS Typesetting Ltd, Wellingborough, Northants
Printed and bound in Great Britain by Biddles Ltd, King's Lynn
www.biddles.co.uk

Contents

Foreword

The fifth edition of this established and influential text continues the strengths of its predecessors. It meets the promise of the title in examining appropriate theory in a way that is relevant to practice; the clear focus on and use of the systems approach to training remains as the essential framework; illustrative examples are frequent and helpful and the coverage of the field is, as in previous editions, both comprehensive and thorough. These features, which were my reason for endorsing the book in the foreword to the fourth edition, are therefore the same source of my recommendation of the book to all potential readers; academics, students and practitioners alike.

There are few lengthy changes in this new edition. However, the new and additional content is welcome. This ranges from addressing innovations such as e-learning to increasingly popular techniques such as the syndicate exercise. It also includes new conceptual material of increasing importance to do with for example adult learning and models of Human Resource Development (HRD). So, as well as incorporating the normal 'updating' of new editions, this fifth edition also adds material missing from earlier editions.

Roger Buckley and Jim Caple have informed the teaching and influenced the practice of training and development since the publication of the first edition of this book. I am confident that will continue to be the case through the wide reading and use that this fifth edition deserves and will achieve. In my judgement, the book remains essential reading for all of those new to the profession.

Professor Jim Stewart
Nottingham Business School

Acknowledgements

The authors would like to thank all of those trainers who have shared their ideas and experiences with them over many years and Patrick Buckley for his assistance in the preparation of material for this edition.

Introduction

Change was the story of the 20th century and will inevitably be the story of the 21st. In order to survive and prosper, organizations in the private and the public sectors will need to respond in a timely and flexible way to social, technological, economic and political change. This means that an organization's survival and growth will depend on its ability to cope with the external and internal requirements that these changes will demand. This implies that existing and new staff will need to acquire new knowledge, skills, attitudes and perspectives on a continual basis.

At one time, most people entered the workforce expecting a job for life, and for the majority that is what they experienced. Very often, members of the same family went to work for the same organization in the same town or city and stayed there until retirement. Some worked their way up from the shop floor to become 'management' while others were content to remain in a safe and stable environment with a regular pay packet. Others sought the 'office job' which they believed gave them status and security for their working lives.

That has all changed. Since the 1970s, there has been a decline in traditional industries and a subsequent loss of many routine and unskilled jobs. The workplace has become highly competitive and will become increasingly so. There is now a global economy to contend with. The West has to face the competition of such countries as Taiwan, Korea, and Singapore where there are low labour costs and where advantage is taken of the new market opportunities created by reductions in trade barriers and technological advances. Employers will be seeking staff with high-level transferable skills, short- and medium-term contracts will become the more common forms of employment and there will be an even greater need for individuals to manage their own learning and careers. The concept of a 'job for life' has become endangered and is nearing extinction.

Gaining or maintaining an edge over competitors has become the priority of organizations, and also for individuals wishing to pursue a fulfilling career. In this competition to achieve success, to keep in the lead or even to survive, organizations seem to have focused on four key areas. These are: the need to diversify, the need to constantly review organizational structures and staffing skills, the need to make best use of technology and the need to focus on the customer.

Diversification has not only meant the updating and modification of existing products and services but the introduction of new products and new ways of providing a service. In addition, it has involved moving into new areas and encroaching upon the traditional territory of other manufacturers and providers. The following examples have now become familiar: building societies have become banks, departmental stores and supermarkets offer financial services, DIY stores offer home insurance facilities, and gas suppliers offer electricity. Various mergers and acquisitions illustrate the diversity within large groups of companies.

Coincidental with this need for, and trend towards, diversification, organizations have had to look at the ways in which they are structured. The processes of what have been described as downsizing, rightsizing, devolution of responsibility and empowerment that started to be introduced in the 1980s have become commonplace. Many organizations found it expedient to regionalize or fragment their operations and functions, allowing individual business units to operate almost as independent companies. The rationale behind such changes was partly that the process was a way of getting closer to the customer. It also gave greater responsibility and accountability to more people, encouraged initiative, demanded business thinking and an orientation towards outcomes, and allowed easier measurement of the effectiveness of the different parts of the organization.

However, towards the end of the 1990s a number of organizations began to move some decentralized functions back to the centre. This was prompted by a number of factors. Kakabadse, quoted by Arkin (1999), suggests that the thinking of the eighties was about getting close to the customer, but that this perceived competitive advantage had been lost and was felt to be greater at corporate level.

The experiences of the authors were that with regard to the training and development function, decentralization has not always been as effective as it was felt that it would be. In order to maintain quality and consistency, and to ensure that money spent on providers is spent wisely, recentralization has been found to be necessary. Kakabadse asserts that organizations move frequently between centralized and decentralized modes of operation and decision making, and both authors have experienced the swing of the pendulum from one to the other many times in the training field, and have had to respond and adapt to the changes that have ensued.

The rapid and unceasing advances in technology, and in particular, information technology, have had an impact on all jobs and the way in which they are done. At all levels in most organizations, staff are expected to be computer literate to some degree or be able to operate technology-driven equipment and processes, as well as having the capacity to keep up with the advances that will be made.

It has been claimed that we are living in a customer-driven society, and this is encouraged further by the flexibility and range of choice that customers have. It has become easier for customers to 'go elsewhere' for better services, and internal customers have the option to 'go outside' if their needs are not met adequately by providers within their own organization. In some cases, training departments have fallen victim to this process, sometimes with justification, but sometimes at the cost of quality and consistency.

Training has always played an important and an integral part in furthering many kinds of human learning and development. If organizations are to make the best of the training function in their response to and promotion of change, the training function will need to be closely linked with business plans. This means that a detailed training policy needs to be agreed and implemented from the top of the organization and supported by management at all levels. It also means that the training and development function has to be accountable in the same way that other functions are.

In this environment where change is frequent, the training function cannot allow itself to become the 'dinosaur' of the organization. It too must explore and introduce new strategies and methods of learning to meet the changing needs of the organization and of its learners. The use of technology and various forms of distance- and open-learning need to be employed when appropriate, and trainers need to examine their own roles and develop them to meet new and differing demands. Trainers have received greater recognition as having skills which enable them, often better than others, to act as agents for change; to become involved in internal consultancy relating to organizational development, quality and performance management; and to develop a learning organization. Line managers have become more involved in the development of staff through coaching, mentoring and assessing competences.

Everyone in the organization, particularly senior managers and directors, should understand the processes and techniques of training and should be able to speak the language of training. Many appreciate the message, 'If you think training and education are expensive, you should try ignorance'. Training cannot be achieved 'on the cheap': it requires a suitable and consistent level of financial support. Those who baulk at this notion must appreciate that in many organizations, the outlay on training should be on a par with other major investment decisions. Some organizations have no doubt rued the fact that they failed to set aside adequate resources for the training function. Their plans for expansion and development would have been severely hampered by the unpreparedness of staff and their recruitment, selection and personnel policies being insufficient to compensate for this shortfall. It follows that training cannot be seen as simply a peripheral function having only a marginal influence over an organization's present and future economic health, for an organization's economic health is determined by, and can only be understood fully, in terms of its ability to adapt to internal and external circumstances.

The world of work continues to become more and more complex and for everyone, including trainers, there are many learning curves ahead. The demands inferred by Senge (1990), 'As the world becomes more interconnected and business becomes more complex and dynamic, work must become more learningful', indicate that there will be a crucial and demanding role for training in the future.

There are many techniques, approaches and theories which can be applied in training and no single volume can do justice to them all. This book is not a stage-by-stage guide to conducting a project in training. All trainers soon come to appreciate that there is no single approach, and that one of the most frequently exercised skills is that of making decisions as to which are the best techniques to investigate performance problems, and which are the most appropriate ways to deliver the training.

What is included in this book is what has worked best for the authors and which it is believed will help others. In our approach to training we have attempted to reflect the sentiments and attitudes expressed in these two quotations:

'There is nothing so practical as a good theory' – Kurt Lewin

'However much thou art read in theory if thou hast no practice thou art ignorant' – SA'DI

Roger Buckley and Jim Caple

1

Training and the Organizational Environment

Before examining how training is initiated and then organized, it is useful to define what we mean by training and to distinguish it from the closely related concepts of learning, education and development. Drawing on a number of sources, the definitions we shall examine and work to are as follows:

Training

A planned and systematic effort to modify or develop knowledge/skill/ attitude through learning experience, to achieve effective performance in an activity or range of activities. Its purpose, in the work situation, is to enable an individual to acquire abilities in order that he or she can perform adequately a given task or job.

Learning

The process whereby individuals acquire knowledge, skills and attitudes through experience, reflection, study or instruction.

Education

A process and a series of activities which aim at enabling an individual to assimilate and develop knowledge, skills, values and understanding that are not simply related to a narrow field of activity but allow a broad range of problems to be defined, analysed and solved.

Development

The general enhancement and growth of an individual's skills and abilities through conscious and unconscious learning.

In the *Glossary of Training Terms* (Department of Employment 1978) the definition of 'training' explains that the words 'learning experience' emphasize that there is no clear dividing line between education and training, and stresses the importance of the integration of these two concepts.

THE DISTINCTION BETWEEN TRAINING AND EDUCATION

Without denying the point about integration and also recognizing the difficulty which is often encountered in clearly separating these concepts, some useful distinctions have been drawn by Kenny and Reid (1986), particularly in relation to training and education. These distinctions have been made with regard to process, orientation, method, content and the degree of precision involved.

In terms of precision, training usually involves the acquisition of behaviours, facts, ideas, etc that are more easily defined in a specific job context. Training is more job-orientated than person-orientated. Education, on the other hand, is more person-orientated, is a broader process of change and its objectives are less amenable to precise definition. In contrasting training and education Glaser (1962) points out that 'when the end products of learning can be specified in terms of particular instances of student performance, then instructional procedures can be designed to directly train or build in these behaviours'. If the skill to be learned is highly complex and the relevant performance is difficult to analyse and to specify, then the student may be educated more generally by providing a foundation of behaviour on which the individual is expected to generalize or to transfer to similar or novel situations.

A second distinction which Glaser makes is related to minimizing or maximizing individual differences. He suggests that, in training, the learning of specific behaviours implies a certain degree of uniformity within the limits set by individual differences. By contrast, education is attempting to increase the

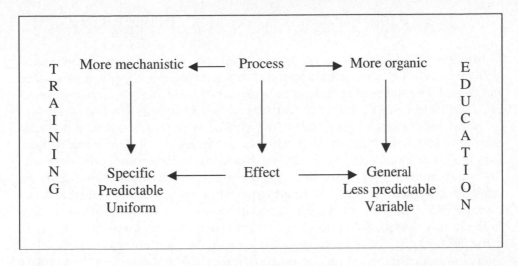

Figure 1.1 The distinctions between education and training expressed in terms of process and effect

variability of individual differences by facilitating learning in such a manner that each individual comes to behave in a way which is particular to him.

Training and education (including development) can be distinguished also in terms of process. In its extreme form, training tends to be a more mechanistic process which emphasizes uniform and predictable responses to standard guidance and instruction reinforced by practice and repetition. On the other hand education is a more organic process bringing about less predictable changes in the individual. These distinctions are expressed in a diagrammatic form in Figure 1.1.

Differences between training and education also can be identified with respect to course or programme content. Training aims to provide knowledge and skills and to inculcate the attitudes which are needed to perform specific tasks. Education usually provides more theoretical and conceptual frameworks designed to stimulate an individual's analytical and critical abilities.

Finally, the effects of training, education and development can be considered on a time scale. The changes brought about by training are often more immediately observable in the short term whereas education and development are more likely to show their influence in the longer term and, possibly, in a more profound way.

TRAINING, EDUCATION AND EXPERIENCE

While considerable emphasis has been placed on the way in which training and education differ, it must be appreciated that they are closely interrelated processes. The ability of an individual to acquire knowledge, skills and attitudes in a training context may depend directly or indirectly on the quality of previous educational experiences. In a similar way, education may be influenced by the skills which an individual has acquired through training and can bring to bear to exploit new learning situations. Furthermore, while concentrating on training and education, a third element which contributes to learning and development, namely planned experience, must not be minimized nor overlooked. This element is a vital concomitant to formal training and education in an organizational setting. For example, management development programmes often have been criticized for focusing, sometimes almost exclusively, on structured training and educational events and ignoring the value of varied and planned inter- and intra-organizational experiences. The advent of action learning, i.e. 'Learning by experience through solving an actual problem of an organization', has done much to redress this particular imbalance.

Training, education and planned experience are interdependent and equal partners with regard to their potential contribution to learning and development (Figure 1.2).

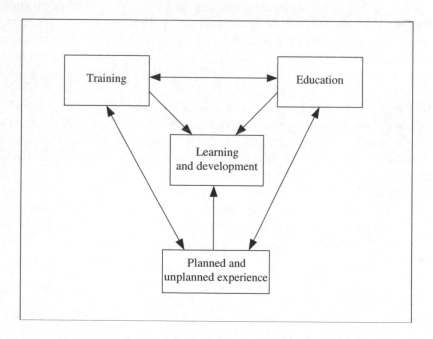

Figure 1.2 Elements that contribute to learning and development

Too often, in the past, training and planned experience have played secondary roles to education. Each should be valued in its own right and their specific strengths in encouraging learning and development should be appreciated. Competently conducted training can expedite the acquisition of specific job-related knowledge, skills and attitudes. Education, when carried out openly and in a spirit of enquiry, can equip individuals with the intellectual perspectives and the tools of analysis that can help to guide them and their organizations through present and future exigencies. Planned experience can integrate and act as the vital catalyst and 'test bed' for the skills, techniques, ideas, etc acquired in formal training and educational settings.

BENEFITS OF TRAINING

Turning now specifically to training, there are numerous potential benefits to be gained by individuals and by organizations from well-planned and effectively conducted training programmes. Individual trainees can benefit in a number of ways. In relation to their current positions, trainees may gain greater intrinsic or extrinsic job satisfaction. Intrinsic job satisfaction may come from performing a task well and from being able to exercise a new repertoire of skills. Extrinsic job satisfaction may be derived from extra earnings accrued through improved job performance and the enhancement of career and promotion prospects both within and outside the organization to which they belong. Benefits for the organization include improved employee work performance and productivity; shorter learning time which could lead to less costly training and employees being 'on line' more quickly; decrease in wastage; fewer accidents; less absenteeism; lower labour turnover and greater customer or client satisfaction.

It follows that in preparing an individual to perform a specific task more effectively, training can contribute to the organization achieving its current objectives. However, it can also play a more long-term strategic role either directly or indirectly. The direct role is pursued through the nature of the actual training content. In this respect training can move away from concern simply for the individual skills, and can deal with leadership, group and organizational issues. Furthermore Stewart (1996) has suggested that the training function can potentially impact in a positive and major way on the management of change. In this respect he has listed a number of key contributions that he feels the training function can make to this process. First, and most importantly, is to make sure that 'people' issues and the implications of change are raised with, and understood by, the organizational decision makers. If this does not occur then there is a serious possibility that planned change will be unsuccessful or take place too late or ineffectively to respond to environmental contingencies and demands.

A second contribution consists of helping managers to develop their capacity to deal successfully with change itself. Training programmes and development activities can be designed to ensure that the necessary abilities to handle the uncertainties associated with change are acquired.

Management development programmes that emphasize the managers' responsibilities for developing their own staff afford the training function the chance to make a third contribution. Linked to this is a fourth contribution, which involves the training of managers at all levels in the knowledge and skills needed to obtain the employees' commitment to change. In addition trainers can provide consultancy services to managers and staff to facilitate this process.

The opportunity for training to make a fifth contribution results from the consequences of change. As these may have created a need for new knowledge, skills and attitudes within the organization, training will make its contribution through the identification of training needs and through the implementation of relevant strategies to meet these needs.

Finally, the training function may make a sixth contribution by being well placed to encourage individuals, groups and the organization as a whole to examine current performance and the operating environment. Trainers are often in a good position to help diagnose the causes of poor performance and to suggest where and how improvements should be made. Stewart cites strategy workshops and team development programmes as examples of training interventions that can be designed to further this critical examination.

Stewart's views accord with the line taken by Frank and Margerison (1978) who emphasize that as trainers we are moving towards providing training interventions which place emphasis on solving organizational problems as well as on developing individual skills.

This kind of approach has been described as Organization Development (OD). By drawing on the definitions offered by Beckhard (1969) and by French and Bell (1984) organization development can be viewed as a long-range, planned, organization-wide effort to improve an organization's health, problem-solving and renewal processes. This is done by focusing particularly on the culture of formal work teams using the theory and technology of applied behavioural science.

Training can also affect an organization's culture in a more indirect way through the management of individual and group training. Cheese (1986) describes the concept and application of cascade training in marketing. This involves training a group at one level in the organization, for example, area marketing managers, and then allowing them to pass on the content and attendant attitudes to others further down the chain. From this it can be seen that cascade training is a form of communication that potentially can have an impact on individual and ultimately on group and organizational values and attitudes.

More important, in some respects perhaps, than the direct and indirect effects already mentioned is the influence that the content and conduct of training can have on attitudes towards the processes of learning and development. This, in turn, can help to create a 'learning organization' that is more flexible and responsive in coping with present and future internal and external demands.

The learning organization

Amongst the many developments that have been introduced to organizations, that of becoming a learning organization has taken on a high profile. It has also led to confusion about what it actually is and some scepticism as to whether it can exist at all. Although it is difficult to define precisely, the description offered by Pedler, Boydell and Burgoyne (1991) encompasses the key sentiments: 'an organization which facilitates the learning of its members and continually transforms itself'. Learning by the organization and by individuals within it is seen as critical to its survival and development. Furthermore, as Senge (1990) suggests, the learning organization 'is continually expanding its capacity to create its own future'.

Drawing upon these descriptions, a profile can be built up to show what a learning organization should be. Any organization that describes itself as a 'learning organization' recognizes the need for change and actively pursues it. This is reflected in its corporate vision and business objectives which are communicated to, and shared by, its members at all levels. In order to realize its business objectives – and, ultimately, its vision – the senior management team should show its commitment to the concept of the learning organization by the comprehensive resourcing of learning strategies and opportunities. These resources should include appropriate rewards for learning, materials, time, support and empowerment.

In order to implement the concept, many would need to develop a new perspective on the way in which they work, their status, their working relationships and their openness. In short, they would have to manage their own change within a change to the organizational culture.

In this new culture individuals should be expected to take greater responsibility for their own development by identifying their own training needs and setting themselves challenging learning objectives. Everyone should be encouraged to learn regularly and rigorously from their work experiences and to seek out opportunities away from the workplace that provide new experiences. This learning should be supported by regular reviews with line managers, team leaders or mentors to monitor and give feedback on individual performances and learning, and to decide upon and plan future learning activities. To fully implement the concept of the learning organization, learning that may be relevant or of benefit to other individuals or to other departments should be shared. The use of technology makes this process easier and quicker once the mental hurdle of being prepared to share has been overcome.

With regard to the organization *itself* learning, the knowledge and experience that individuals have about their own roles and their own departments, together with what they know about other organizations, can be drawn upon and put to good use by contributing to the corporate vision, objectives and strategies. Many examples can be found of people in operational roles who have discovered ways of improving processes and procedures that have resulted in an organization saving on money and materials, developing a faster reaction time or producing an improved product or service.

To tap into this valuable source of ideas and initiative, individuals should be encouraged to challenge, without fear, the traditional way of doing things, and the organization should be open to any suggested change or innovation which can realistically be implemented. This could lead to opportunities to contribute to policy or strategy formulation. To further and to strengthen this approach, a continual open dialogue should take place between units and departments within the organization to exchange information and ideas, and to give feedback on the goods or services that they receive from one another. The success of this approach assumes that invisible barriers have been broken down and that an open rapport has been established.

From what has been discussed it can be seen that, essentially, learning organizations have to operate as open systems (in all senses of that term) in relation to their internal and external environments. Burgoyne (1999) believes that an organization cannot be converted into a learning organization in one grand project, but that the concept should be used to guide specific projects. However, for the concept to become a reality, a number of issues need to be addressed.

In order to overcome the barriers that are likely to be created by internal politics, constitutional forms and systems need to be introduced to give people the opportunity to question and to challenge existing practices and beliefs, and to try out new ideas in a blame-free environment so that the organization is continually improving itself. Safeguards need to be incorporated to prevent the learning organization from being used as a cover for something else, e.g. downsizing, that could be made to look more respectable if introduced as a strategy within the framework of the learning organization. There needs to be a synergy with the stakeholders and any conflict between them must be resolved. Strategies need to be developed to enable collective learning to take place in circumstances where functions such as human resource management have been separated or devolved from a central function, or where there is a multi-site operation.

With regard to the acquisition of knowledge, there needs to be an understanding of where the collective learning processes take place and where the subsequent collective knowledge is kept, i.e. in people's heads, in technology, in procedures, in cultures, in traditions and in the curricula of training courses and events. The nature of intellectual property and its ownership also needs to be addressed. Burgoyne sees the need to clarify the ownership of competence and intellectual property between the organization and the individual. The issue of who pays for and who receives education, training and development 'are usually hopelessly confused in the psychological contract surrounding development, with the result that it is mismanaged or not done at all'. In addition, processes and strategies need to be developed to deal with the interaction between tacit and explicit knowledge. The concept of whether or not it can be shared needs to be settled. Very often professionals perpetuate the notion of a mystique in their discipline and use technical language or jargon to avoid sharing knowledge.

The introduction and development of the concept of the learning organization has had many implications for the trainer. The swing from trainer-centred learning to a more learner-centred approach will make demands upon the range and availability of learning materials, increase the need for individuals to develop learning skills and strategies, and encourage the development of the wide range of skills that people at all levels will need in order to function effectively in the environment of a learning organization.

THE IMAGE OF TRAINING

It is easy to follow and to appreciate the logic which demonstrates how organizations and those individuals who work in them could benefit from well-planned and well-directed training programmes. It could be said that one doesn't have to make the case for training. In fact, many who occupy senior and executive positions have publicly endorsed the claims that can be attributed to training and extol the competence and the contribution of their own training departments. However, this leaves us with something of a riddle because a close examination of the staffing, function and status of training departments does not always reflect the apparent views and attitudes of organizational chiefs.

It is worth spending a little time considering the factors that might explain this conundrum. An indication of the status of training departments or sections is often found by a glance at the organizational chart. Usually, training is placed in a box which is remote from the main operational functions or sometimes it shares a box with another function in the general area of human resources. Furthermore, the level of the manager who heads training is rarely equivalent to that of other managers with whom he has to plan and negotiate for resources and staff. It is rare, for example, to find training to be represented directly in the boardroom.

The attitude adopted by a number of line managers towards training is reflected in their failure to appreciate the limitations of training and the complexities of the learning process in general. These managers see training as some kind of panacea for all the performance deficiencies of their staff. They often abrogate their responsibility for thoroughly analysing the causes of these deficiencies. In many cases they ignore the fact that the causes could be attributed to organizational or environmental factors such as poor supervision, inefficient work practices or poor motivational strategies rather than to a shortfall in individual knowledge and skill. However, despite this oversight, training is still blamed for the lack of improvement in performance. Furthermore, even when the causal analysis has been undertaken effectively and appropriate training has been delivered, some managers do not appreciate the important role they play in ensuring that the post-training environment is conducive to reinforcing and consolidating the learning that has taken place on the training programme. The consequent skill loss and poor performance is still laid at training's door.

Another factor relates to those who have been recruited into training positions. There are still many training or human resource development managers who have been appointed because they may not have been amongst the better performers in operational areas and have been moved into what are wrongly perceived as less critical roles. For some, appointments to the training department have been pre-retirement jobs. A glance at their career paths plus the evidence from their performance, their lack of knowledge, qualifications and experience in training and development, together with the low morale that this engenders in their training teams, challenges the wisdom of such moves.

On the other hand where 'high flyers' have been selected for training they have endeavoured to make their stay as short as possible for fear of jeopardizing their career prospects in the operational functions. It is hardly surprising that attitudes to training have been influenced by experience of these kinds of situation.

There is also a concern about the effects of training. By comparison with other departments which may be involved with production, sales and marketing, there has always been some question about the measurable effect on individuals who have participated in training programmes. On the basis of their research Mangham and Silver (1986) suggested that the incidence of training was not always related to company performance and that some companies which were doing no training at all were as likely to be successful as those who did a great amount. This is supported in a study of 80 of the largest business organizations in the United Kingdom in which Hussey (1985) found that only 33 per cent of the respondents felt that there was a direct link between training and the achievement of corporate objectives. Very few of these organizations assessed the full cost of training activities and therefore were unable to evaluate the benefits.

If these kinds of situation are common then one can understand why training has been seen as a cost to the organization rather than an investment and why it is that the training department is the first to suffer when there is a recession or when cuts have to be made.

Another part of the riddle which impacts on the training department is the pressure on, and the demands made of, operational departments. Line managers are faced with a dilemma when they acknowledge the value of training, recognize the need for their staff to be trained but cannot spare them the time away from the job to undertake the training. In many cases this has led to apathy all round and this has been supported by a number of staff in training departments who have admitted that their organization's training programmes, particularly those in management development, are little more than cosmetic – an internal public relations exercise. This gives credence to the Franks Report (1963) which claimed that industrial management was just about the only profession which could be practised without training.

The Coopers and Lybrand report 'A Challenge to Complacency' (1985) highlighted differences between organizations in the United Kingdom and their European counterparts in their approach to training. In a number of ways the report threw down the gauntlet to company chiefs and to trainers to change their attitudes to training and to make greater efforts to make it more effective.

Research by Ashton, reported by Woodcock (1991), led him to conclude that, in fact, there has been a change in attitude in recent years, particularly among larger companies. This view was supported by the findings of a survey carried out in the United Kingdom by Harbridge Consulting Group (1991). They revisited a number of large organizations which they had first surveyed in 1982. In over 50 per cent of the sample of 57, their overall impression was that training and management development activities were more closely integrated with corporate strategy and objectives than had previously been the case, and that there was more top management involvement in these functions.

Organizations responded by making new demands on their training depart-ments which will test their professionalism and should bring their activities more clearly into line with achieving their organizational objectives. For example, the traditional long courses, which last several weeks, have lost favour. While it is appreciated that such courses have considerable value in changing and developing attitudes, they are time-consuming and costly. Now, there is a much greater call for short skill-based courses, for training to be delivered on demand and for trainees to be given the skills of learning so that they become more responsible for, and more in control of, their own develop-ment. In a number of instances this means that the workplace will become the centre of training activity because it is here that the equipment to provide training can be found and it is here that the knowledge and skills that have been learned will be put to the test. Above all there is a demand for value for money.

Even so, the Skill and Enterprise Briefing document (1999) drew attention to the fact that, in 1998, the proportion of adults in the UK with qualifications at the technician level and above was only half that of Germany, mainly because of the large number of Germans who had undertaken apprenticeship training. The proportion of UK adults qualified to intermediate level and above was also well below that of France.

Training departments can no longer work in a vacuum and be judged by the stability of, and the number of courses they run, the low budgets upon which they can operate and a stack of 'happy sheets' recording the end-of-course reactions of former trainees. Training courses must become linked closely with corporate objectives and training will have to be judged by the effectiveness of those who have been trained to perform the jobs which contribute to achieving those objectives. This, in turn, should bring training into the board-room.

All of this means that the trainer will have to develop a new role which demands a much higher level of professionalism. Traditionally, the theory which underlies approaches to training implies a thorough but pedestrian process. As a result training has often been accused, not without cause, of being too slow to react to organizational demands. By the time training had responded, the game had moved on and something different was required.

What is needed now is a different approach. The training department cannot stand still while change is going on all around it. Trainers need to modify their attitude towards the demand for speed of response. They might react initially to this by describing speedy response as being 'quick and dirty'. However, this censure can be accepted only in part because trainers must work towards being 'quick and clean'. The days of the leisurely approach are unlikely to return. This does not mean that a less skilful approach is called for nor that there should be a neglect of proper practice. Trainers need to be more adept in taking calculated risks and short cuts and in drawing upon their own experience and that of their colleagues. This means that the trainer has to be even more knowledgeable in order to appreciate the level of such risks and the size of the short cuts.

Therefore, a thorough understanding of the 'ideal' approach and the theo-retical aspects of training become even more important. In the past trainers have tended towards caution to guard against being the 'whipping boys' when things have gone wrong, but it must be recognized that without a new profes-sional approach the whip could be even more painful.

Speedy response is not the only factor in influencing a more effective and more influential role for the training department. Trainers need to be able to plan and mesh with the organization's long-term plans for marketing, financial and operational concerns and to take on new and additional responsibilities as human resource needs become more complex and varied.

Trainers also must be able to provide more in-house consultancy as organiza-tions pursue programmes of motivation and creativity and they must become more involved with the investigation of different organizational problems. As mentioned earlier, there is an important role for trainers to play in the manage-ment and administration of organizational development. This means that trainers should play a more proactive role in making a company effective rather than simply maintaining existing systems.

In addition, a closer relationship must be established with operational functions. Trainers must become more sensitive to what works best for managers at the 'sharp end' rather than concentrating on what is best for trainers and what always has been done in the past. In turn, being closer to the operational functioning of the organization, trainers are able to spot trends in the socio-technical system, e.g. absenteeism, turnover, etc, and help to seek solutions through research in the areas of job engineering, job enrichment, etc.

TRAINING AND CORPORATE STRATEGY

The short-, medium- and long-term effects of training referred to in previous sections can only be experienced to the full if training is not only managed professionally but also is linked clearly with the corporate mission or purpose. Lynch (1968) describes the corporate purpose as a goal towards which the activities of all sections in an organization are directed. From this goal more precisely defined objectives can be set and passed down the organization to form the basis of divisional, departmental, and unit objectives and ultimately objectives for individuals. The methods used to achieve these corporate objectives and subsequently the corporate purpose form the basis of corporate strategy.

Hussey (1985) argues that any new corporate strategy must be looked at in the context of a number of factors or variables that affect the way in which the organization works. The relationship he sees between these organizational variables is shown in Figure 1.3.

The clear connection which Hussey forges between strategy and the organization lead him to formulate two basic premises. Firstly, that because an organization's activities in the education and training of management can be used to alter the organizational variables, they should be regarded as an aspect of strategy. Secondly, that because these activities in the education and training of management have the power to make a positive contribution to the implementation of strategy, training objectives and training initiatives should be reviewed periodically by top management and specifically when a major switch in strategy is planned.

These premises are applicable equally to broader aspects of training and indicate that training plans should be related closely to corporate strategy and built into a training policy. This policy should describe in detail the organization's commitment to training, the needs of both the business and individuals, together with opportunities for individual development. Also included should be details of budgeting, priorities, roles and processes. The assessment of training needs should be considered also from the top of the organization downwards rather than being a mainly individually orientated bottom-upwards process.

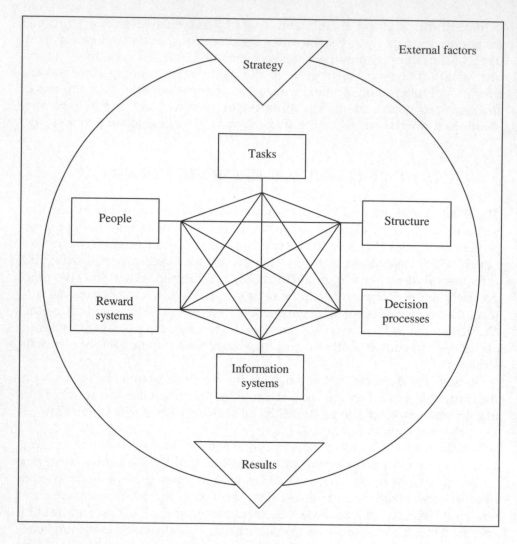

Figure 1.3 Strategy, environment and organizational variables

Reproduced with permission from Hussey, 1985

Romiszowski (1981) illustrates the top downwards relationship between corporate objectives and training objectives and how this relationship can be measured by the use of an objectives matrix (Figure 1.4).

The matrix shows how a single lesson objective within one particular course contributes to the achievement of objectives at higher levels. There is less likelihood of conflict or incompatibility between objectives when they are generated from the top of the organization.

System Level	Necessary input conditions from environment	Desired outputs	Standards (criteria)	Measuring (evaluation instruments)
Electronic industry	Continued 5 per cent pa economic growth (GNP)	Increased sales of electronic equipment	Ten per cent pa increase production and sales (total value)	Study of nationally published statistics
Organization X	Necessary bank approval for loans Necessary recruitment for manpower	Increase in colour TV production sales and after sales service	Twenty per cent pa for next three years	Production department statistics
Training Department of organization X	Necessary manpower resources New recruitment and selection policy etc	TV Maintenance engineers	Forty per annum next year rising to 60 per annum in two years' time Capable of repairing 20 typical faults per working day	Training department statistics On-the-job performance evaluation
Course	The necessary prerequisites in trainees Laboratory and workshop facilities	Trainees can – locate – identify – repair faults in a colour TV	Average 10 minutes per fault Location 100 per cent; identification 100 per cent; repair 80 per cent correct	Using a special TV set programmed to simulate faults manufacturer's models A, B and C
Lesson	A fault of type X in a colour TV model A	Identify the type of fault	Correctly in under one minute	Practical labora-tory test of faults simulator model A
Individual lesson exercise	A live circuit and a multi-test meter	Measure the voltage and resistance between any two points	To 5 per cent accuracy 10 seconds per measure taken	Practical test using real test meter and a variety of standard circuits

Figure 1.4 Extract from an objectives matrix for a hypothetical training design project (Romiszowski, 1981)

The Japanese experience seems to lend support to the preceding argument. On the basis of discussions with a variety of large- and medium-size Japanese companies, Brown & Read (1984) attributed their relative success in terms of productivity, by comparison with companies in the United Kingdom, partly to the fact that:

> Manpower and training plans were said to be constructed in the same context and by the same process as the business plan and viewed in direct relation to it.

Much depends on how HRD is practised in the organization. Garavan (1997) identifies five possible models which are based on the organization's perceptions of the meaning of training, development and education.

In the rudimentary model a single individual takes responsibility for the HRD function but his or her activities relate mainly to operational needs, while line managers and those in professional grades look after development and education. Working to this model often results in sporadic and unstructured learning activities.

The intermediate model is representative of moderate sized organizations. The HRD function is a department in its own right but the reporting line may not be to a head of HRD but to another function or indirectly to the chief executive. The range of its work is likely to include giving information about training and development activities and presenting training and developmental programmes.

The specialized model is more sophisticated. It has a centralized HRD function and is self-sufficient to a large extent. It is staffed by full-time specialized trainers who enjoy the benefits of being well funded to offer a wide range of general and specialized activities.

The developmental model puts an emphasis on continuous learning, with learning objectives being identified from real organizational problems. The model recognizes that learners direct their own learning rather that being directed by and dependent on a trainer. However, Garavan points out that there may not be a direct strategic link.

Garavan's fifth model is described as the strategically linked model. This model, as its title suggests, ensures that HRD is integrated into strategic planning and that HRD practices are accepted and used by line managers as part of their everyday work.

The difference that Garavan sees between this model and the others is that the previous models are focused on the maintenance of organizational stability whereas this one places an emphasis on management of change.

Training and performance management

The notion of linking or relating corporate considerations, i.e. mission, strategy and objectives, more closely to individual performance is a critical feature of what has come to be known as 'performance management'. This approach has been adopted by a growing number of organizations. Armstrong and Baron (1998) suggest 'performance management' is an imprecise term. In their view, it involves 'a strategic and integrated approach to delivering sustained success to organizations by improving the performance of the people who work in them and by developing the capabilities of teams and individual contributions'.

The performance management process begins with the senior management team developing corporate objectives and a business strategy which support the organization's mission statement. These are cascaded down the organization and are reflected in individual performance plans agreed between job holders and their line managers.

At appropriate times during the year and usually at the end of a year, performance reviews are undertaken when individuals and their line managers consider how far objectives for task improvement and personal development have been met. During these reviews the discussion is likely to cover what has or has not been achieved, what helped or hindered the achievement, whether new priorities need to be set, whether new needs have emerged, and an assessment of overall performance. At the end-of-year review the cycle of preparing a new development plan begins again.

In some performance management systems the formal end-of-year performance assessment of appraisal goes towards determining the level of financial rewards for staff.

TRAINING AND SYSTEMS THINKING

From what has been discussed it would seem obvious that the trainer must adopt a wider, macro perspective and, as implied in Figure 1.3, accept that training is an integral part of the organization's system. But what essentially is a system? Buckley (1968) describes a system as 'a whole which functions as a whole by virtue of the interdependence of its parts'. Interdependency or interaction of its component parts is thus a prime characteristic of systems and organizations. In addition, there are a number of other features of systems which have been encapsulated in diagrammatic form by French and Bell (1984). Figure 1.5 shows that the system receives *inputs* from sources in the external environment. The *transforming mechanism* acts upon these inputs and creates *outputs* for *users*. The system may have a number of *feedback* mechanisms that either regulate its current output or require changes in the nature of the outputs.

The organization as a whole may be described in systems terms or its component parts, e.g. training, recruitment, etc may be characterized in the same way.

Looking at training as a sub-system of the organization, it receives personnel, materials and information from other functional sub-systems such as marketing, from other more general sub-systems such as the one that decides and

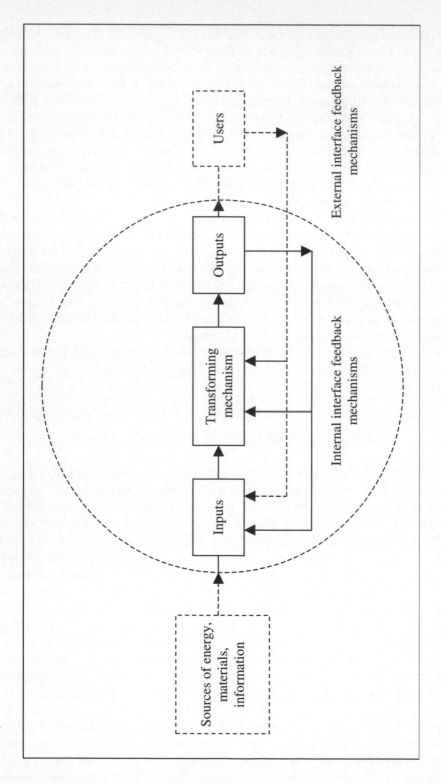

Figure 1.5 Diagram of a system in interaction with its environment (French and Bell, 1984)

communicates corporate objectives, or from externally generated feedback. The transforming mechanism in this training sub-system produces outputs that include the knowledge, skills and attitudes acquired by trainees. The users, i.e. other sub-systems, should then provide the training system with appropriate feedback. This kind of model is essentially an 'open' training system which requires a proactive approach from the trainer. A 'closed' system would confine itself more to the activities contained within the circle in Figure 1.5.

In the past, too much training has been of the 'closed' system variety which has made it unresponsive to organizational needs. To operate effectively in an 'open' system trainers have to be aware of and alert to, the realities of, and the changes in, other sub-systems and organizations beyond their own which may impact on the form, content and conduct of their training efforts. For example, the launch of a new product may affect not only the knowledge content of a course in sales but also the selling skills that a sales representative needs to acquire and to exercise.

In addition, the trainer must consider both the direct and planned outputs and the possible side effects of training that may influence behaviour back in the place of work. A training course which has been designed in a particular way, e.g. using a questioning, consultative approach, may give rise to expectations in the trainees which are subsequently frustrated when they return to their work situation. Such an experience may then create negative attitudes and feelings which become part of the input to future training initiatives. This is not to suggest that constraints should be placed on particular styles of training, but rather to show that trainers should be aware of certain contextual factors which may affect the application of skills and knowledge and that these factors should be a vital input to the training system.

All parts of the organization react to the inputs from other sub-systems and the external environment in their own way depending on their function. It follows that each specialized function has its own particular approach within the general framework of the organization. Training is no exception and trainers have developed their own logical or systematic approach.

2

A Systematic Approach to Training

The terms systems approach and systematic approach are used widely to describe how trainers apply themselves to the training function. This has caused some confusion and frequently the question is asked as to whether these terms have the same meaning.

Drawing upon systems theory, Atkins (1983) makes a distinction between the use of the words 'system' and 'systematic'. He suggests that the term systems approach can be interpreted in two ways. It can be used to describe an approach that views training as a sub-system interacting with the other sub-systems upon which an organization depends for its progress and its survival. This was the context in which training was placed at the end of the last chapter. This approach enables an observer to obtain a wider picture of training functioning within the system or within the organization as a whole. It gives a broader and possibly a different perspective of factors, influences and problems and the way in which they impact not just upon the training function but upon all parts of the system.

Another way in which the term systems approach can be interpreted is as a logical relationship between the sequential stages in the process of investigating training needs, designing, delivering and validating training. Atkins believes that the emphasis on logical and sequential planning and action makes it more appropriate to describe this process as systematic.

While it might appear that a systems approach and a systematic approach are quite different, they are not incompatible when they are applied to training

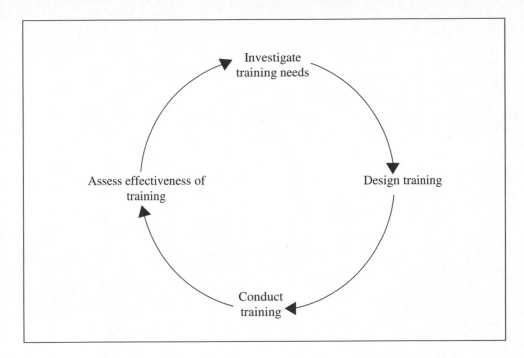

Figure 2.1   A basic model of a systematic approach to training

at different levels. A systems approach can be applied at organizational level to examine the broader issues of the aim, function and appropriateness of training. A systematic approach is applicable directly to the day-to-day functioning of the training department.

The diagrammatic representation of a systematic approach is a working tool and as such it should be expected that trainers will draw up a model which is comfortable for them to use as individuals or as members of a training department who need to monitor the progress of their training projects. A close study of such models will show that they all contain the same activities even though they may be presented in different formats. Whatever the format, all models are likely to have individual variations around four main activities which are shown in their simplest form at Figure 2.1.

The model which follows (Figure 2.2) has been developed by the authors as an outcome of their experience. It is not intended to be the definitive model for all trainers but it is a practical guide to the complexities of training. In addition, it can serve to illustrate to managers the process which has to be followed if effective training is to be achieved.

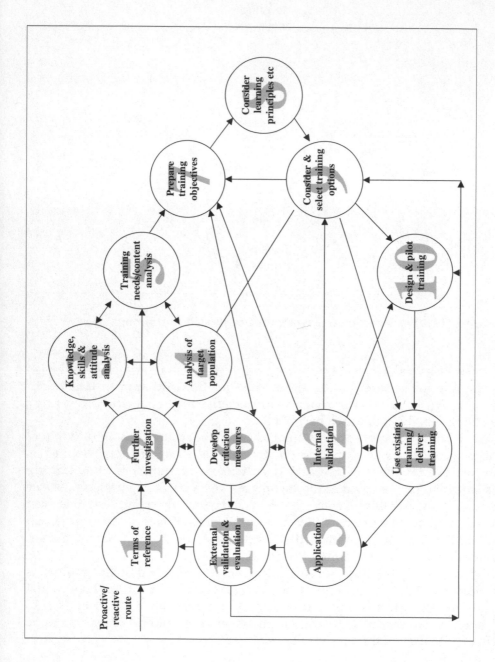

Figure 2.2 A systematic approach to training

STAGES IN A SYSTEMATIC APPROACH TO TRAINING

A systematic approach is applied when training is seen as the best way of overcoming a performance problem. There will be occasions when the trainer has to invest some time in analysing the nature of the problem to ensure that there is a logical route leading to the first stage of the process. The two routes that lead to this stage can be described as the **reactive route** and the **proactive route**. In this chapter each stage of the process shown in the model is described in outline only. The chapters that follow are dedicated to discussing key areas in depth.

Stage 1: Establish terms of reference

Before any work begins, it is important to establish terms of reference. The client must specify and agree with the trainer exactly what has to be done and thus indicate a commitment to, and an ownership of, the project. Line managers who do not have a background of training are likely to find it difficult to frame terms of reference and it is appropriate that the trainer should be involved in negotiating and framing them. This means that time, cost, manpower resources, physical constraints, etc can be clarified at the outset so that the expectations of both the trainer and the 'client' can be seen in a realistic light. At this stage, or soon afterwards, a reporting system and an action plan should be devised so that the trainer can work within sensible bounds and so that clients can be kept involved.

Stage 2: Further investigation

The process or processes that helped to identify training as the solution to actual or predicted performance problems also may have generated sufficient relevant information for the trainer to move on to subsequent steps in the systematic approach. However, it may be that the investigation has been incomplete, insufficient, inconclusive or unconvincing. It may be that the trainer has not been involved up to this point. When this is the case, which it often is, there may be a need to confirm previous findings or to undertake a further study of the training requirements. A number of analyses could be carried out at this point.

Job analysis has been described as the process of examining a job in detail in order to identify its component tasks. It involves collecting information about the jobs or positions being examined and subsequently a detailed analysis of the information. During the collection stage a variety of sources and techniques may be used. These include observation, interviews, questionnaires, group discussions, an examination of documents and materials used on the job. These are some of the main methods used although there are several others, some of which require special techniques, such as those used in work study and in work measurement. The choice of the most appropriate technique will depend on such factors as the nature of the job being studied, the numbers doing the job and their geographical location.

During the analysis stage, information will be gathered which identifies the main objectives of the job, the conditions under which it is performed, responsibilities, main and subsidiary tasks, difficulties and distastes, anticipated job changes, etc. Consideration would need to be given to such factors as the importance or the difficulty of the tasks and how frequently they are performed. This would help to decide the nature of the training which needs to be undertaken or by what other means the performance gap could be filled. The information gathered during the analysis is used to draw up a job description.

In addition to job analysis, part of the further investigation might include a close examination of data provided by reviews or previous training programmes which were designed to tackle the performance problem currently being studied.

Stage 3: Knowledge, skills and attitudes (KSA) analysis

A natural extension of the preparation of the job description is the job specification. When drawing up a job specification the trainer uses information which has been confirmed or collected previously and analyses the knowledge, skills and attitudes (KSA) associated with each task that makes up the job. This form of analysis is essential if the trainer is to make appropriate decisions about the nature and type of training that may be required. Other forms of analysis, such as task analysis, faults analysis and skills analysis which reveal more detail or which identify critical features of the job, may be undertaken at this stage.

The extent and scope of the analysis will depend upon the job being examined and how much further information is required to determine the extent of any actual or potential training requirement.

Stage 4: Analysis of the target population

Allied to the need to undertake analyses of the job is a need to assess the capabilities of, and to determine other features of the target population, that is, those for whom the training is to be designed. This might include an examination of the current training and development programmes being undertaken by the trainees and the effectiveness of such programmes. In addition, at this stage the trainer might be giving some preliminary thoughts to solutions and strategies which might be appropriate to match the characteristics of the target population. These characteristics would include age, experience, previous training and attainment.

Stage 5: Training needs and content analysis

As a result of the various forms of analysis which are likely to be undertaken, a substantial amount of data will be collected about jobs and tasks and the people who perform them. This should reveal an actual or a potential 'gap' which could be the basis for identifying the training need and the training content. In many circumstances it will not be possible to include everything and often it is not desirable to do so. There needs to be an identification of the 'need to know' and the 'nice to know' aspects of the job. This, in turn, would have to be balanced against the constraints which were identified earlier while establishing the terms of reference.

This stage is an important reporting point and may lead to the trainer and the client negotiating to ensure that the best possible training content is agreed.

Stage 6: Develop criterion measures

While various forms of analysis can indicate what the content of a job should be, this is of no real value by itself. The standard or level of performance expected of a competent job holder has to be clarified to ensure that training can be designed to achieve that level, or at least the level at which an individual can begin his or her progression to the standard of the experienced worker.

These criteria are likely to be considered during the early stages of investigation and the data will be incorporated in the objectives later and before any training strategies can be considered. Contributions by the job holder, supervisors or immediate managers give the most reliable data to establish the performance criteria for the job.

Stage 7: Prepare training objectives

Training objectives must be written to provide unambiguous statements which describe precisely what trainees are expected to be able to do as a result of their learning experience. Normally an objective is presented in three parts. The first part states the performance which is expected of the trainees to show that they have acquired the skills and knowledge which make up the content of their job. The second part describes the conditions in which the performance is carried out and includes details of equipment, job aids, environment, etc. The third part lays down the standards of performance which trainees are expected to achieve by the end of their training. For example,

Performance	*Conditions*	*Standards*
Inflate a car tyre.	Given:	
	Wheel with flat tyre.	To ± ½lb psi of correct
	Foot pump.	pressure shown on
	Tyre pressure gauge.	chart.
	Chart of tyre pressures.	

All of the information which is needed to write objectives is obtained during the investigation stage from the analyses of knowledge, skills and attitudes and from the criterion measures which are established in liaison with those in close contact with the job. Objectives are the key to the design of good training and are essential to assessing its effectiveness.

Stage 8: Consider principles of learning and motivation

Having identified earlier the knowledge, skills and attitudes which trainees need to acquire, the trainer should then be concerned with creating a suitable environment to ensure that the training objectives can be achieved. A part of that training environment is the methodology which the trainer can use. Another part includes such factors as physical arrangements, time of day, resources, etc. However, consideration must be given, at this stage, to the principles of learning and motivation such as knowledge of results, reinforcement, rehearsal, practice, etc that may need to be embedded in the training environment.

Recognition and the application of these principles form a rational link between writing objectives and the consideration and selection of training methods. In addition, this link helps to ensure that objectives are realized. The trainer also needs to consider the different ways in which people learn according to their individual differences in personality, age, experience, etc which as far as it is possible help to identify their learning styles. The training environment often can be modified and adjusted to take account of such styles.

Stage 9: Consider and select training methods

A number of options are available to the trainer when it comes to selecting the most appropriate form of training. It is to be expected that some ideas will have begun to form as the investigation and the analyses have progressed. In addition, some direction on methodology is likely to have been given within the terms of reference that places constraints on the number of options open. However, it is important to try to keep an open mind and not to be orientated towards one particular method of training from the outset. Many trainers have fallen for the 'flavour of the month' approach and adopted the current fashionable methodology as a panacea to meet all training needs.

Close attention must be given to constraints, target population, objectives and sometimes 'political' implications when deciding between such options as internal and external courses, various forms of open learning and on-job and off-job training.

Stage 10: Design and pilot training

The design of training involves the translation of objectives and strategies into a balanced programme of instruction and learning. This does not necessarily mean a course; it could be a learning package, a video, computer-based training, etc, or it may include a number of different methods and strategies.

In addition to the nature of the content, consideration has to be given to the principles of learning and learning styles. Furthermore, the design should not ignore pre-training and diagnostic tests if they are relevant to ensuring that students have a common base before they begin training.

Piloting training is a stage which the trainer is often under pressure to leave out. Clients who are anxious to have their staff trained quickly are prone to declaring their total confidence in the trainer and prompt him to forge ahead. This should be resisted whenever possible and when it cannot be, clients need to be made aware of the possible shortcomings of such a move and trainers must take it into consideration during the validation stage.

Piloting of every aspect of the training programme including administration should be planned in detail and executed with an eye for minutiae.

Stage 11: Deliver the training

The selection of, or the systematic design and development of training content is no guarantee of success; training programmes have to be delivered properly. Everyone appreciates the need to have technically competent tutors to present training material. However, the skills which are needed by the trainer to present the training are often overlooked. Technical competence is not sufficient in itself. Trainers themselves must be trained to use a range of teaching techniques, particularly those involved in one-to-one training where a common misbelief has been that by simply observing an expert doing the job, learning will occur by some form of psychological osmosis.

The use of various forms of open learning which might include computer-based training, video and learning packages also need the support of a trained tutor or supervisor. It is not sufficient merely to supply trainees with material resources and leave them to manage their own learning. It has been found in a number of organizations that open learning is most effective when the learner has the support of a trainer or, at least, someone whether it be a manager or a workmate, to take an interest in their progress and generally act as supporter.

While considering training strategies there is a danger of 'reinventing the wheel'. It is always of value to review existing training programmes within the organization and those provided by outside organizations. Sending people on courses whether internal or external is not an end in itself. The trainer has a responsibility to monitor feedback gathered from internal training and to debrief those who attend external courses so that a detailed profile can be assembled of the resources which have been used.

The practice of debriefing individuals and work teams on completion of projects or various types of operation fulfils a similar purpose. Participants are encouraged to air reasons for success or failure and to offer suggestions for improvement in an open and honest environment. The purpose is to learn from the experience, to improve performance and, coincidentally, to provide information for trainers to act upon. Trainers should ensure that they have a look at the debriefing documents and, when appropriate, attend debriefing sessions themselves.

Stage 12: Internal validation

Internal validation is the process of measuring trainees' performance to see if they have achieved the objectives of the training. Information to make this assessment needs to be obtained in two ways. Firstly, a series of tests, exercises and assessment instruments should be designed and used to examine objectively or to check on the progress of trainees. Secondly, trainers need to seek the views of trainees on their training programme including such factors as the performance of their tutors or instructors, the learning materials and the environment.

Information from these two sources together with the tutors' end-of-course review should assist with the identification of areas of success and failure and suggest changes and modifications to the existing programme.

Stages 13 and 14: Application and external monitoring of training

Once the training has been delivered and learning has taken place, the trainees should be able to apply their knowledge and skills to the job. When the former trainees have had sufficient opportunity to put into practice what they have learned during their training, the process of external monitoring should be introduced. This process involves the external validation and the evaluation of the training.

External validation is the assessment of whether the objectives of the training have met the needs of the trainees so that they are able to perform specific tasks, or the total job, to previously identified and acceptable standards. A follow-up study should be undertaken in the job environment to establish whether the training was designed with the job requirements clearly in mind. If it was, then all things being equal, job performance after training should be satisfactory. On the other hand, information gathered from such a study could lead to amendments being made to training content or methodology.

Evaluation is the assessment of the total value of training. It differs from validation in that it attempts to measure the overall cost benefit of training and not just the achievement of specified objectives. The term is used also in the general judgemental sense of continuous monitoring of a training programme or of the training function as a whole, i.e. what the total value of training is in both financial and social terms. In other words, it attempts to measure cost benefits, social and individual benefits as well as the operational effectiveness of training.

Conclusion

The intention here has been to concentrate on a systematic approach to training. While this approach, which has its parallels in other disciplines, may seem to be common sense, a number of criticisms have been levelled at trainers for adopting it. In the past this has been due to confusion about the meaning of the words 'system' and 'systematic'. However, the process itself has attracted more specific criticism. The number of stages and the nature of the work undertaken at each stage of the process imply that it is slow and costly in terms of resources and, while it is seen as a sound idea in theory, it is believed that the investment in time cannot be justified. As a specialized function, training has developed its own technical language which has left it open to the criticism that it is creating barriers by using jargon which renders the whole process too complex for non-specialists to understand. Training involves a consideration of individuals and their personal development which allies the training function very closely to the social sciences, particularly to psychology, and as a result trainers sometimes attract the same kind of criticism which has been directed at some social scientists. This generally includes comment that people are being manipulated, too much theory is involved, too much emphasis is placed on individuals or conversely everything is far too general to be of specific value. There is also the criticism that a systematic approach is too cold and clinical and is void of any consideration for the individual as a human being. Diagrammatic representations of the systematic approach have often attracted the comment that all trainers seem to be working to a different format therefore how can anyone be sure which is the correct one.

There are many senior managers to whom the explanations do not have to be given because training has become a well-established and integral part of their organizations, but explanations, if not justification, still have to be given in some organizations or to those who are lower down the managerial chain.

The logical, common-sense or systematic process is not necessarily a time-consuming activity. It allows the trainer to plan and to work realistically within the constraints which may be placed on time, the availability of staff and of other resources. As a logical process it ensures that nothing is overlooked accidentally and when short cuts have to be taken and some stages have to be abbreviated, the trainer is aware of where this has been done and is conscious of the likely effects. This is an aid to future diagnosis and problem solving should the need arise.

There is no need to make any form of apology for drawing upon the social sciences. Trainers need to be interested in both individual differences and group similarities so that they can use or recommend the use of training techniques which will contribute to the speed and ease of learning thus meeting the needs of the individual and of the organization.

The model of a systematic approach to training has been presented here, as a number of stages which have been arranged in a sequential order. However, it does not necessarily represent the sequence in which trainers approach every project. Depending on the nature of the project the trainer could start at any point in the model once terms of reference have been established. For example, if a large number of staff need to be trained to perform an existing job for which no training exists, then all stages of the model would have to be applied. However, if the trainer is faced with a situation in which trainees using an existing training programme appear to be performing badly, the trainer is most likely to begin an investigation by examining the training objectives, the course content and the instruments used for validation.

The way in which the trainer enters the systematic approach will depend largely upon how and why the training department has become involved – that is, by which route the decision to involve training was reached.

In reality a great amount of consideration has to be given to this issue. It is important to appreciate the circumstances which indicate whether or not training is required and there is a need to be thoroughly familiar with the methods, approaches and forms of analysis that have to be used in order to reach the decision to implement training. The criticality of this process cannot be over emphasized bearing in mind the consequences that might arise for organizations which provide too little training or no training at all when a real need exists.

Davies (1971) contributes some of the following consequences:

- Additional on-job or other forms of supplementary training.
- The slowing down of production and the under utilization of machines and equipment.

- An increase in the proportion of work rejected on inspection for not meeting the standards laid down.
- An increase in the wastage of materials and in the damage to equipment.
- Increased demands on supervisors' time.
- An increase in injuries and possibly fatalities amongst personnel.
- Job dissatisfaction because the worker is inadequately prepared to do the job. This may lead to an 'induction crisis' for new staff and to higher turnover.
- Slower or poorer service resulting in an increase in customer complaints and in a decrease in customer loyalty and interest.
- Decrease in sales and hence a reduction in profits.
- Adverse financial and other organizational repercussions that stem from any of the above consequences which may cast doubt on the continued or future viability of an organization or a unit within it.

The converse of the problem, that is, too much training, also has its consequences and this will be examined later.

When deciding whether or not to train, the first matter of importance is to define what constitutes a training need. It is suggested that a training need can be assumed to exist when the following two conditions are met:

Condition 1. Training, in some form, is the most effective and the most appropriate means of overcoming a current or an anticipated shortfall in performance.
Or, all things being equal, training will result in current or in future performance objectives being achieved more economically, thus allowing resources to be freed for alternative organizational objectives to be pursued.

The first part of condition 1 implies two things: first, that performance problems may be caused by one or several of a variety of factors other than the lack of ability of the job holder(s), and training may not be a viable solution to such a problem; and second, that training is only one of the possible learning and development processes, along with education and planned/unplanned experience (see Figure 1.2), for meeting the critical need(s) identified.

Condition 2. Present or future job objectives are clearly linked to the organization's corporate objectives.

This condition or pre-condition underlines the fact that if a job is redundant or is a 'non-job' in respect of current or future organizational requirements, then it is quite inappropriate to regard a performance deficiency on such a job indicating a training need.

To expand on this explanation, training can be initiated in response to two kinds of training need; one may be described as reactive and the other proactive. The former arises out of an immediate and urgent on-job production or productivity shortfall for which a behavioural cause has been identified and separated from other possible causes. By contrast, proactive training may be closely associated with an organization's corporate strategy and manpower plan. It is very much future orientated and may come about for a number of reasons such as anticipated technical developments, the results of management development and personal replacement action and policies, etc. These two sets of needs can be contrasted also in relation to the concept of change. Boydell (1976) emphasizes that:

> Current needs are due to faults in the present situation; to solve such needs will, of course, involve change, but this change occurs after the need is identified. Future needs on the other hand, will arise as a result of change.

Apart from this present – future dichotomy another valid way of clarifying training needs is by the level at which the needs occur within the organization. A number of writers have suggested a tripartite classification:

At the organizational level
When general performance weaknesses have been observed or are anticipated in functions at or across divisional boundaries.
At job or occupational level
When distinct groups of employees have been identified as having a common need for training, e.g. staff within departments or functional units.
At the individual level
When performance weaknesses have been found in individual members of staff anywhere in the organization.

Level \ Time/Response	Performance problem/Training need	
	Present/Reactive	Future/Proactive
Organizational		
Job/Occupational		
Individual		

Figure 2.3 Classification of performance problems and training needs

In order to clarify future reference to levels of need and to systematize the ideas, etc on performance problems and training needs, this classification of levels can be drawn together in schematic form (Figure 2.3).

It must be emphasized that the divisions shown in Figure 2.3 are, to a degree, for convenience of explanation only, because performance problems and training needs cannot always be categorized as clearly and conveniently as the schema might suggest. This should become apparent in what follows which describes how training can be identified as the best means for overcoming current or potential shortfalls in performance.

3

The Reactive Route into Training

Training could be an extremely expensive way of attempting to remedy a human performance problem if it is not the most appropriate strategy to use. Mager and Pipe (1970) make the point that:

> Solutions to problems are like keys in locks; they don't work if they don't fit, and if solutions aren't the right ones, the problem doesn't get solved.

It is unfortunate that, too often, insufficient analysis is undertaken in order to determine whether or not training is an appropriate solution to a shortfall in performance. Additionally, there may be pressure from line managers to implement a training solution to whatever performance difficulty they may encounter. In many cases they attribute the cause of the problem to the people who operate within the system rather than to the system itself or to environmental or organizational factors.

Similarly, the anticipation of any future shortfall, inadequacy or deficiency in performance, is most likely to be attributed to personal factors. In this kind of situation it is important that the trainer is involved in clarifying the nature of the problem, identifying the cause of the problem and evaluating possible solutions to the problem.

In order to fulfil this function, trainers must be familiar with the questions and issues that need to be addressed in conducting this 'front-end analysis' which Romiszowski (1981) has described as analysing performance problems

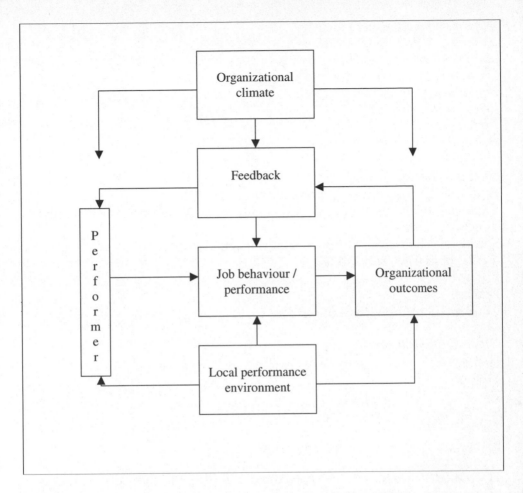

Figure 3.1 A model of human performance (Boydell, 1976)

'at the front end of the instructional design process in order to avoid the possibility of developing training where no training is needed'.

The use of a model of human performance in front-end analysis is a recommendation made by Zemke and Kramlinger (1982). They suggest that working with a model of human performance, which is organizationally relevant, greatly helps to choose the appropriate factors to study and the methods by which to study them. In addition it provides a framework for analysis and for reporting the results to management. The model shown in Figure 3.1 is based on the work of Zemke and Kramlinger (1982) and of Campbell *et al* (1970).

The main factors affecting job performance and organizational outcomes which are shown in the model are:

Performer characteristics
Abilities, skills and aptitudes
Attitudes, values, needs and motives
Knowledge
Personality
Physique and health
Gender
Perceptions

Local performance environment
Physical: lighting, heating, space, location, etc
Technical: equipment, procedures, resources, task demands, task standards, directional data
Social/psychological: support, supervision, expectations, rewards, punishments, objectives, role models

Feedback
Confirmation: knowledge of results

Organizational climate
History
Mission
Goals
Strategy
Tactics
Plans

The model makes the obvious and common-sense point that performance may be affected by factors other than those associated with the performer. It also suggests, at least in theory, that one factor in isolation could have an adverse affect on performance.

However, in reality, it is far more likely for there to be multiple and interacting causes within the individual and between the individual and the environment. Boydell (1976) demonstrates the potential complexity of interacting causes by considering the simple interdependency of the health, skill level and aspirations of an individual (Figure 3.2).

The health → skill causal link is really self-explanatory. An individual's current state of health may interfere directly, or indirectly through the medium of motivation, with his or her ability to exercise a normal repertoire of skills. The reverse of this, the skill → health link, also could come into play as changes in skill level may, for psychosomatic reasons, affect an individual's health. Aspirations could have a positive or a negative impact on health through the same kind of psychological process. Finally, someone with high aspirations may be prepared to expend the effort needed to acquire new skills or vice-versa.

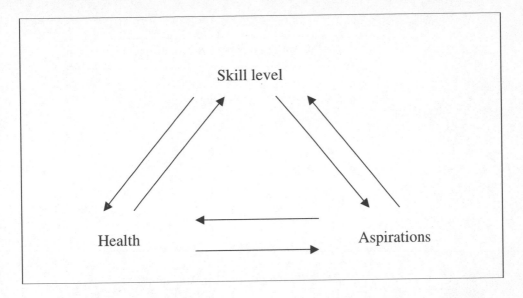

Figure 3.2 Interdependence of human factors (Boydell, 1976)

On the other hand, a realistic appraisal of current skill levels, in the light of previous opportunities, etc, will doubtless influence future aspirations.

It is suggested that by considering a model of human performance, it is more likely that causes will be separated from effects and symptoms and that potentially viable solutions will be generated.

In addition to studying problems by using a performance model, it is quite likely that a number of different forms of analysis would have to be undertaken before a decision on training could be made. In some cases the analyses may have to be fairly crude because the urgency of events determines that the performance problem has to be resolved quickly. In other cases, circumstances may allow more time to be spent on analysis or the nature of the problem may demand that sufficient time is allowed to conduct a thorough analysis. When time allows a detailed study, each successive form of analysis could be regarded as a finer filter which helps to isolate those features of the problem that could be solved by training (Figure 3.3).

Undoubtedly, there are likely to be occasions when training is very clearly the solution to the performance problem and the trainer is able to identify and confirm this very quickly. The filtering process in this kind of situation is likely to be very limited in its application. There will be many occasions when the trainer must be prepared to accept a speedy identification of the problem and how it should be remedied. Slavishly plodding through unnecessary analyses is not to be recommended as it might lead to what has been described as 'analysis paralysis'. This may, in turn, reinforce the negative image of training which is held by a number of line managers. However, not to ignore this

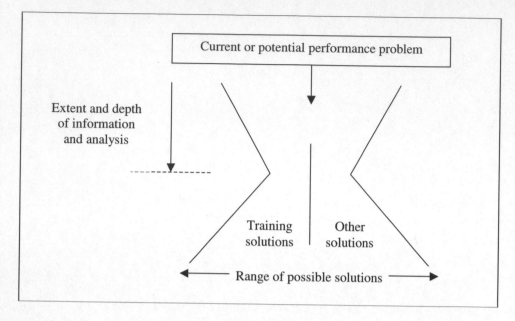

Figure 3.3   A filtering process to find solutions to performance problems

possibility, it is still important for the trainer to ensure that thorough analyses are undertaken when the circumstances merit it. This often means working methodically through a number of logical stages of investigation (Figure 3.4).

Stages in investigating performance problems

Stage 1: Problem identification and definition

A performance problem is first noticed when performance fails to reach prescribed standards. The symptoms of the problem may be observed in the activities undertaken by the performer, by the quality and quantity of the goods and services produced or by other indicators such as time taken to learn or to perform tasks, accident rates, absenteeism, delays, disputes, customer complaints, labour costs, labour turnover, etc. Sources of information which can alert the trainer to such symptoms include:

- Work planning and review systems
- Performance appraisal
- Customer and organizational surveys
- Monitoring indices

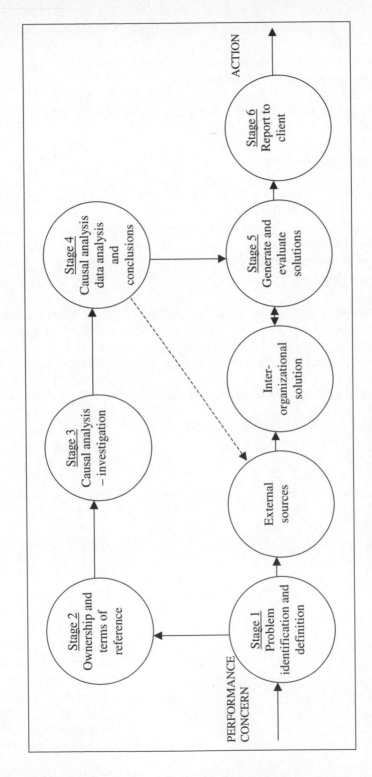

Figure 3.4 Stages in investigating performance problems

    organizational climate indices: turnover, grievances, suggestions, attitude
    surveys, etc
    analysis of efficiency indices: wastage, productivity, down time, equip-
    ment utilization, costs, quality control, etc

- Exit interviews
- Management requests, interrogations or proclamations, e.g. 'Something's wrong here'
- Probation reviews
- Validation of training reports

Naturally, the performance problems that arise within an organization will be dependent on the nature of the organization, the objectives it is attempting to pursue and the commercial, physical, etc, environment in which it operates. However, the first practical step towards eliminating any particular perform-ance problem is understanding the nature of it. Kepner and Tregoe (1981) suggest this can be done by:

- Defining the deviation in performance as precisely as possible and avoiding vague phrases, such as: poor communication, poor morale, excessive complaints. The aim should be to quantify where possible.
- Realizing that the problem presented may only be symptomatic of the real cause(s).
- Defining the problem more fully by posing the following questions:

What is the problem?	What isn't the problem?	What's distinctive about the actual problem?

(i.e. What is the difference between what is being done and what is expected)

Where is the problem?	Where isn't the problem?	What is different about this particular place?
When did the problem occur?	When did it not occur?	What's different about or what's changed in the period the problem occurred? What is distinctive about the time when the problem occurred compared with the rest of the day or year?

To whom or to what is the problem attached?	Who or what hasn't got the problem?	What's different about the person or object with the problem?
How often does the problem occur?	How often doesn't the problem occur?	What's distinctive about the frequency of its occurring?
How big is the problem?	How big isn't the problem?	What's distinctive about the size or growth of the problem?

At this stage it is necessary to discuss with the key client, or the person who is most closely concerned with the problem, how the problem is perceived. Information obtained from external sources which may provide comparative data on other organizations about quality of products, customer complaints, etc needs to be put into perspective. Information obtained from within the organization which may include observations, reports, statistics, etc needs to be examined for trends. As part of this process the client could be asked to consider why the problem or the discrepancy is important and what would happen if it was left alone. It may be found that the client has to be persuaded to accept either that there is no problem or that the problem is unimportant and should be ignored. This could be an extremely sensitive undertaking if the client happens to be a member of the senior management.

Alternatively, it may be necessary to examine, in more depth, the nature of the problem as it was presented. Unsatisfactory answers to the questions 'What is my evidence?' and 'How reliable is it?' may point to the need to ask for resources to carry out a preliminary enquiry in order to establish a more secure data base on which to structure the discussion with the client.

Even at this early stage, another organization or an external factor may be pinpointed as the cause of the problem and it may be possible to consider a solution which requires co-operation between organizations. For example, if pollution created by another organization is affecting the performance of staff then the solution lies in liaison between the two organizations.

Stage 2: Establish ownership and terms of reference

If internal factors begin to emerge as the possible cause of the problem, it is important that the client accepts ownership of it and of the solution when it emerges. It may be necessary for trainers to use powers of persuasion to get the client to accept this responsibility whilst resisting attempts to have solutions forced upon them. In this respect, trainers need to make a realistic appraisal of their positional power and their personal power in the event that they have to refuse to accept efforts by the client to off-load both the problem and the solution. For example, if the client believes that the problem is caused by inadequacies in the job holder as a result of poor training, then the 'solution' is believed to be obvious and a convenient and plausible answer to any future failings. In these kinds of circumstances it may be necessary for trainers to show just a little moral courage to stand by a refusal to accept such a solution.

When it has been decided that a project to investigate the problem should go ahead, then it is important at the outset to establish terms of reference or objectives with the client. False expectations by either party may hinder the process of reaching a satisfactory conclusion. It is well worth remembering Frieson's principle quoted by Zemke and Kramlinger 'When it comes to doing studies of the problem, keep it "Short and Sweet".'

Also their rule of thumb is worth bearing in mind 'In 20 to 40 working days you can conduct 99 per cent of all the performance studies you are ever called upon to perform.' Because of the dynamic nature of organizational life, it is possible that the problem could have disappeared or altered radically before a lengthy study has begun or presented its findings which, by then, will be out of date.

Stage 3: Causal analysis – problem investigation methodology

When the decision has been made to examine the problem in more depth, consideration has to be given to the methodology to be used in the study. At the planning stage it is important not to fall into the trap of 'reinventing the wheel'. The problem under investigation may have been examined by someone else and possible causes may have been identified already. Ideas and approaches may have been suggested which could be an influence on the form of the investigation being planned and it could be that an effective solution has been identified and tested.

Much of the planning stage is concerned with developing a detailed set of questions that will help to direct the investigation and which is in line with the model of human performance that has been adopted. Both the model and the set of questions which relate to it serve the purpose of helping to 'delineate our problems before we rush into a solution' as Gilbert (1982) explains in relation to his own PROBE Model.

The questions that follow, which relate to the human performance model, can be used to examine jobs and tasks. In drawing them up, liberal use has been made of questions from the PROBE Model and from the checklist produced by Mager and Pipe (1970).

Job/Behaviour/Performance

Tasks

- What are the major job objectives?
- Into what major tasks does the job break down?
- Why are the tasks done?
- What is the frequency, importance and difficulty of each task?
- How are the tasks and task elements sequenced?
- How long do or should tasks/task elements take?
- Where are the tasks done?
- Who are the tasks done for?
- What methods are employed to accomplish the tasks?
- What job aids and equipment are used?
- What assistance is given to enable tasks to be completed?
- Who gives assistance?
- What standards of performance are required?

Responsibility (to)

- To whom is the job holder responsible?
- What is the frequency and degree of supervision?

Responsibility (for)

For what is the job holder responsible in terms of:

- People (numbers, level, frequency of supervision, degree of authority)?
- Money (amount, frequency of responsibility)?
- Equipment (type, location, value, action in event of breakdown)?
- Materials (type, quantity, value, action in event of loss or shortage)?
- Time-keeping, target setting, deadline setting/meeting?
- Policy making (extent of authority)?
- Organization image?

Relationships

- What contacts (formal/informal, structured/unstructured) does the job holder have within the organization/outside the organization?
- What is the frequency of contact?
- What numbers of people are involved?
- What are the grades/levels of people involved?

- How is contact made (person to person, telephone, meetings, etc)?
- What are the purposes for the contact?

Judgement

- What judgements does the job holder have to make?
- What discretion does the job holder have to exercise?

Physical working conditions

Under what physical conditions is the job holder working in terms of:

- Environment (place of work, lighting, heating, noise, vibration, humidity, cleanliness, danger, hazards)?
- Physical workload (weight of materials, equipment, etc)?
- Psychological load (stress, vigilance, decision making, etc)?
- Posture (standing, sitting, bending, walking, stretching)?

Social working conditions

What is the nature of the social conditions in which the job holder operates in terms of:

- Size of work group, level of work group, cohesiveness of work group, attitudes of work group?
- Nature of rewards affecting work group?

Economic working conditions

What are the economic working conditions in terms of:

- Length of employment contract?
- Hours of work (full time, part time, overtime)?
- Pay (average earnings, salary scale, nature of and reasons for increases, method of determining basic pay)?
- Additional remuneration (bonuses, danger/dirt money, long service awards, profit sharing, payment by results, etc)?
- Payments (to medical schemes, social clubs, pension schemes, etc)?
- Holidays?
- Absenteeism?
- Fluctuations in availability of work?
- How do the job holder's economic working conditions compare with others at a similar or a lower grade?

Prospects

- What are the future prospects for the job holder?
- What opportunities for advancement does the job offer?
- What are the opportunities for transfer?
- What are the opportunities for further training?
- Does the organization have an appraisal and a career development scheme?

Training

- What training is made available to the job holder?
- What is the organization's training policy?
- When is training available?
- Who does the training?
- Where does the training take place?
- Is full pay given during training?

Job holder's performance

- What are the stated difficulties, distastes and satisfactions of the job and what are the apparent consequences?
- What is the nature of unsatisfactory performance? In what terms is it expressed (qualitative or quantitative, i.e. time, money, numbers etc)?
- How does the stated nature of unsatisfactory performance compare with the standards of performance required?

The performers

The performers' knowledge and skills

- Could they do the job if they really had to?
- Could they do the job if their lives depended on it?
- Did they once know how to perform as required?
- Have they forgotten how to do what is required?
- Are their present skills adequate for the required performance?
- Do they understand the consequences of both good and poor performance?
- Do they grasp the essentials of good performance?
- Do they understand concepts to perform well?
- Do they have sufficient basic skills, e.g. reading, etc?
- Do they have sufficient specialized skills?
- Are good job aids available?

Mental, physical and emotional capacity

- Do they have the physical and mental potential to perform as required?
- Do they have the basic capacity to learn the necessary perceptual discriminations with accuracy and with speed?
- Are they free from emotional limitations that would interfere with performance?
- Do they have sufficient strength and dexterity to learn to do the job well?
- Are they over-qualified for the job?

Motives, needs and perceptions

- Do the job holders seem to have the desire to perform well when they enter the job?
- Do their motives endure, e.g. is the turnover high?
- Do they perceive desired performance as being geared to penalties or rewards?
- Does performing the job to the required standard matter to the job holder?
- Are the procedures based on sound methods?
- Are the procedures appropriate to the job and skill level?
- Are the procedures free from boring and tiresome repetition?
- Are adequate materials, supplies, assistance, etc usually available to do the job well?
- Are there sufficient accurate, readily available data to direct an experienced person to perform well?
- Are there conflicting demands on the performers' time?
- Do they get a source of satisfaction for performing well?
- Are they able to take a pride in their performance as individuals or as a member of a group?

The local performance environment

Physical

- Is the physical environment, i.e. lighting, heating, space, etc, interfering with performance?

Technical

- Are the necessary tools/implements usually on hand to do the job?
- Are the tools/implements reliable, efficient and safe?

- Are the procedures efficient and designed to avoid unnecessary steps and wasted emotion?
- Are clear and measurable standards of performance indicated to the performers?
- Do they accept the standards as reasonable?
- Do they know when to do what is expected of them?

Social/psychological

- Do performers have the authority to command the resources to meet the requirements of the job?
- Do they receive sufficient supervisory or managerial support?
- Are there good models of job performance available?
- What do they gain from their present performance in terms of reward, prestige, status, etc?
- Is there a favourable outcome for performing well?
- Is there an undesirable outcome for not performing to an adequate standard?
- Is there a source of satisfaction for performing well?
- Do the performers get more attention for performing badly than for performing well?
- Is irrelevant behaviour being rewarded while crucial behaviour is overlooked?
- Are the performers 'mentally inadequate' in that the less they do, the less they have to worry about?
- Are they 'physically inadequate' in that the less they do, the less tired they become?
- Is the pay for the job competitive?
- Are there significant bonuses or pay increases based on good performance?
- Does good performance have any relationship with advancement?
- Are there meaningful non-pay incentives (e.g. recognition) for good performance?
- Is the frequency of non-pay incentives so frequent as to lose meaning or so infrequent as to be valueless?
- Is good performance rewarded by absence of punishment?
- Is the balance of positive and negative incentives in favour of good performance?

Feedback: knowledge of skills

- Is feedback provided that is 'work related'? (i.e. are results and behaviour compared with standards?)

- Is feedback immediate and frequent enough to help people to remember what they did?
- Is feedback selective and specific? (i.e. is it limited to a few matters of importance and free of 'data glut' or vague generalities?)
- Is feedback educational, positive and constructive so that something is learned from it?
- Exactly how do they find out how well they are doing?

Organizational climate

- Are the performers restricted by policies or traditional approaches such as a 'right way of doing it' or 'we've always done it this way'?
- Have there been any changes in organizational policy or circumstances which directly or indirectly affect the performers personally?

Naturally, not all of the questions listed may be applicable to any given situation. For example, questions about the job may be redundant because sufficient information may have been obtained already. Nevertheless, the questions do provide useful cues as to the line that data collection could take and should prove sufficient to guide most investigations in the analyses of performance problems.

In addition to preparing a repertoire of questions, three other considerations have to be taken into account when planning the methodology of an investigation. These are, methods of collecting data, sampling and the actual implementation of the study.

Methods of collecting data can be divided broadly into observational techniques and non-observational techniques. The former literally involves observing people in their work setting and then analysing the observations according to a pre-determined schema. Observational techniques include task listings, time and motion study, algorithms and behavioural analysis. The non-observational techniques include one-to-one interviews, discussion groups, questionnaires, telephone, critical incident techniques and scrutinizing the organization's records. The main methods, together with the criteria for selecting them, are enlarged upon in Appendix 1: Methods for Obtaining Information.

When deciding which method or methods to employ in the investigation, the trainer should choose the most appropriate method to serve the purpose of the investigation rather than the easiest or the most convenient method. For example, in some circumstances, there is no substitute for direct observation. The trainer should also use more than one method whenever possible. Each method has its particular strengths and weaknesses and therefore employing more than one method in an investigation can serve both as a compensatory 'belt and braces' mechanism and as a valuable cross-check on information which has been gathered. Whenever possible, focus should be placed more on the actual behaviour of theoretical or of practical interest and less on verbal behaviour. The ease with which the trainer can separate fact from opinion or objective data from conclusions could be the factor which indicates the best method to use.

If the problem which has to be investigated is considered to be widespread then the number of personnel or the number of locations covered should be sufficiently large to ensure that it is representative of the whole target population. It is also important that as well as including personnel who are not performing satisfactorily, the sample should include individuals who are performing satisfactorily so that a comparative analysis can be made. Kepner and Tregoe (1981) argue that 'regardless of the content of a problem, nothing is more conducive to sound analysis than some relevant basis of comparison'. Guidelines on using sampling as a technique are contained in Appendix 2.

It is sound practice to undertake a pilot exercise prior to conducting the main investigation if time and resources permit. This gives the opportunity to test and, if necessary, to modify the methods for collecting data and the procedures which have been planned. In addition, a review should be carried out of the general strategy and tactics which it is planned to use. Intermediate reviews also could be used during the course of the main investigation to monitor progress and to help to decide, on the basis of data collected, whether larger numbers should be included in the sample or whether the study should be enlarged to include the total population.

Stage 4: Causal analysis – data analysis and conclusions

The forms of data analysis should have been decided upon during the planning stage. They range from simple qualitative analysis to forms of quantitative analysis. Qualitative analysis involves examining raw data in order to identify common themes and evidence that may reveal the causes of the problem. This form of analysis may be appropriate when the sample is unavoidably small; when the problem lies with a very few individuals or when it is too difficult to convert the qualitative data through some form of coding.

With regard to quantitative analysis it is best to keep things simple. Zemke and Kramlinger (1982) suggest that in a substantial majority of the studies they have conducted, a good job can be done in problem analysis by using simple descriptive statistics (e.g. average, median, mode, kinds of skew, standard deviation, correlations, etc). They advocate the use of the 'Inter Ocular Trauma Test' – 'If the results hit you between the eyes, they probably have practical import'. It is worth remembering that the difference between successful and unsuccessful groups may be 'significant' in the statistical sense but without being particularly dramatic and, therefore, may be of minimal practical importance.

Problem analysis should now continue with a series of questions. First, pose the question 'What is distinctive in the information or data which has been collected?' Answers to this question should reveal important clues about the cause of the problem. If a distinction has been revealed, the second question can be asked – 'How could this distinction (or this change) have produced the performance deviation or shortfall?' This should help to generate possible causes. A third question can be asked in relation to each possible cause – 'If this is the true cause of the problem then how does it explain each shortfall in the specification?'

In other words to test for a cause-and-effect relationship involves lining up information about likely causes against information about the observed effect or symptom in order to assess how the cause could have had that effect. Kepner and Tregoe (1981) point out that it is an exercise in logic. It identifies the most likely cause that explains the poor performance but cannot prove it beyond doubt. Definitive proof could only be obtained if a systematic laboratory or field experiment was set up but this is highly unlikely in a work setting. A practical alternative could be an 'on-going' evaluation of the solution or solutions which it has been decided to implement.

Stage 5: Generate and evaluate solutions

The outcome of Stage 4 should be the identification of the causes underlying the problem. These causes, together with the problem, need to be shared with, and accepted by, the client in order to obtain their involvement in the generation of a solution. As a matter of course, in some cases the solution will be suggested directly by the causal analysis. However, where several factors are involved or when the problem arises from more deep-rooted causes, then both the client and the trainer must be prepared to commit more time to develop a solution. The trainer may find it appropriate to drop out at this point if it is felt that there is only a limited role for training to play. This may be the case when it is felt necessary to bring in expertise from outside the organization. Naturally, whatever solution, or solutions, finally are proposed it is important that the environmental, organizational and individual considerations in the causal analysis are reflected in the possibilities which have been generated. These could be made up of action plans relating to work restructuring, team building, organizational development, motivation, communication, selection or training.

The solution or solutions which have evolved need to be analysed in terms of feasibility by a comparison of their relative advantages and disadvantages. Factors which would have to be considered include cost, time, manpower requirements, acceptability, materials, ownership by the client and political consequences. Romiszowski (1981) categorizes these factors under four main headings: those affecting the value of a solution, those affecting the cost of solving the problem, those affecting the practicality of system development and those affecting the practicality of system utilization.

When jobs are close to the production 'sharp end', the value of a solution often can be estimated in terms of its contribution towards minimizing lost productivity, costs of error, etc. It is more difficult to make this kind of estimate as the job becomes more distant from the production context. However, even in this kind of situation, it may be possible to compare the relative value of different solutions in terms of tangible and intangible benefits.

The main costs that need to be taken into account are the development and running costs. The former are incurred in relation to the form and content of the solution and in relation to the depth of analysis required to isolate potential difficulties that may be experienced by those who will become subject to the solution, e.g. learning difficulties if the acquisition of new knowledge and skills is part of the solution.

The availability or non-availability of certain kinds of resource will affect the practicality of developing some solutions. These resources might include:

- time available for system development
- financial and material resources
- human resources
- back-up facilities (technical, administrative, etc)
- adequate test facilities.

Romiszowski emphasizes the importance of the quality of human resources to determine the practicability of human utilization. In addition, he highlights the fact that the prevailing political, ethical, philosophical and attitudinal climate in the wider system may be profoundly influential. The solution which might be recommended to a client may depend largely on the trainer's assessment of these more intangible factors. This underlines the need to adopt both a systems and an historical, organizational perspective.

Stage 6: Reporting to client

At the end of an investigation it is usual to make a written or an oral presentation to the client. Such a presentation is vital if the substantive content of the report is to be accepted. The report must separate clearly, findings, interpretations, conclusions and recommendations. The recommendations should be formulated in a way that helps the client to instigate a subsequent course of action.

Above all, the report and presentation must be persuasive. The presenter will go a long way towards achieving this aim provided that close attention is given to the audience, their needs, motives, concerns and prejudices. This process will be assisted further if the trainer has kept closely in touch and communicated with the client as the investigation has progressed.

There are several sound reasons for nurturing this liaison. It will increase the client's feelings of ownership and involvement. It will afford the trainer opportunities to question the client about interim findings and interpretations and about the feasibility of proposed solutions as they emerge. If the client is keyed into the politics of the organization he or she will know who else should know about the report and what would be the most effective means of informing them about it.

Putting things into perspective

What has been described in this problem-solving approach may seem to be reasonably straightforward in theory. There is a clear, rational outline of the important stages to be gone through and guidelines as to how they should be carried out. Unfortunately, in practice, things are not always as easy. The trainer may find that the senior managers who are involved pay only cursory attention to the first two stages of identifying and defining the problem and establishing ownership and terms of reference. In addition, the identification of the problem often has to be incorporated with the third stage – causal analysis. Organizational power may dictate the dynamics and the results of establishing ownership and framing terms of reference. In addition, the trainer may have to exercise a great deal of patience and tolerance in order to cope with the inevitable frustrations that arise. There are few trainers who have not been faced with some of the following dilemmas:

- Who really is the client? A question that may be difficult to answer if the hidden agenda are in operation and organizational politics have been instrumental in initiating demands for an investigation in the first place.
- Lack of action, or demand for action, at critical points on the part of the client and other interested parties, which require the trainer to resist firmly.
- Wider organizational problems and issues may be revealed in the course of the investigation which are studiously ignored by the client.
- The client's reaction to the results, conclusions and recommendations of the investigation may be less than enthusiastic. The trainer should never expect to be welcomed as the new Messiah when bringing what may be seen by some as bad news. 'Shoot the messenger' may be one possible response. However, not to present too gloomy a picture, the more likely reaction from 'interested' parties in circumstances such as these, are remarks which imply that the trainers are naive, inexperienced or just incompetent, e.g. 'Training people don't really understand. . .' 'What do you really know about this industry?' 'It takes a long time to understand our culture.'
- While it is important to record, in the report, the constraints which have been encountered, e.g. time, manpower, etc, it could be a mixed blessing. It may justify the nature of the investigation and the report, but at the same time, by stating the constraints, the trainers can create rods for their own

backs because it may allow the 'opposition' to criticize the conclusions or opt out of implementing the solutions.

It is possible to address circumstances such as these by displaying professionalism and patience and by recognizing the client's appreciation of, what may be for them, a radical change which would have to be implemented over a comparatively long period. The enthusiasm of the trainer and a few interested parties cannot change an organization overnight.

4

The Proactive Route into Training

In addition to the reactive route, other equally important routes into training come from a variety of proactive procedures and future-orientated considerations which make up part of an organization's 'horizon-watching' activities. Unlike the methods of investigation which were described in the problem-solving approach, these processes are not initiated in response to specific performance problems. They may come about because there are to be internal organizational changes that will demand markedly different performances from employees in the future. They may come about because of changes that will occur outside the organization and which will have implications for individuals or groups on how they perform their jobs.

Another route into training is through on-going personnel or other organizational functions which monitor performance to identify current or potential training needs. The results of this last method, in particular, may lead to setting up a full performance investigation. However, irrespective of which of these routes suggests the possibility of a need for training, it is still important to bear in mind a number of questions posed in Stage 3 and the factors set out in Stage 5 of the problem-solving model before making a final decision.

Naturally, solutions other than training may emerge from the proactive approach which are summarized in diagrammatic form in Figure 4.1. The processes and considerations which give rise to these outcomes are worth further mention.

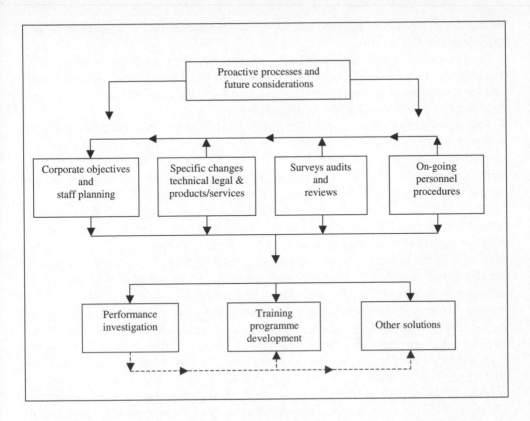

Figure 4.1 Outcomes of proactive processes and future considerations

Corporate strategy, training and manpower planning

It has been shown already how training is linked to an organization's corporate purpose and objectives through the medium of the corporate strategy. In many instances training may be an integral part of such a strategy either directly or in a less direct, long-term fashion through the process of manpower planning. Hussey (1985) describes three cases which illustrate how training was of direct value in helping to implement a shift in corporate strategy. The example of the UK operation of a foreign cosmetic manufacturer is particularly worthy of mention.

The company wanted to gain a larger brand share in their sector of the toiletries market. The shift in strategy required some changes to be made in the channels of distribution it was using. This consequently required the sales force and the tasks of a number of the representatives to be reorganized. Top management were convinced that their new strategy would be more likely to succeed if the sales force was committed to the change and had the requisite knowledge to handle the different types of wholesaler and retailer they would encounter in the future.

To achieve this commitment and to build an improved knowledge base, Hussey developed a short course. The course partly revolved around a case study, comprising authentic market data, which allowed the representatives to discover the reason for the new strategy.

The course also covered specific training to help the sales force to cope with situations that they would encounter once the change got underway. As Hussey emphasizes 'the point of the example is that the annual training needs assessment could not have revealed the gap except in retrospect, by which time, the implementation of the strategy might have been threatened'.

Another example of the direct link between training and corporate plans is found in a major UK bank in which training was again closely linked with a shift in corporate strategy. The bank was concerned about the income that it was not getting from the business of operating the accounts of corporate customers. It decided to become more assertive in securing higher and more realistic commission fees for providing this service.

A group of top-level managers who were examining this issue felt, on the basis of their experience, that training should form part of the solution to the problem of ensuring that branch managers had the requisite knowledge, skills and attitudes to implement the new strategy. As time was at a premium, the broad training needs had to be established quickly. This was done over a relatively short period mainly by group discussions which was by no means ideal but fitted in with the time constraints that had been imposed. The training needs which had been identified were met by workshops of two-and-a-half days in duration. The whole exercise, from beginning to end, including the training of over 1,500 managers, was carried out in less than twelve months. Subsequent performance figures confirm the impression that the training programme had a major impact on the managers' on-job behaviour and the 'bottom line'.

To understand the relationship between corporate strategy and the identification of longer-term training needs within the organization requires an appreciation of the manpower planning process. Lynch (1968) suggests that manpower planning has two interrelated functions. The first of these is an on-going function that should provide information about current manpower resources and capabilities. This will allow short-term plans to be developed in order to meet current needs which have been created by changes in the organization's internal and external environment. The second function is that of anticipating longer-term future requirements that are affected by changes in the organization's plans which, in turn, have been determined by internal factors such as restructuring, modification of corporate objectives, etc, and by an awareness of changes in the macroeconomic, commercial, technological, social and political fields. Essentially, Lynch believes that manpower planning should

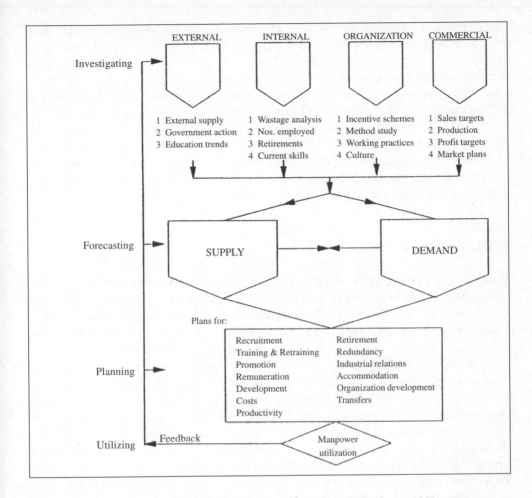

Figure 4.2 A framework for manpower planning (Bramham, 1982)

attempt to ensure that an organization has 'the right numbers of employees, with the right level of talent and skills, in the right jobs at the right time; performing the right activities; to achieve the objectives to fulfil the corporate purpose'. These functions and intentions are realized in the main phases and activities which make up the manpower planning process. This is well illustrated in Bramham's (1982) framework for manpower planning (Figure 4.2).

In looking at this framework in detail, it can be seen that before attempting to formulate future manpower plans, it is imperative that information should be obtained that either will dictate or will have a vital bearing on the forecasting of manpower supply and demand.

It has been emphasized by manpower specialists that manpower planning can be effective only when it is an integral part of the business planning process, i.e. corporate strategy. Those who are responsible for manpower planning must be familiar with sales targets, profit targets, marketing plans, social responsibilities of the organization, changes in the level, nature and organization of production activities, etc. Ideally, these business plans and objectives should be presented in a style which can be interpreted in terms of manpower involvement, i.e. the numbers of employees needed in specific jobs and the levels of skill which they need. Other factors which need to be taken into account include details of how it is intended to organize productivity, and the work methods, practices and incentives that will be used. Chadwick (1983) adds that manpower planning should work hand-in-hand with studies of productivity and with other studies of the utilization of manpower.

Manpower reviews

Basically, there are two phases to an internal manpower review. First, a manpower inventory should be prepared setting out the current situation. A manpower inventory is a form of stocktaking which identifies numbers of employees by department, sex, age, length of service, qualifications, total manpower costs shown in terms of salaries, wages, pensions, etc.

Part of this inventory might take the form of a skills inventory which focuses on the professional and technical skills, educational and formal qualifications, and work experience of present employees. This kind of survey is usually undertaken by using questionnaires and interviews.

The second phase of the manpower review should concentrate on the analysis of past and present ratios and trends in the staffing of the organization and in particular those areas identified in the skills inventory. These analyses should help to reveal or highlight potential problems or opportunities for staff development in connection with retirement patterns, promotion policies, skill shortages, experience gaps, etc. This, in turn, might determine the feasibility of projects and initiatives that have emerged from business planning or it might indicate what recruitment and training would be needed to make up the shortfall in skills.

The external manpower review should be designed to find out what is the potential supply of people with relevant experience and skills from outside the organization. Bramham (1982) suggests that there are three influences that may have a bearing on the availability of skilled and experienced manpower. The government manpower policy could have a substantial impact on the numbers of people available to any particular organization. Availability of manpower can be influenced by the expansion, contraction and change in local labour markets. In addition, the qualifications, skills and abilities of people entering the labour market are determined largely by the aims of the educational system.

The manpower demand question is 'What does the organization want?' and the manpower supply questions are 'What does the organization have and what can it get?' It must be appreciated that none of these questions can be answered with a high degree of certainty, particularly as the time scale extends. However, despite this reservation, organizations must make attempts to predict manpower supply and demand patterns if they expect to have any control over their futures.

From the point of view of demand, it has been shown that current manpower requirements must be understood fully before any attempt is made to identify future needs. In addition, the time scale, the amount of detail, and the assumptions about political and economic forecasting must be made clear.

Given this information, it is possible to make either objective or subjective forecasts. Objective forecasts involve the use of statistical techniques applied to trends over a period of time, ratios of productivity, etc. Subjective forecasts may rely on intelligent 'guesstimates' which can be improved upon if full use is made of all available information and statistical data.

Turning to considerations about the supply of manpower. This is an area where, again, statistical and diagrammatic techniques can be used to analyse the future availability and supply of manpower. Age distribution and trends, promotion and transfers, succession planning, recruitment patterns, wastage, etc need to be examined to draw up a picture of the future supply situation. As with the demand forecast, it is important to clarify the time scale, the amount of detail needed and underlying assumptions before such an examination is begun.

A comparison of supply and demand should expose any potential difficulties, discrepancies and opportunities which might affect the organization's manpower strategy. The policies that are developed from the strategy in relation to each personnel activity should be interrelated and integrated. In some cases they may function in a compensatory manner, for example, a poor quality intake of new employees may have to be made good by increasing training resources. Finding a workable balance between the various personnel policies which might be available, ultimately will be a matter of judgement.

Plans may need to be developed in any of the areas shown in Figure 4.2. These plans which involve training and re-training should relate closely to overall manpower plans and have a major influence on management development and organization development. When the plans are implemented, an assessment of their effectiveness provides feedback so that the manpower plan can be adapted to meet changing circumstances and demands.

Specific changes and training needs

In discussing manpower planning, emphasis was placed on the interrelationship between various phases, procedures, functions and influences. The perspective which was adopted was that of a systems approach. The organization's internal and external environment are usually in flux to some degree and a change in one area is assumed to have direct or indirect effects on other functions in the system. Manpower planning and corporate strategy essentially deal with the broader picture. However, certain changes and considerations which may have specific implications for training in the short term, could have a significant influence in the longer term on the organization's manpower training. These might include the introduction of new technology, new products and services, new legislation, and the results of different surveys, audits and reviews.

New technology

The introduction of new technology usually will bring about a number of training needs. This technology may be used operationally in such processes as packaging, manufacturing, quality testing, money transmission, etc or it may be introduced in the information retrieval systems used by management in its control of the functions of the organization. The training needs may arise directly from the knowledge, skills and attitudes needed to operate the new technology or from the 'spin-off' effects that may have changed working practices and influenced social interactions and relationships. In particular, the relationships between managers, supervisors and the workforce may need to be re-examined. This might, in turn, result in a need to change management style and roles within the line structure in order to promote the openness and speed of response that often accompanies new technologies.

New products and services

The introduction of new products and services may lead to training needs across a broad range of jobs. If the product is manufactured, there might be a need for the development of existing skills, the acquisition of new skills and knowledge of new processes and procedures for those involved in making the product. In addition, it is quite likely that product knowledge and selling skills are best developed through the education and training of marketing and sales staff.

It should be possible to anticipate the need for training and education at the conclusion of the development phase of the new product or service. Failure to do so has, no doubt, foiled at least in the short term, the efforts of many organizations to extend their services or increase their range of products with the impact that they might have wished.

New legislation

There are numerous examples of how new legislation has imposed statutory obligations on organizations which have had implications for the training function. In the United Kingdom the Health and Safety at Work Act (1974) required every employer to provide 'such information, instruction and supervision as necessary to ensure, as far as is reasonably practicable, the health and safety at work of his employees'. The Race Relations Act (1976), the Sex Discrimination Act (1975), the Data Protection Act (1984), the Disability Discrimination Act (1995), the Working Time Regulations (1998) and numerous subsequent directives and guidelines have had important influences on the way in which organizations should plan and conduct a number of their operations and functions. Training has been recognized clearly as one of the means by which the statutory requirements of these acts can be met. For example, no current course on recruitment and selection would be seen to be complete without coverage of the relevant sections of the legislation on sex and race.

It requires little imagination to appreciate the pervasive influence that the introduction of decimal currency in 1971 and the 'big bang' of 1987 must have had on training activities in the financial sector in the United Kingdom. On occasions economic or financial changes announced by the Chancellor of the Exchequer in his budget have had a knock-on effect for training, e.g. the introduction of value added tax. The message seems fairly obvious. All new legislation, which has implications for organizations, must be scrutinized carefully to identify any features that might create a training need.

Surveys, audits and reviews

Training needs survey

These surveys are normally 'in-house' studies which aim to find out what employees feel that their training needs are in general or what they are in relation to specific aspects of their work. Most surveys are conducted by questionnaire but when small numbers are involved, interviews and group discussions can be used.

Employee-attitude survey

This kind of survey is usually organization-wide in its scope and lends itself to the use of questionnaires. Training needs may not be the main focus of attention but they are likely to emerge from answers to questions about job satisfaction and dissatisfaction, feelings about supervisory and managerial attitudes and styles, etc. Furthermore, it may not be only the training needs of the respondents that are highlighted. The needs of groups within the organization could be identified, for example, the training programmes of supervisory and managerial personnel are sometimes partly based on the results of employee-attitude surveys.

Consumer surveys

There are few organizations that have not experienced the negative feedback that customers are prompt to volunteer when they are not satisfied with a product or a service. How much notice is taken of complaints varies and some customer service departments exist for the sole purpose of appeasing those who are aggrieved. However, much more positive use can be made of feedback from customers by the use of surveys to gather information on the quality features of products and services as well as finding out about the negative aspects.

It is a known fact that customers are quick to complain but slow to praise. This is because, rightly, they expect high quality and good service to be the norm. The onus for seeking positive feedback lies with the organization and a number of techniques can be used. In the United Kingdom, gas fitters leave a pre-paid post card for the customer to complete after the work has been finished. The questions asked relate to promptness, courtesy, cleanliness, quality of work and other such values which make up a good service. Some garages telephone customers after their cars have been serviced to see how satisfied they were with such things as reception arrangements, cleanliness, quality of work etc. Customer contact staff are used in banks and other financial organizations as well as supermarkets and shopping malls to talk with customers and seek their opinions of, and ideas for improving, the products and service that they receive. Restaurants, particularly on main motoring routes, invite customers to answer questions about the service that they have received by printing a short questionnaire on the reverse of the bill. In addition, postal questionnaires can be sent to customers who have made recent purchases of such things as electrical appliances or who have made recent use of a particular service.

The data gathered from all sources must then be collated and fed back to different parts of the organization in such a way that all departments can benefit from it – and that includes the training department.

Functional audit

Periodic audits may be conducted to investigate or examine the effectiveness of any functional unit in the organization. Such audits may highlight both the unsatisfactory features of current operations and warn of future impending problems. Sometimes, specialist units such as organization and methods inspection units are established to undertake this kind of work. The remit of these audits can be very broad and the methods of investigation may include observational and non-observational techniques. Some of these may be designed specifically for an individual unit within the organization. Unless the audit is concerned with a training unit or a management development unit, it would be uncommon for the trainers to be involved directly. Therefore, it is important, in these cases, for trainers to liaise closely with the auditors and to be conversant with their findings, conclusions and recommendations if they are to identify, at an early stage, potential problem areas that may need a training involvement.

Benchmarking

Benchmarking is designed to help an organization to improve its performance and ways of working. It is a systematic process of comparing specific operations and outcomes of an organization against those of an external competitor, non-competitor or an internal performer and then drawing lessons from the comparisons. The non-competitors do not have to be in the same business, but they may have similar functions such as distribution, marketing or customer service against which comparisons can be made. The comparisons may indicate a need for change in the organization's mission, aims, objectives, structure, culture, processes or employee competencies.

Boydell and Leary (1996) suggest that benchmarking covers six steps:

1. Define the processes and operations of production or aspects of concern about performance.
2. Draw a flow chart describing the critical stages in the process or operation.
3. Establish measures of quality or productivity in those areas that are the subject of concern.
4. Identify the organization against which to benchmark.
5. Collect relevant data in order to make a valid comparison.
6. Determine the gap between the measures of quality or productivity.

The amount and the quality of the information that is obtained will depend upon the relationship between the organization benchmarking and the organization being benchmarked. If a 'significant' gap is found, then it would be appropriate to undertake a causal analysis, which may lead to the identification of training needs.

Organizational review

Kenny and Reid (1986) suggest that, what they term an organizational review, might be undertaken when planned training is being introduced or re-introduced to the organization as a whole or to parts of it. Generally, its purpose would be to assess strengths and weaknesses of the existing approach to training and to look for ways to make it more effective. The review might be part of an organization's manpower planning process and, to reiterate a familiar exhortation, it should be set in the context of the organization's corporate purpose, policies and plans.

Up to a point, an organizational review is similar to a training survey, but it is wider in its scope covering such issues as the extent and costs of training, plans for training present and future employees, quality of current training, training standards, appraisal of trainees, attitudes of line managers to training and the extent of their knowledge of, and commitment to, organizational training policy. Information about these issues might be obtained by interview, questionnaire, discussion, direct observation and the examination of policy statements and departmental personnel records such as training reports, accident records, turnover figures, grievances, etc.

On-going personnel procedures

Within most medium- and large-sized organizations a number of on-going personnel procedures have been established either to help to identify current and potential training needs or, in the course of their operation, to explore work problems for which training may be an effective remedy. Several of these procedures initially focus attention on the problems and needs at the individual level in contrast to the other proactive and future-orientated approaches which are concerned mainly with occupational and organizational levels (Figure 2.3). However, in the more sophisticated systems, data that has been collected on individuals would be collated and fed into the manpower planning process either directly or through regularly up-dated personnel records. These personnel procedures include performance appraisal, career planning and development, management development, succession planning, probationary reviews, exit interviews, on-job training and coaching, and achievement or proficiency testing.

Performance appraisal

Performance appraisal systems formalize the comparatively natural and straightforward process of a manager and a subordinate periodically discussing together what the subordinate has achieved over the preceding period and then setting targets for the next period. The outcome of the discussion could result in one or more types of action plan – remedial, maintenance or developmental. Remedial and developmental programmes are more than likely to give rise to training. In the case of remedial programmes, training is initiated to help an employee to meet current job requirements and standards. In developmental programmes, training may be one of the means to enable the employee to cope with new tasks, new assignments, new and increased responsibilities, etc. These types of developmental activity are either part of management's effort to enrich an existing job or part of an individual's career or management development plan.

Career planning and general development

Most responsible organizations are concerned about making the best use of their manpower potential. With this in mind, some of them have created career planning and development systems. At particular stages in an individual's career a 'stocktaking' exercise is undertaken with a number of aims in mind:

- to profile competencies, abilities, skills and knowledge;
- to find out the individual's ambitions and aspirations;
- to review past employment, experience and performance;
- to profile abilities, skills and knowledge;
- to review future possible and probable moves and responsibilities;
- to prepare a personal or self-development programme which might include training and planned experience.

This stocktaking may involve no more than talking through the items listed above with someone qualified in personnel or career development. However, many organizations have taken a further step and have designed career development centres, at which the stocktaking process may be extended over a period of two or three days.

The outcomes have seen the introduction of personal development plans, which are often linked with appraisal, the use of learning journals, the promotion of the concept of 'lifelong learning' and the more extensive use of mentors.

Management development

Management development is similar in a number of respects to career development. It is a process by which organizations try to ensure that they have sufficient managers of the right calibre by establishing a systematic scheme to develop the performance and potential of managers by the use of training, education and planned experience. The training needs of managers are normally identified by performance appraisal procedures and more recently by the use of assessment centres.

The term 'assessment centre' should imply a method or a process rather than a place. It consists of a series of individual and group activities designed to generate information about an individual's personal and managerial strengths and development needs. These activities are likely to include psychological measures, interviews, simulation exercises, discussions, business games, case studies, etc. The information that has been collected is then used to give feedback to the participants and to suggest programmes to assist to develop their skills.

Succession planning

Succession planning is closely associated with all of the procedures which have been discussed so far in this section. Basically, it involves identifying and preparing people to take up jobs or positions in the future. These may become vacant fairly predictably through retirements and organizational changes or less predictably as a result of illness, death or termination of employment. Such planning would require knowledge about what pattern of promotion and experience was required for a particular job or position. Additionally, information about current performance and an appraisal of potential would be needed for those who might be considered as possible candidates for these jobs.

From this it should be possible to specify suitable programmes, courses, transfers, secondments, assignments, etc for the development of those who have been identified as 'successors'. Naturally, the programme and those participating in it would need to be kept under review so that modifications and adjustments could be made to meet unexpected changes and unanticipated opportunities.

Probationary reviews

It is common practice in many organizations for certain categories of staff to complete a probationary period before being taken on to the permanent staff. During the probation period, the performance of the new members of staff is monitored and should it fall short of the standard which is required, then where it is appropriate, remedial training may be given. Even at the end of the period of probation, when an individual is confirmed as meeting basic requirements, there may still be a recommendation for further training related to performance weaknesses which have been identified during the probationary period.

Exit interviews

Responsive and sensitive organizations are always interested to know why their employees decide to find employment elsewhere. The exit interview is used to investigate the reasons for their leaving. Very often this kind of exploratory interview can help to reveal a variety of training needs. Interviews of this type can draw a number of honest, if not blunt points of view which bring to light aspects of working conditions, management styles and training needs which might not be voiced by those remaining with the organization.

On-job training and coaching

Sometimes the training needs of individual employees become apparent during the guidance, coaching and training sessions which they have with their line managers, supervisors or mentors.

Achievement and proficiency testing

Achievement and proficiency tests are used to assess the amount of knowledge and the level of skill of job holders. This can help to prevent training being given when it is not needed and it can indicate the extent of training which may be needed in the future. Usually, the tests are actual tasks which make up the job. Sometimes, the tests can be the complete job. Examples of such tests include driving, first aid, marksmanship, operating equipment, etc. In a number of jobs, employees have to prove their competence periodically in order to receive 'qualification pay'.

A competence-based approach

A competence-based approach to training in the UK has been surrounded by controversy since its introduction was formalized at national level by government initiative in 1986. There has been confusion about the concept, its application and its administration. Levels of concern about the outcomes and value of a competence-based approach have been raised and a continuous debate has opened across education and training.

An immediate confusion is caused by the meaning of the word 'competency'. Woodruffe (1991) believes that Boyatzis (1982) made the word popular, even though few were certain what it meant, and points to the fact that some have described the whole area of competency as a minefield.

Competency is used to describe either the required outputs (competences) or the desirable inputs (competencies). In the latter sense it is viewed by Boyatzis (1982) and Spencer, McClelland and Spence (1992) as 'any individual characteristic that can be measured or counted reliably and that can be shown to differentiate significantly between superior and average performers. . .' and could include personal skills, values and attitudes. Woodruffe (1993) sees competencies as sets, dimensions or repertoires of behaviours that underlie competent performance, e.g. self-confidence. In his opinion, required outputs or areas of competence refer to key aspects of an individual's work. For instance, staff management would be an area of competence against which to assess the work performance of most managers. Figure 4.3, drawing heavily on Woodruffe (1993), attempts to depict the relationship between these different versions of the concept of competency.

Over the years many organizations have developed competency frameworks to help them to integrate their human resource processes. The frameworks may have included both competences and competencies but, as Whiddett and Hollyforde (1999) suggest, it is far more common for descriptions to be behaviour-based rather than solely task- or job-output based.

Within each competency the behavioural indicators may be grouped into levels in order to cover a wide variety of jobs that are subject to different

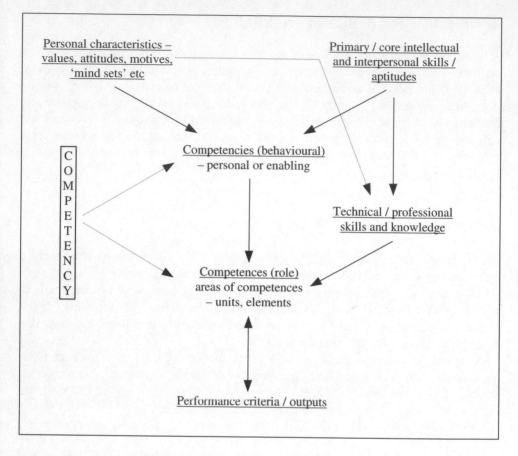

Figure 4.3 The relationship between different concepts of competency

demands and requirements. In the view of Whiddett and Hollyforde, there are two key benefits to be derived from establishing a common set of competencies that makes a competency framework. The first is that a common language and understanding can be developed in different functions and at different levels in the organization. Secondly, there is likely to be a greater consistency when assessing performance for selection, appraisal or training purposes.

In the context of performance management, a competency framework can be used to help to identify training needs. This can be done by enabling a competency profile to be identified through an analysis of the key tasks and performance objectives for a job holder's current position, and by comparing a job holder's on-going performance against the profile. In addition, consideration should be given to the implications of any new demands resulting from the changing priorities or initiatives emerging from business plans.

Present/Reactive	Level	Future/Proactive
Questionnaire survey Organizational records	Organizational	Corporate objectives Manpower planning Attitude survey Consumer survey Functional audit Organizational review
Telephone Group discussion Behavioural analysis Algorithms	Job/Occupational	New technology New products and services New legislation Training needs survey Functional audit Succession planning Exit interviews
Critical incident technique Structured/Unstructured review Observation Participation	Individual	Performance appraisal Career planning and development Management development including assessment centres Probation review On-the-job training – coaching Achievement/proficiency testing

Row label (vertical): P E R F O R M A N C E I N V E S T I G A T I O N

Figure 4.4 Training needs: routes, methods, means and procedures

SUMMARY AND CONCLUSIONS

It has been seen that there are two major routes into training – the present/ reactive route and future/proactive route. There are a number of methods, means and procedures associated with these routes which can help the trainer to investigate performance problems and to identify training and development needs. Figure 2.3 introduced the concept of a classification of methods etc, which has been developed in Figure 4.4 to show how the methods, means and procedures might be classified in relation to the reactive and proactive routes. It is not possible to make a rigid classification because some of the methods could be used at more than one level depending on the nature of the performance problem or future need and on the size of the organization.

Irrespective of the route into training there should be a clear link between the needs which have been identified and corporate objectives. In reality such a level of sophistication is unlikely to exist in many organizations. Nevertheless, by adopting some of the approaches and through an understanding of the perspectives which have been described, trainers can make a positive contribution to organizational effectiveness even though their understanding of the corporate mission and objectives may not have been conveyed to them directly. Furthermore, the trainer may be limited by a number of unforeseen or uncontrollable constraints which may not allow a fully comprehensive study of behavioural problems or training needs to be undertaken. In circumstances such as these, the trainer may have to employ very basic methodology and take a number of short cuts that may not be very satisfying.

However, there are many situations when a series of swift, professionally conducted interviews is all that is needed to find the critical issues and needs. Success on short projects that have an impact can gain a considerable amount of credibility and kudos for the trainer which can be put to good use when asking for more time and resources for other projects. As trainers we should not always be prepared to give in to the 'quick and dirty' approach. Whatever the outcome of training projects, the trainers are accountable at all levels of their involvement; memories are short when it comes to remembering success and trainers are quick and easy targets when it comes to directing blame. It is not unrealistic to recommend that trainers should be responsible for familiarizing senior managers with the tools of the trainer's trade.

5

Analyses for Training

Ideally, the decision to use training to overcome an actual shortfall in performance or to prevent a shortfall occurring in the future, should have been taken after the trainer and the client have studied the results of some form of reactive or proactive investigation. The trainer is then able to address the basic and critical issues:

- What should be the specific content of the training?
- How should the training be organized and implemented?
- How, in terms of effectiveness, should the training be evaluated?

This chapter will concentrate on the first of these issues – What should be the specific content of training? In turn, this will lay the foundation for answering the third question on how training should be evaluated.

The systematic approach shows that determining the content of training (Stages 2–5) will normally require a series of analyses beyond, or in addition to, those that may have been carried out already in the earlier stages of the investigation. These further analyses have been developed to ensure that the training which is to be introduced is fully relevant and that the potential problem of including redundant training is avoided. Davies (1971) argues that high costs may be incurred as a result of too much training because:

- More training is being organized than is really necessary.
- Courses and training programmes are longer than they need to be.
- More instructors/tutors and equipment are employed than the job demands.
- Students, who may be perfectly competent in performing the job, fail the training because it is too theoretical rather than practical in its nature.

- Irrelevant criteria may be used to select students for training resulting in potentially suitable students being excluded from the programme.
- Job dissatisfaction can result from the worker being prepared for a higher calibre job than the one being done. In turn this could lead to higher turnover of personnel, poorer performance, etc.

Naturally, because of the time and expense involved, the trainer must give very careful thought to the scope and depth of any further analyses. In considering the question of scope, Kenny and Reid (1986) suggest three approaches that are particularly appropriate to organization training: comprehensive analysis, key-task analysis and problem-centred analysis.

Comprehensive analysis

As implied by the title, in this approach all aspects of the job are scrutinized. The intention is to produce a comprehensive and detailed list or record of every task and sub-task that make up the job together with the knowledge, skills and attitudes which are needed to perform the tasks and sub-tasks effectively. As this approach is very likely to be costly and time-consuming, certain criteria should be satisfied before the trainer undertakes such a study. Kenny and Reid suggest the following criteria:

- The tasks are unfamiliar to trainees or potential trainees, they are difficult to learn and the costs of failure or error are unacceptable in terms of expenditure of money, time and human effort.
- Resources are available to carry out such analyses.
- The training programme that results from this approach will be used frequently and should, therefore, be cost-effective.
- The tasks comprising the job are laid down in a tight and closely prescribed manner and the right way of carrying them out must be learnt and adhered to.
- Management understand and accept the need for this type of approach to be adopted.

The circumstances or situations that are likely to warrant this level and extent of analysis are:

- The introduction of new equipment, technology or procedures that necessitate either the creation of entirely different jobs or the acquisition of an extensive range of new skills, etc.
- Thorough update of training in a particular functional area where current training has been allowed to 'drift' and general performance has become poor.
- Creation of a new position as a result of changing market conditions.

- The introduction of planned training into a functional area where no formal training has existed previously but changing technical requirements and developments make it imperative for the manpower concerned to be 're-fitted' and updated.

Key-task analysis

This form of analysis is concerned mainly with the identification and detailed investigation of key or primary tasks within the job. It has particular relevance to managerial and supervisory positions that consist of many tasks of which not all are critical for effective performance. It is also relevant to jobs that change in emphasis or content leading to a need to establish priority tasks and to identify the knowledge and skills which are required and to establish an acceptable standard of performance. Kenny and Reid reinforce the point that a fully comprehensive analysis of managerial and supervisory jobs would be too expensive and unwieldy to be viable. Key-task analysis would probably result in a job description that only highlights key or critical tasks and an outline of the knowledge, skills and attitudes required to perform the job.

Problem-centred analysis

This approach is effectively an extension of the reactive route into training which was described in Chapter 3. Attention is focused neither on the whole nor necessarily on all of the critical or key tasks but on those aspects of current performance that are below standard. In cases such as these it will have been decided already that training is an appropriate way to overcome the problem or difficulty which has been identified and that a more extensive analysis is unnecessary because the performance of the job holders is quite satisfactory in other respects.

Beyond the concern about the scope of the investigation, the trainer then has to decide upon the specific analyses that have to be carried out and what associated analytical methods and techniques should be used. Figure 5.1 illustrates diagrammatically the sequence of stages or steps that a trainer may have to follow in order to determine the content of training. The direction of the arrows in the diagram are intended to indicate that the different types of analyses are not mutually exclusive nor independent and that data gathered at an early stage may reduce the extent of, or even the necessity for, subsequent analyses. For example, information stemming from the reactive route into training may mean that only a limited job analysis needs to be undertaken. Again, a thorough job analysis which produces a detailed and comprehensive job specification may suggest that any additional analyses can be by-passed.

The analyses referred to in Figure 5.1 and the associated analytical techniques and methods can now be looked at in more detail.

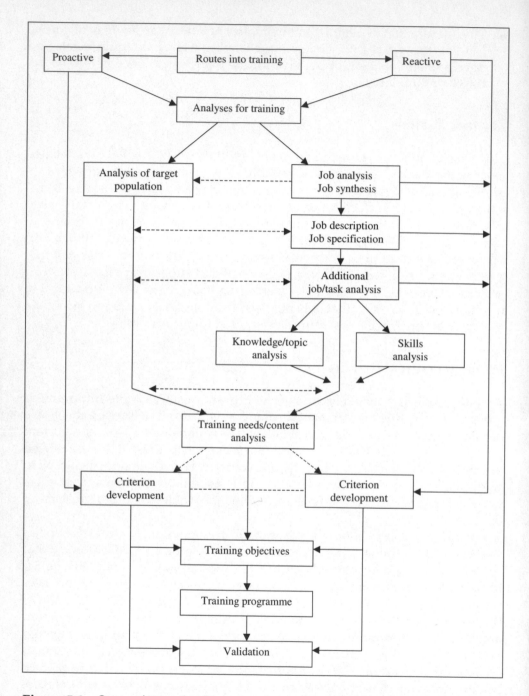

Figure 5.1 Stages/steps leading to training needs/content and beyond

JOB ANALYSIS

Job analysis can be used for a number of different purposes which include personnel selection, job evaluation and training. *The Glossary of Training Terms* (Department of Employment, 1978) describes job analysis as:

> The process of examining a job in detail in order to identify its component tasks. The detail and approach may vary according to the purpose for which the job is being analysed, e.g. training, equipment design, work layout.

The different purposes for which the job is being analysed may include the identification of performance problems and therefore it is likely that some form of job analysis will have been used in the filtering process which was described earlier (Figure 3.3).

To many, the process of job analysis has associations with time-and-motion studies and may appear to be a lengthy, dull and uninteresting activity. To employees it is often viewed with suspicion, like many other forms of analysis, and they feel that there is a hidden or secret motive which could threaten their livelihood. There are some who use the term job analysis as being synonymous with training-needs analysis and gain the false impression that all analyses of training needs involve lengthy procedures before any hint of training is given.

Ideally, a job analysis should only have to be done once in the lifespan of a particular job. Many diagrammatic representations of a systematic approach to training show job analysis as an early stage in the process of training design. All such systems are intended to be self-regulating so that any changes in the job procedures or equipment, etc should be fed into the system so that the information held by the trainers can be updated. In theory this is a sensible and logical process but in practice it is all too rare. The usual outcome of a job analysis is a job description or the more detailed job specification and these should be the documents that a trainer should want to look at first. In many cases, job descriptions are out-of-date, thin on content or non-existent, while some human resource departments review job descriptions annually and indicate that they have been either 'revised' or 'reviewed' on a specific date. When this is the case, the trainer's job becomes easier. When it is necessary to undertake a job analysis, many of the techniques which have been described already may be used, such as the structured interview, observation, questionnaire, etc.

Other forms of analysis which often are used interchangeably with job analysis are task analysis and skills analysis. In essence the trainer has to delve deeper into jobs in order to find out more about the duties or tasks which make up the job description so that suitable training can be designed. *The Glossary of Training Terms* defines task analysis as

A systematic analysis of the behaviour required to carry out a task with a view to identifying areas of difficulty and the appropriate training techniques and learning aids necessary for successful instruction.

This definition points much more clearly to the training function than that of the job description. Pearn and Kandola (1988) deliberately avoid the use of the term job analysis because of what they see as its self-perpetuating dull and uninteresting image. They prefer to use the term job, task and role (JTR) analysis as a research tool that has many more applications for managers.

In order to provide the degree of detail which is needed in a job specification, further analyses may have to be carried out and the trainer has the choice of using one or more of those techniques shown in Figure 5.1 to look more closely at the various tasks and skills which make up a job.

JOB SYNTHESIS AND FUTURE-ORIENTED JOB ANALYSIS

The notion of future-oriented job analysis has been discussed by Hall (1986) in relation to succession planning for executive positions. This process would first of all involve an examination of an organization's corporate objectives and strategies. From this examination the anticipated executive job demands and the necessary skills required by future executives to meet these demands could be derived. As Hall points out, 'Thinking through this link between the organization's basic objectives and need for future top executive skills is the core of strategic succession planning' and must be the basis for identifying the future training and development needs of these individuals.

When a job is new, when it has been changed greatly or when new tasks have been added to it, it is not possible to write a job description or a job specification using the same analytical techniques. It should not be regarded as an appropriate method to throw job holders in at the deep end and wait until they have mastered the job before any analysis begins. The end result could be very costly to the organization. However, that is not to say that some trial and error should not be involved in the way that the job develops.

Job synthesis is the technique by which a new job or task can be examined in order to produce a job specification and, subsequently, appropriate training. A number of people are likely to be involved in developing the new job or task and in many cases it would be them to whom the trainer would turn to assist with an analysis.

The products or outputs would provide a first indicator of what the job is about; for example it might be a new piece of machinery, a new technique of food preparation or a new service. It is possible that there are other jobs which are related to the new one, the holders of which can contribute to the structure of the new job or task.

When this is not the case, it may be possible to tap the experience of those in other organizations or to recruit new staff with relevant experience. In organizations which are large enough to have an organization and methods department, much of the trial-and-error work will have been done by them. Where this is the case the trainer should have been involved at an early stage in the development. Subsequently, the involvement of managers and supervisors can contribute through technical conferences and trials with job holders to build up a picture of the knowledge and skills, and the activities or tasks which must be performed to achieve the results required.

It is unlikely that the job specification will be perfect at the first attempt and all training developed through job synthesis should be monitored carefully and reviewed frequently.

The first products of a job analysis or job synthesis of particular relevance for training are a job description and a job specification.

A job description

This has been defined as a general statement of the purpose, scope, responsibilities and duties which make up a particular job. The layout of a typical job description format, including any explanatory notes, is set out below:

1. *Job title* Generally speaking the job title should be succinct and, as far as possible, a realistic reflection of the nature of the job.
2. *Division/Department/Section* This information will help to identify where the job 'fits' in the organization.
3. *Location of job* This refers to where the job holder normally performs the duties, etc which make up the job. If the job is peripatetic then that feature may be mentioned here.
4. *Main purpose of the job* It may be valuable to have a brief statement of the main purpose or general aim of the job in order to appreciate how it helps to fulfil unit, section, departmental or divisional objectives.
5. *Duties/Responsibilities/Tasks* The duties and responsibilities provide the main headings and sub-divisions of the job. Under these should be listed the specific tasks to be performed. For example:
   Job: Personnel Manager
   Duty/Responsibility: Recruitment and selection of clerical grade staff.
   Tasks 1.1 Check and, if necessary, amend after discussion with current job holders the job description and personnel specification.
   1.2 Compose a recruitment advertisement for placement in the local newspaper, etc.
   It is recommended that the task descriptions should be terse, in the present tense and each sentence should begin with a crisp action word.

6. *Responsible to* This should state the position of the job holder's immediate superior and sometimes include the frequency and closeness of supervision. Ungerson (1983) suggests 'this first, apparently simple, piece of recording can give warning of fundamental weaknesses or muddle in the organization'.
7. *Relationships*
8. *Judgement*
9. *Physical working conditions*
10. *Social working conditions*
11. *Economic working conditions*
12. *Prospects and current training/Developments opportunities*
13. *Difficulties/Distastes and satisfactions*
14. *Reasons for failure*

What might be included under items 7–14 inclusive is indicated by the questions listed in Chapter 3.

Even if the scope of the analysis, referred to previously, is limited only to problem areas it may still be necessary in some circumstances to produce a description covering all aspects of the job under review. This should enable the trainer to see features of the problem in a wider context and thus possibly get a better understanding of the training requirements. Furthermore, provided the job has been legitimized in terms of organizational objectives then a briefly constituted job description should help to avoid time and effort being wasted on peripheral and irrelevant matters. In addition a description of the physical, psychological and social environment in which the job has to be performed may have clear implications for training programme design.

A job specification

This is a detailed statement of the knowledge and the physical and mental activities required to carry out the tasks which constitute the job. A job specification pro forma might have the following headings:

Duty/responsibility and task/task element

A task/task element is a clearly definable activity forming part of a main duty or responsibility.

Knowledge/comprehension

What the person undertaking the task must know or understand in order to carry out the job to an adequate standard and would cover:

Organization/company knowledge Products, departmental structure, policies, procedures, wage and salary structure, etc.

Task knowledge/comprehension 'Headwork' necessary for successful performance, theory the job holder will put into practice, materials used, equipment available, work method, quality, standards, safety, team working, etc.

Skills/abilities

A series of behaviours or acts that form the task and which require practice in order for the task to be performed satisfactorily. The skill or ability may be psycho-motor (manual), social/interpersonal or intellectual.

Attitudes

In this context attitudes refers to the feelings or emotional reaction towards or against something or someone, which may affect job behaviour in a positive or negative way.

An example of a job specification, which has been drawn up along the lines outlined above, is set out in Figure 5.2.

In respect of training the main benefits of drawing up a job specification are:

- It helps to ensure that the training provided is relevant to the real needs of the trainees.
- It gives the trainer a clear picture of all the possible training requirements, including those items that might have been ignored.
- It can be used as a checklist for identifying specific individual training needs.
- It can be an invaluable aid to the trainer when he is looking to identify an appropriate method of training for a particular task or task element.

The derivation of the essential knowledge, skills and attitudes necessary for the effective performance of specific tasks/task elements is a difficult undertaking. Leaving aside certain statutory knowledge or skill requirements the trainer would normally rely on logical or rational inferences based on one or a combination of the following sources of evidence:

- The actual nature of the work involved or as it is synthesized or described in a technical/procedural manual.
- The physical, social and psychological conditions under which the tasks/ task elements are, or are intended to be, carried out.
- Recommendations emerging from some form of investigation coming out of either the reactive or proactive routes into training.
- Reports from job holders and their immediate superiors about the perceived difficulties and distastes of performing the tasks/task elements.

Title: Representative Sales

Department: Sales

Function: To increase the profitable sales of company products to potential customers in the area

Reports to: Field Sales Executive

Duties and responsibilities:

1. To plan work
2. To make sales to. . .
3. To send in orders
4. To seek new business/customers
5. To assess competitor activity
6. To carry out various analytical tests
7. To liaise with company personnel
8. To assist with deliveries
9. To deal with certain financial matters
10. To deal with complaints and queries
11. To attend various meetings and courses
12. To keep abreast of all developments and up-to-date

Task/Task element	Knowledge	Skill	Attitude
1. To plan work			
1.1 To make cycle plan	Square number and company breakdown of area; location and availability of customers; customer records; location of potential customers; market days and early closing days; sales targets and budgets	Time estimation Map reading Record keeping	Must value the relationship between planned (efficient) activity and profitability
1.2 To use telephone to sell, and to book and cancel appointments	Telephone service and costs; customers' telephone number; secretaries/ receptionists' names. (All record cards must be complete at all times.) Most suitable times for telephone bookings	Telephone techniques Listening technique	
1.3 To write letters to book appointments	Letter construction Company procedures	Letter writing	
1.4 To use diary to record appointments and work schedule	Diary record system		

Figure 5.2 Extract from job specification drawn up by the Chemical and Allied Products Industry Training Board

- Personnel records, including performance appraisals, leaving interview reports, etc, that highlight why present and past job holders are, or were, dissatisfied with, or failed on, the job tasks/task elements in question.

The job specification may also include an analysis of the competences relevant to a particular position in order to identify the skill, knowledge and attitudinal elements that make up the competency.

FUNCTIONAL ANALYSIS

Functional analysis has been defined by Lloyd and Cook (1993) as a 'technique for arranging a hierarchy of functions so that you can best describe an occupational area from its overall purpose down to the individual contributions needed for the fulfilment of that purpose'. This brings together all of the interactions that take place between work, workers and the organization. Therefore such an analysis involves input and commitment from staff at all levels to ensure that every job and each task within it are related to the ultimate purpose or function of the organization as a whole. It is another way of arriving at a job description.

This form of analysis is very much a 'top down' approach and should begin by establishing what the organization's function or key purpose is. For example the key purpose of an electrical manufacturing company might be 'Supply a range of domestic electrical kitchen products to meet current and estimated future needs'. The next stage in the analysis would be to identify all of the different occupations within the organization. These could include sales, manufacturing, distribution, after-sales service, finance etc., all of which should be linked to the organization's key purpose by a key purpose of their own. For example, the key purpose of the distribution department might be – 'Co-ordinate and plan the dispatch of products to retail outlets to enable them to respond promptly to customer needs'. Further down the line, individuals will have a key purpose for each of their key roles and functions. For example, a packer in the distribution department could have a key purpose of 'Protect electrical goods with pre-formed polystyrene packaging to prevent damage in transit'.

As each function or job is analysed, its main components can be grouped together into Units which can be broken down further into Elements which relate very closely to actual work practices.

Having established the structure of the key roles, the analysis can be taken further to identify the scope of the tasks which is described in terms of Range Statements. These statements list the different conditions which might apply to the performance of a task. For example, the packer described earlier may have to use different types of protective material for a range of different items such as toasters, microwave ovens, washing machines etc. In order to ensure that the task is done properly a set of performance criteria are identified which list what is expected in the way of competent performance. Again, in the example of the packer, it would be expected that there would be reference to the appropriate pre-formed material being selected, where protective material is located in or around the equipment etc.

The process of breaking down a key role or function into its component parts is likely to draw upon a number of analytical techniques. At the outset, brainstorming can be used to define key purposes. As the analysis becomes more detailed then some form of hierarchical task analysis or procedural analysis are likely to be of use. Both of these techniques are described in the following pages.

Hierarchical task analysis

Hierarchical task analysis is a technique developed by Annett and Duncan (1967) which has the advantage of being applicable to a wide range of jobs. It is a process by which tasks can be broken down into operations and sub-operations and presented in a format which resembles a family tree of all the duties, tasks and sub-tasks that make up a job or a main task within it (Figure 5.3).

It is not crucial to use the same terminology used in Figure 5.3, the important factor here is to understand the concept of breaking down tasks level by level so that the operations which make it up can be identified clearly. The example at Figure 5.4 illustrates the value and flexibility of using this technique.

It is noticeable that all of the words used to describe the operations at each level of the hierarchy are 'behavioural'; that is, they describe what the operator actually does rather than give a general heading for the activity. The description 'Change engine oil' is of far more use than 'Engine oil'. While it is accepted that in this instance 'Engine oil' could give a clear idea of what is required, it is good practice always to use verbs so that there is no chance of confusion.

For example, in this partial analysis of a clerical task a number of questions need to be asked.

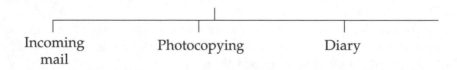

What is actually done with the 'incoming mail'? Is it opened? Sorted? Filed? Is it replied to or are draft replies prepared? Does the 'photocopying' have to be done? Sent? Collected? Checked?, etc. It is not difficult to imagine the confusion that could be caused for other members of the training team if one of its number analyses a task in this way.

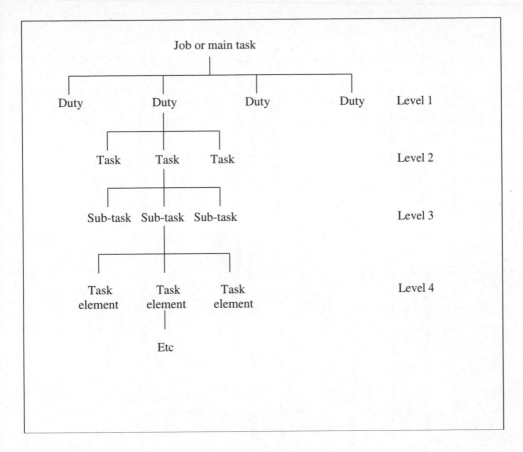

Figure 5.3   Family tree or hierarchy of tasks

Another feature of the hierarchy is that activities can be arranged sequentially when it is needed. The analysis of changing engine oil (Figure 5.4) provides a suggested sequence in which the tasks are carried out.

Hierarchical task analysis is valuable for the trainer because it can present the job in its entirety, it can give a picture of the simplicity or complexity of the job, it helps to identify tasks and jobs which overlap (e.g. a number of tasks and more than one job may involve operating a photocopier) and because tasks can be presented sequentially it provides an aid to the learning process without reference to the principles of learning.

A problem which trainers have encountered in using this technique is knowing when to stop analysing. It has been envisaged that tasks could be analysed down the levels ad infinitum. In many cases it becomes obvious when to stop and it is not unusual to see some tasks which do not have to be analysed further than sub-task level while others need more in-depth treatment. It is useful in these instances to 'rule off' or to indicate in some other way that the

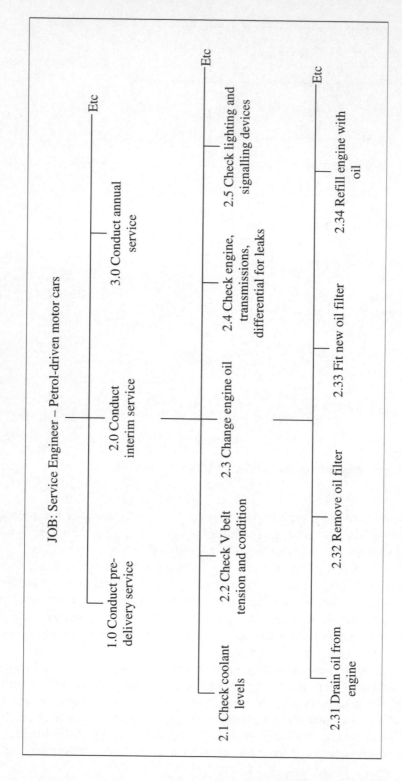

Figure 5.4 Example of hierarchical task analysis

analysis is complete. This overcomes the problem which might arise later of not knowing whether that part of the analysis has been finished.

Apart from the detail contained in the hierarchical diagram, it is quite likely that a number of supplementary notes and observations will be made. In order to avoid cluttering the diagram and causing confusion, notes can be kept as separate documents and numbers or some other form of coding can be used on the diagram as a reference. This information could include references to operating manuals, to legislation, to job aids, to other forms of analysis, etc.

Annett and Duncan suggest two criteria to judge how far the analysis should go. Each operation should be looked at in terms of:

- What is the probability *without* training of inadequate performance?
- What would be the costs to the system of inadequate performance?

The probability of failure on each performance or operation is represented by P and the cost of inadequate performance is represented by C. The decision is made by examining the criteria in terms of P × C and when the outcome is considered to be unacceptable then the analysis should continue.

Procedural analysis

It has been shown how hierarchical task analysis can indicate the sequence of tasks and sub-tasks when those tasks are ordered serially. However, not all tasks follow a serial pattern and there are points within the hierarchy when the trainer may need to continue the analysis in a different format. This happens when there is no predetermined sequence and when the job holder is faced with circumstances which involve decision making which could result in any of a number of options being taken. The algorithm or decision tree has been found to be a useful way of recording this data. The example at Figure 5.5 illustrates this technique.

The technique can be extended to apply to procedures where there is more than one person involved in the operation. For example, in a production process an item may be passed through a number of operators before it is complete. This could involve finishers, checkers, etc. In the same way documents can be handled by a number of people before the procedure has been completed. Using the decision tree, links can be made between the work of different operators which might help to reveal problem areas in the procedure, e.g. too many links in the chain rather than performance problems on the part of the individual or individuals. An example of how jobs can be linked is shown in an extract from a decision tree in Figure 5.6.

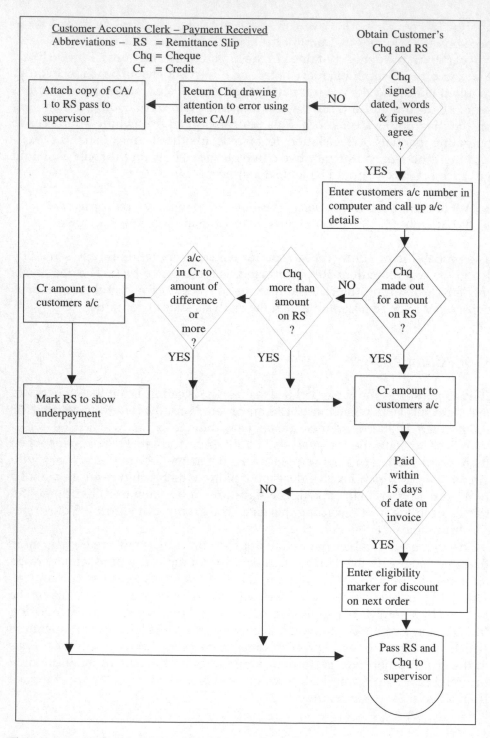

Figure 5.5 Example of an algorithm or decision tree

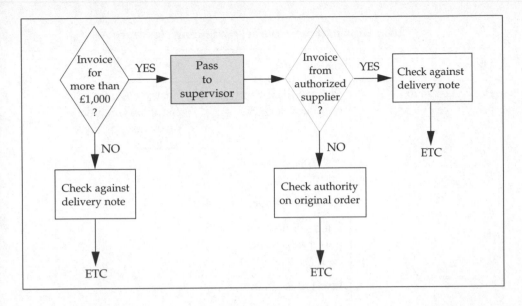

Figure 5.6   Example of algorithm/decision tree showing link between jobs

Key points analysis

This form of analysis is suitable for straightforward jobs and simple tasks for which no great amount of time needs to be spent on training. The outcome of such an analysis could be a simple job aid for the job holder or a guide for consumers similar to those issued with self-assembly products.

The analysis focuses on three main aspects of a task – the sequence or stages in which it is performed, the instructions which describe how the task is done and the key points which have to be emphasized so that the operator does not make mistakes. All of this information can be presented in the form of a chart as shown in Figure 5.7.

Faults analysis

Faults analysis could be used as part of a more detailed form of analysis or it could be used in its own right when the trainer is operating in a reactive mode in response to investigating performance problems as a result of feedback on quality control, customer complaints, etc.

In the first of these two approaches the trainer is usually concerned with analysing where problem areas are likely to occur, what the causes are likely to be, what might be the consequences of error and how the faults can be prevented. In this respect the trainer is being proactive, up to a point, and

Task: How to wrap a parcel containing glassware		
Stage	Instructions	Key points
Pack glass item in protective cylinder	Place cylinder upright on a firm surface	Ensure cylinder is big enough to include sufficient polystyrene packing
	Seal top with card insert	
	Reverse cylinder	
	Put 5 cm layer of polystyrene chips in base	
	Insert glass item	
	Fill around and over glass item	Make sure adequate packing is placed around the item
	Seal with card insert	
Wrap in brown paper	Place sheet of paper on table	
etc		

Figure 5.7 Example of key points analysis

Symptom	Cause	Remedy	Preventive measure
Brakes pull to one side	Soft tyre on one side	Check pressure and adjust	Check and adjust pressure weekly and before long journeys
	Worn or contaminated brake linings	Overhaul brakes	Ensure vehicle is serviced regularly

Figure 5.8 Example of faults specification

subsequently will be able to build into any job aids, training guides or lesson notes as indicators which will give advance warning to the trainees of possible problems, the symptoms of the problem and the appropriate action to take or what to do to prevent it from happening. This might be presented in the form of a faults specification as either a table or as a decision tree or algorithm.

A number of motoring manuals contain a form of faults specification as a self-help guide to motorists (Figure 5.8).

DIF (difficulty, importance, frequency) analysis

This form of analysis helps the trainer to decide between the 'need to know' and the 'nice to know' content of training. In its simple form (Figure 5.9) it could be used to help to decide how far one should continue with the hierarchical task analysis.

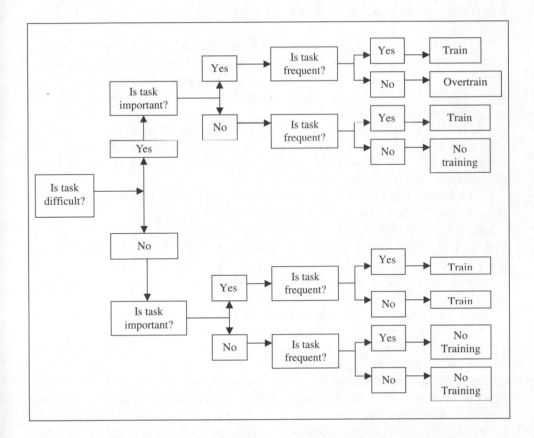

Figure 5.9 Example of DIF (difficulty, importance, frequency) analysis

It can be seen from the diagram that there are three criteria by which the decision to train is made – the level of difficulty of the task, the importance which is placed on it and the frequency with which it is performed. The diagram shows that when a task is difficult, important and performed frequently then training must be given. By contrast, when a task is not difficult, not important and performed infrequently then there is no need to train because it is quite likely that it can be learned while doing the job. One task which is worthy of note, is the task which is difficult, important but not performed frequently. The diagram indicates that in these circumstances the trainee should be over-trained. This does not suggest an unnecessary amount of training which one might associate with over-training. In this case it indicates that because the task is performed infrequently, the trainee must be trained to such a level in terms of skill or knowledge retention that there is little chance of under-performance when the event occurs. Emergency procedures would fall into this category.

Naturally, not every task needs to be measured against these criteria. In many cases the 'train' or 'no training' decision is clear. DIF analysis is a useful tool when the decisions are difficult to make and represents an approach for the trainer rather than a set of rules.

The DIF analysis technique can be enhanced by building in different degrees of difficulty, importance and frequency and by introducing levels of training which give, for each task, an indication of the priority and the standard to be achieved. Figure 5.10 provides an example which has been developed from the basic model.

The levels of training shown in Figure 5.10 are shown on a scale of 1–5.

Level 1 indicates a very high priority for training to a standard which will ensure that a high level of skill and knowledge is retained without the job being done frequently. In effect this is 'over-training'.

Level 2 sets a high priority for training to a standard of competence that will ensure that the task can be done without further training.

Level 3, being the mid point of the scale, sets the priority level at average and to a standard which will ensure that the task is done efficiently. Further training or practice would be required to enhance performance.

Level 4 sets a low priority for training at a standard which provides no more than a basis for on-job training and practice.

Level 5 indicates that no formal training is required and that the task should be easy to learn whilst doing the job.

One of the problems which the trainer encounters in applying this form of DIF analysis is deciding how difficult tasks are and their relative levels of importance. Job holders and their supervisors often see the job from different perspectives and there is always the tendency for all job holders to enhance the importance of their jobs.

The degree of importance which is attributed to any particular job or task needs to be measured against specific criteria; these might include danger to

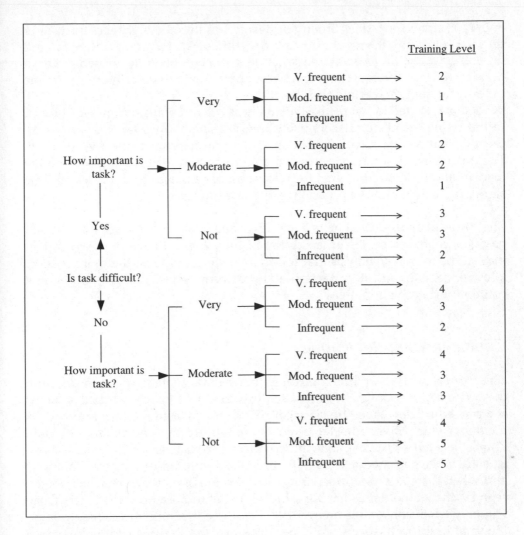

Figure 5.10   Example of DIF analysis and levels of training

life, costs of failure to the organization, etc. Care has to be exercised in assessing level of difficulty because the skilled, long-serving operator could have forgotten how difficult the tasks were for him to learn. Similarly, some job holders may feel that it is a reflection on their performance if they admit that a task is difficult or that they do not do it. Sometimes the trainer will have to apply considerable skill in questioning to assess tasks at the correct level and continually focus on 'what do you think a newcomer to the job would find difficult?' The degrees of difficulty, importance and frequency also need to be decided carefully by the trainer. There is no set scale which can be applied to all situations. Figure 5.9 indicates that difficulty is looked at in terms of 'Yes' and 'No'; either the task is difficult or it isn't. In some circumstances the trainer may wish to show the task as being 'very difficult', 'of average difficulty' and 'of no difficulty'. In looking at frequency, a three-point scale is used – 'very', 'moderate' and 'infrequent'. It might be appropriate to describe this variable in terms of 'daily', 'weekly' and 'less than. . .'

The data needed to complete a DIF analysis can be obtained from job holders, recent trainees and supervisors using interviews and questionnaires. Some of the information may have been obtained at an earlier stage in the investigation. The outcome is that the trainer is in a better position to make decisions on the content and design of training, the allocation of resources to priorities and the standards which must be set as a target for training.

The forms of analysis that have been described in the first part of this chapter have concentrated on the organization of the job and the tasks of which it is made. The forms of analysis that follow will concentrate on the more specific knowledge, skills and attitudes needed to perform the tasks and the subsequent content of training initiatives.

Critical incident technique

This form of analysis or technique for gathering information can be used within the process of most of the forms of analysis that have been described so far. It is a procedure developed by Flanagan (1954) for collecting information about incidents which have proved to be critical to the effective performance of a job. That is, incidents that have contributed directly to success or failure. It has been a useful tool when conducting a DIF (difficulty, importance, frequency) analysis and when there is a need to separate a large number of activities which are all seen by the job holder as having a high level of importance. It is particularly valuable when constraints on training time force the trainer to concentrate on the vital or critical aspects of job performance. Similarly, it is of value when studying tasks that are not performed frequently, such as emergency proce-dures, or which cannot be observed directly because of physical constraints or lack of access to the job environment, such as working in a confined space.

Information can best be collected by individual and group interviews. A pre-formatted response sheet might also be used but this could prove difficult if the trainer does not have sufficient knowledge of the job. Using a tape recorder during interview sessions ensures that the flow of description is not inhibited by the trainer trying to make copious notes. Those participating should be asked to describe incidents which have resulted in success or failure in achieving job objectives, to place these incidents into a context and to relate precisely what they did to bring about the successful or unsuccessful outcome. For example, the failure to ask probing questions at a critical point in a disciplinary interview could lead to problems with industrial relations.

Similarly, failure to check a replacement part number for a piece of sensitive equipment could lead to costly damage. On the more positive side, being alert to the need to ask probing questions and to check part numbers could be seen as critical for a successful outcome. It follows that there is likely to be a natural reluctance on the part of individuals to 'confess' to the remainder of the group, or in private, that they have made bad mistakes. Therefore, confidentiality must be guaranteed for all participants.

Once the information has been gathered it can be categorized as appropriate to the needs of the study and checklists can be produced for further investigation. However, the categorization of all data based on anecdotal experience is liable to be subjective to a greater or lesser degree and it is important that trainers are in agreement over their approach, especially as they will need to record and categorize a large number of incidents in order to gain a clear picture of the job that they are analysing.

Repertory grid technique

This form of analysis or technique is similar to the critical incident technique in that it examines and compares good with poor performance. The repertory grid technique can be used in a number of ways. These include:

- Identifying training needs.
- Evaluating the success of training courses.
- Exploring management's opinion of the training function.
- Examining the marketing of training products and services.

The technique is based on a system which examines what have been called *personal constructs* or ways in which we view the world. The repertory grid is a method in which these constructs can be drawn out. As with the critical incident technique, the interview is the tool by which the trainer obtains the information to build up the grid. However, the interview is much more highly structured and interviewers need to be well-trained in order to avoid the bias that could be placed unwittingly on the responses given by the interviewees. This technique is particularly useful in probing the areas of interpersonal skills and, unlike some other techniques, a considerable amount of information can be gathered from a small number of people.

Interviewees are asked to think carefully of aspects of job performance which are referred to as *elements*. Basically the elements chosen should depend on the purpose of the study or project being undertaken. However, beyond this general criterion, there are several guidelines for selecting specific elements:

- Use objects, people, events or activities and make them as discrete as possible.

- Do not mix classes of elements; objects, people, events or activities should not be muddled up.
- Do not have an element as a part or sub-set of another element, e.g. tea as one element and darjeeling tea as another element.
- Avoid elements that are evaluative or might be construed in an evaluative way, e.g. involvement, controlling, etc.
- Do not use abstract nouns, e.g. 'the perfect boss'.

The elements for a training manager could be the trainers or instructors for whom he or she is responsible. In order to examine the nature of good and poor performance as an instructor or tutor, the following procedure should be followed with the tutors:

- Write the name of each instructor or tutor on a card and arrange the cards into two piles. One pile should contain the names of those who are good at their job and the other pile should consist of those who are not as good or poor at their job.
- Two names are selected from the 'good' pile and one name from the 'poor/ bad' pile so that comparisons can be made between them. First, those who have been described as good are compared for similarities and then they are compared with the less able performer for differences.
- Having noted the differences the next stage is what is called *laddering*. This involves picking out specific behaviours which are important to the job in the eyes of the interviewee and probing each one for detailed information. This will identify the key behaviours which contribute to good performance. This stage is vital if we are to avoid vague statements which cannot be used for any practical purpose.

An example of probing might follow this pattern:

One of the differences between the good performer and the bad performer is given as their ability to deal with individual learning problems. The interviewer can then probe this answer and subsequent responses by asking such questions as – How can you tell that they are good at dealing with these problems? Are there any other problems that they can identify in the same way? etc.

- Replace the cards into their respective piles and repeat the process. It does not matter if some of the names selected are the same as before.

The area contrasts between tutors can then be probed in more depth by interviews with the training manager to consider how and why these contrasts have come about.

KNOWLEDGE AND TOPIC ANALYSIS

In its simplest form, knowledge analysis involves supplying greater detail about the knowledge items in the job specification. This additional information may need to be presented in the form of notes, diagrams, maps, photographs, samples, procedural sequences, etc.

A more complex form of knowledge analysis is that of topic analysis which, in addition to factual information, covers comprehension and intellectual skill. A variant of topic analysis has been described by Davies (1971). In this analysis, a topic is first broken down into its smallest constituent parts or elements and these are then set out in a hierarchical form. It is important to limit the topic and to try to ensure that it is as self-contained as possible.

Davies refers to the elements making up a topic as 'rules'. A rule is basically 'a statement of generality, a definition, a factor, an item of information'. He suggests that to identify the rules, which form the building blocks of a topic, the analyst should ask the following questions:

- What does the analyst expect the trainee to do to demonstrate that he has learned the topic?
- What questions does the analyst expect the trainee to answer?
- What tasks, procedures and techniques does the analyst expect the trainee to perform, and to what standard of performance?
- What discriminations does the analyst expect and in what terms does he or she expect these discriminations to be made?
- What total changes in behaviour are expected and how will they be observed and measured?

In addition, Davies emphasizes the importance of ensuring that the rules are carefully written and sequenced and that:

- They comprise only a single factor or idea.
- They are composed at the same level of generality as preceding rules.
- They take the form of simple, core sentences.
- They avoid negative forms, qualifications and conjunctions.
- They contain only one active verb.
- They are critical and essential to performing the task.

Every effort should be made to ensure that the rules follow a logical and natural sequence, each rule leading on to the next in an easily understandable way. Davies points out that the traditional 'laws' of sequence should be borne in mind when arranging the order which the rules should take, i.e.:

- Proceed from known to unknown.
- Proceed from the simple to the complex.

- Proceed from the concrete to the abstract.
- Proceed from observation to reasoning.
- Proceed from a whole view to a more detailed view to a whole view.

Wherever possible rules should be arranged so they dovetail – 'a word, topic or a concept introduced in one rule, is built on or expanded upon in the next'.

A more detailed coverage of topic analysis has been described by Romiszowski (1981). He elaborates on the notion of categorizing and arranging topic elements by reference to the work of Bloom (1956) and Gagné (1965). The former drew up a taxonomy of educational objectives in the cognitive or thinking domain ranging from knowledge objectives (e.g. knows common terms, facts, basic concepts, etc) through comprehension, application, analysis, synthesis to evaluation, e.g. judging the adequacy with which conclusions are supported by data, etc. Further mention will be made of Bloom's taxonomy in Chapter 6 when the subject of training objectives is examined.

The notions of learning hierarchies and learning prerequisites described by Gagné (1977) also have a bearing on topic analysis. First of all he suggests that there are five varieties of learning (Figure 5.11).

Gagné maintains that when a learning outcome or capability has been clearly described and categorized it is then possible to undertake a form of learning analysis which should identify 'the prerequisites for the learning of the capability represented by the task description'. By prerequisite Gagné means 'a capability of prior learning which is incorporated into new learning'. For example to learn Pythagoras' Theorem in geometry would necessitate that the learner had already acquired an understanding of and facility with more basic rules and concepts, e.g. right angles, square roots, etc. Generally speaking, in terms of intellectual capability, within a topic or subject area higher levels of learning cannot be fully mastered unless relevant lower level forms of learning have already taken place. In other words, in order to learn a designated topic it may be necessary to acquire a hierarchy of prerequisites related specifically to that topic.

Finally, it must be emphasized that because topic analysis can be extremely time-consuming then all the knowledge/intellectual features set out in the job specification should not be looked at in this kind of depth. Rather, it is a form of analysis that would, in practice, take place after the areas of deficiencies in knowledge and intellectual skill of the target population had been identified. Topic analysis could then be employed to determine more precisely the training need or content by continuing the target population analysis to a greater level of detail, so that the task elements or information elements that do not need to be taught can be identified.

Capability (learning outcome)	Examples of performance made possible

Intellectual skill
   Discrimination
   Concrete concept
	Demonstrating symbol use, as in the following:
	   Distinguishing printed m's and n's
	   Identifying the spatial relation 'underneath';
	     identifying a 'side' of an object

Defined concept rule	Classifying a 'family', using a definition Demonstrating the agreement in number of subject and verb in sentences

Higher-order rule	Generating a rule for predicting the size of
	   an image, given the distance of a light
	   source and the curvature of a lens

Cognitive strategy	Using an efficient method for recalling names;
	   originating a solution for the problem of
	   conserving gasoline

Verbal information	Stating the provisions of the first Amendment to US Constitution
Motor skill	Printing the letter R Skating a figure eight
Attitude	Choosing to listen to classical music

Reproduced with permission from *The Conditions of Learning* by Robert Gagné, copyright © 1977 by Holt, Rinehart and Wilson Inc., reprinted by permission of the publisher.

Figure 5.11 Five major categories of learned capabilities, including subordinate types, and examples of each (Gagné, 1977)

MANUAL SKILLS ANALYSIS

This form of analysis is used to examine those tasks which involve a high degree of manual dexterity and perception. It has a wide range of application and could be used to analyse the skills used, for example, by a lathe operator, a word-processor operator or someone working in the crafts such as weaving, pottery, etc. In these skills the analyst would observe and record the movements of the hands, the fingers, the eyes and other senses. Examples of the use of the senses in the practice of skills include taste for wine connoisseurs, hearing for musicians, touch for pastry cooks to gauge the consistency of dough, etc. The concept of dexterity can be extended to include the use of the feet. The operator of a crawler crane is likely, in some of the manoeuvres he has to perform, to use hands and feet to drive and to operate the gib, vision to gauge the position of

Task: Cut timber to size					
Task element	Left hand	Right hand	Vision	Other senses	Comments
Select piece of timber	Reach to pile of prepared timber, grasp with 1, 2, 3, 4 and T and place on top of bench		Confirm timber not damaged or warped	Touch – either hand to confirm timber	Unaccepted timber placed on reject pile is smooth
Measure and mark timber	Grasp measure 1, 2, 3, 4 on top T underneath and place on timber	Grasp pencil 1, 2 and T and mark timber at appropriate length	Check measure placed at end of timber, identify specified distance on measure. Confirm pencil mark on correct position		
Place saw in position to cut timber etc	Palm on flat surface of timber	Grasp saw 2, 3, 4 and T around hand grip. 1 along side of handgrip pointing forward. Place saw on pencil mark	Confirm saw in correct position		

Note: T = thumb; 1, 2, 3, 4 = fingers

Figure 5.12   Example of manual skills analysis

the gib and attachments such as buckets or hooks, the vision to look out for signals from those guiding operations, hearing to listen for the note of the engine, etc.

All of these movements and sensory functions can be recorded in a tabular format the layout of which will depend on the skills which have to be analysed. The analysis of a carpenter's skill shown at Figure 5.12 is presented purely as an illustration of how the technique can be used and is not taken from any training document.

SOCIAL SKILLS ANALYSIS

In examining interpersonal or social skills it may be necessary to undertake some form of behaviour analysis. This involves classifying on-going social interactions into discrete oral and non-verbal units or elements. The purpose of this type of analysis is to identify those behaviours that constitute effective and ineffective performance in particular social situations. Rackham and Morgan (1977) describe a methodology for arriving at such critical behaviours.

The application of their methodology begins by developing a behaviour analysis system which is appropriate to the social situation that is being examined. A typical list of categories which might form the basis of such a system is set out in Figure 5.13. However, it should be noted that the non-verbal categories are not included in Rackham and Morgan's list. There then need to be developed the criteria or measures that could be used to pinpoint individuals in that social situation whose performances are regarded either as effective or ineffective. It is then possible to identify and to observe particular individuals who are seen as high and low performers when measured against the criteria. The behaviour analysis schema can be used either to record or to describe the frequency of incidence of the different behaviours. From this the critical behavioural dimensions, that help to distinguish high and low performers, can be identified. For example Rackham and Carlisle (1978) identify the behaviours that characterize skilled negotiators as being: behaviour labelling, testing understanding, summarizing, seeking information, feelings commentary, etc. By contrast the less skilled or average negotiator tends to use: irritators, counter proposals, defend/attack spirals.

The one-to-one or group situations in which the above type of analysis might be applicable include: interviewing – selection, discipline, appraisal, counselling; coaching and training (including telephone sales); group problem-solving; team negotiation; chairing meetings.

ANALYSIS OF THE TARGET POPULATION

There are basically three phases of this form of analysis:

1. Deciding who should constitute the target population, i.e. trainees who may be drawn from inside and from outside the organization.
2. Determining the levels of knowledge and skill together with the attitudes of the target population prior to their entry to the training programme.
3. Identifying any characteristics of the target population, e.g. age, experience, intelligence level, etc, that might have a bearing on how the training should be conducted.

This section will concentrate on phases 1 and 2. Phase 3 is more appropriately covered in Chapter 7 that deals with learning principles and conditions.

Phase 1 follows on fairly naturally from either the proactive or reactive route into training. Normally it should take place after some form of job analysis/

Behaviour category Verbal behaviour	Description
Proposing	Puts forward an idea or a course of action as a definite statement or announcement, i.e. 'We must. . .' 'We should. . .'
Suggesting	Similar to proposing but tentative and expressed as a question, e.g. 'May I suggest. . .' 'Could we consider. . .'
Seeking proposals/suggestions	Inviting other participants to contribute
Building	Extends, builds on or adds to a proposal or suggestion
Supporting	Involves a clear declaration of support or agreement with another individual's views or opinions
Seeking clarification	Requesting that there is a recap of a previous contribution in order to check understanding
Seeking information	Seeks facts, opinions or classification of another person through questioning
Summarizing	Summarizing or restating in a succinct form the content of a previous discussion or consideration
Giving information	Offering facts, opinions or classification to others
Bringing in	A positive effort to involve another individual
Feelings commentary	Expressing feelings about what is taking place in the here and now
Disagreeing	Flat declaration of disagreement, difference of opinion or criticism of another person's views
Defending/attacking	Attacks another person or defends own position – often has emotional overtones

Blocking	Raises an objection to or places a block in the path of a proposal without offering an alternative
Shutting out	Excludes or attempts to exclude another person by interrupting, talking over, or ignoring them
Difficulty stating	Pointing out the snags associated with another person's proposal or suggestion – not actually a disagreement
Behaviour category Non-verbal	Description
Body contact	Caressing/stroking – touching – greeting/ farewell contacts
Proximity and positioning	Distance at which people sit or stand from each other – give clues to the degree of intimacy
Posture	Physical position – slumping or inactiveness
Facial and gestural movements	Hand movements, facial expressions – grimacing, etc. Attitude or emotion indicator
Gaze direction	Eye contact – used to establish level of intimacy

Figure 5.13 Categories of behaviour (after Rackham and Morgan, 1977; and Argyle, 1969)

synthesis has been completed and before any of the in-depth analyses described above, e.g. DIF, skills analysis, topic analysis, have been carried out. The criteria used for the selection of the target population should be based on clearly defined and rationally determined factors. For instance, if the trainees come to training via the processes of personnel selection, transfer or promotion then they should have been matched successfully against a personnel specification. This is an interpretation of the job description, job specification, other informa-tion emerging from the job analysis or synthesis and/or additional personnel data, in terms of the kind of person suitable to perform the job or tasks in question when given appropriate training.

The additional personnel data referred to might be obtained from existing personnel and training records, from specially commissioned in-house research, or from a review of previous intra- and inter-organizational personnel or training research. It is common in selection for the qualities, attitudes, experience, attainments, etc on the personnel specification to be listed under two headings 'essential' and 'desirable'. Those placed under essential are just that! A candidate would have to be rejected if he or she failed to meet just one of these essential requirements. Other requirements would have to be regarded as 'nice to have' and as desirable only. The relationship between job analysis/synthesis, job description, job specification, other data and the personnel specification is shown in Figure 5.14.

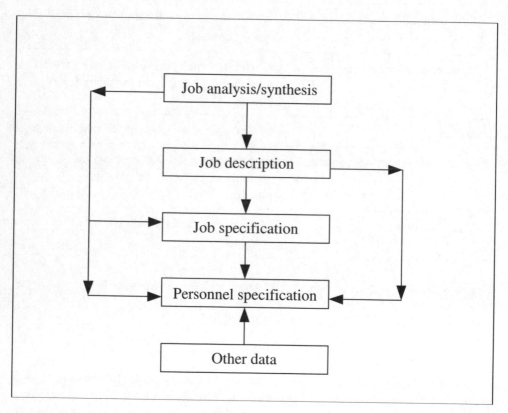

Figure 5.14 The relationship between personnel specification and other processes, documents and sources

It must be appreciated that a 'full blown' personnel specification may not always be necessary and, in some situations, even undesirable. Nevertheless where new forms of training are being established it is extremely important for those responsible for selecting the target population to have defined very clearly the minimum entry requirements in terms of intelligence, previous attainments, experience, current levels of skill, basic aptitudes, etc, otherwise subsequent training efforts may go badly wrong.

To conclude this first aspect of phase 1, it is critical for trainees to understand that a personnel or 'entry level' specification is unlikely to be 'cast in stone' and may depend on the supply and demand, internally and externally, for particular kinds of people.

In a 'tight', competitive labour market the quality of entrants may be such that they need extensive training to bring them up to the required standards. On the other hand in more favourable conditions training may play a minor or a far more limited role, because those performing the tasks have some, if not all, of the necessary abilities, etc. This example of the interaction between training and other organizational processes illustrates how necessary it is for trainers to maintain a systems perspective throughout the implementation of the systematic approach to training, as emphasized in Chapter 2. Therefore trainers must question any assumptions that they may make about the entry level of the target population because of the 'knock on' effect of other internal or external changes to the organization.

The second aspect of phase 1 is concerned with assessing the potential trainees against the criteria established earlier. The methods of assessment range from those of a fairly general nature, as for instance in performance appraisal, to those of a more objective kind associated with systematic assessment procedures, e.g. psychometric tests of special aptitudes – spatial, mechanical, numerical, etc – for selecting engineering apprentices; assessment devices and methods employed at assessment centres for awarding management traineeships or making promotion decisions.

In the case of some jobs, particularly those that need manual skills and hand–eye co-ordination skills, there may be good reasons, when labour is in short supply, to develop a trainability test. This is a validated test designed to assess whether a job applicant has the potential to reach a satisfactory standard after training.

The applicant is required to perform an appropriate, carefully designed, short task after being given prior instruction. The short task might involve making a simple work item, operating a machine or performing part of a work process. However, as Downs (1985) has emphasized, the 'workpiece' or 'process' must include those critical aspects of the job and those elements which give the trainees difficulty during their training. How successful applicants are on the test is then regarded as a firm indication as to how well they would cope on the actual training programme.

Turning now to phase 2, estimating the training 'gap' is, to a certain extent, a matter of comparing what is set out in the job specification with what the target population has learned already and is competent to perform. It should, or it is very likely to be the case, that, at a general level, information about the target population's competencies will be known already to the alert trainer. For as Romiszowski (1981) points out, the trainer must keep the trainee in mind throughout the process of instructional design. He emphasizes that it is never too early in the process to begin to analyse the characteristics, needs, habits, levels of knowledge or skill, etc of the trainee. Of course, in addition, the knowledge, skills and attitudes that the trainees bring to the training situation may have been identified or determined by what occurred in phase 1, particularly if a clearly defined personnel or 'entry level' specification has been developed.

However, despite the foregoing it may still be necessary to obtain more general supplementary information about the potential trainees. This can be obtained through either questionnaires, surveys, interviews with a sample of the target population and, for internal candidates, discussions with their immediate supervisors or managers or by examining previous training and personnel records.

TRAINING NEEDS/CONTENT ANALYSIS

From the phase 2 target population analysis it should now be possible to isolate those features of the job specification that might comprise the broad content of any subsequent training. However, this content can be further narrowed down by reference to the outcome of a DIF analysis either undertaken earlier or even at this stage, which may indicate that only the KSA associated with some of the tasks or task elements will require the training treatment. The resultant training needs that emerge could be subject to a topic or skills analysis, which might then be used to obtain more specific information about the potential trainees by serving, as suggested at the end of the knowledge/topic analysis section, as the basis for the development of diagnostic procedures or entry tests.

By this stage, if the preceding analyses have been performed effectively, the trainer should have an extremely good idea of what is the real training specification. However, this may still not constitute the ultimate training content. For, as mentioned in Chapter 3, this may be the point at which the trainer and the client review what has emerged to date. In this review consideration should be given to any constraints in cost, time, social or political influences and organizational priorities that might necessitate some selective pruning of the initial plans for training content.

TRAINING CRITERIA AND STANDARDS

Having decided on the training content, and with all the necessary preceding analyses completed, the trainer should now be in a position to tackle one of the most important and vexed issues that has to be faced in adopting the systematic approach to training, namely choosing or developing criteria. These are the dimensions, factors or measures against which a trainee's performance, or the effects or results of that performance, are assessed.

How the trainee performs on certain criteria at certain times will be the means by which the effectiveness of the training effort finally must be judged. Goldstein (1986) claims that the most carefully designed study, which employs all the sophisticated methodology available, will stand or fall on the basis of how adequate the chosen criteria are. Consequently in selecting or developing such criteria the trainer will have to answer several interrelated questions. These include:

- When and why should the assessment/measurement take place?
- How, and against what specific criteria, are training and the subsequent effects of training, i.e. on-job performance and results, going to be assessed?
- In what form should the standards of acceptable training and on-job performance be couched?

To consider the first two questions, the points in the training sequence when criterion choices should be made and the reasons for employing them at these particular junctures are set out in Figure 5.15.

The nature of the actual criteria adopted at different stages in Figure 5.15 sequence will vary. Examples of the types of criterion measures that have been used are:

Knowledge How well can the trainees:

- Retain/recall facts and procedures?
- Recognize and select appropriate procedures?
- Demonstrate analytical abilities and understanding of concepts and principles?

Skills How effectively can the trainees:

- Apply concepts and principles through solving problems, e.g. numerical calculations?
- Perform straightforward procedures, i.e. conform to certain prescribed actions, followed in a particular sequence within a specific time limit?
- Perform physically skilled actions that meet qualitative and quantitative standards? (see below)
- Handle certain sorts of interpersonal and group situations by employing a range of appropriate social behaviours?

Attitudes To what extent have the trainees changed or modified their attitudes as indicated by the actions they take, the behaviour they display or their professed intentions?

Point in the training sequence	Reasons
Pre-training	To form the basis for constructing entry level tests for assessing whether or not potential trainees meet training entry requirements.
	To enable diagnostic tests to be developed that will help to reveal a trainee's pre-training profile of knowledge, skills and attitudes.
	To aid the formulation of terminal and enabling training objectives.
During training	To help in the assessment of trainees at each stage of training to ensure they reach requisite levels and standards on the enabling objectives.
Immediate post-training	To allow a check to be made that all the objectives of the training programme have been realized.
On-job: short to medium term	To assist the trainer to ascertain whether or not, in the short to medium term (one week to one year) the actual or potential performance gap has been closed and that training has transferred credibly to real on-job conditions.
On-job: medium to long term	To help the organization in its assessment of whether or not training is contributing towards meeting its corporate, economic, strategic, social or political goals.

Figure 5.15 Criterion choices at points in training

An attitude may be defined as a predisposition or tendency to behave towards an object, e.g. particular people, or issue, in certain ways based on thoughts and feelings about that object or issue.

Quantitative measures How well can the trainees perform in relation to:

- Units produced per designated time interval?
- Units sold within a specified time period?
- Number of tasks completed, applications processed, etc within prescribed time period?

- Turnover?
- Wastage or time taken to produce items or services?
- Error rates?
- Cost-effectiveness?
- Numbers of new clients taken on?

Qualitative measures How well can the trainees produce items or services in terms of:

- Meeting physical measurement specifications/tolerances?
- Satisfying client needs by minimizing complaints and maximizing positive feedback?
- Enacting or carrying through certain behaviours or procedures?

Some of the criteria will undoubtedly be more closely associated with specific on-job tasks and others with the knowledge, skills and attitudes identified as being necessary for these on-job functions to be performed to the requisite standards. Therefore criteria will change as the trainer moves through the training sequence. However, they always must be connected directly or indirectly to the task/task elements and KSA set out in the job specification and with one another.

Although it is difficult to forge clear links between the various stages, it is an essential enterprise if the systematic approach to training, being advocated in this book, is to have any credibility within organizations. The connection between the job/task and the criterion staging points is illustrated in Figure 5.16.

Thus the criteria that are used at particular stages should depend on what training need is being addressed and at what point in the training cycle it is being considered. If, for example, the training need was concerned with selling a particular service or product, one of the on-job short- to medium-term criteria could be the number sold in a designated period of time, e.g. one-month/three-month/six-month period. The during-training and end-of-course criterion measures might cover product knowledge and comprehension, letter-writing skills, and skilled selling and negotiating behaviours.

In addition to choosing or developing the criteria to be applied at different stages in the training sequence, the trainer also must decide what minimum standards the trainees are expected to achieve on these measures. This process may need to be carried out in liaison with the client, particularly in relation to the immediate post-training and the on-job short- to medium-term criteria.

Furthermore, in choosing or developing criteria and standards, the trainer will need to bear in mind the following issues:

Criterion-referenced and norm-referenced measures Criterion-referenced measures and standards enable trainees' performance to be assessed in some absolute

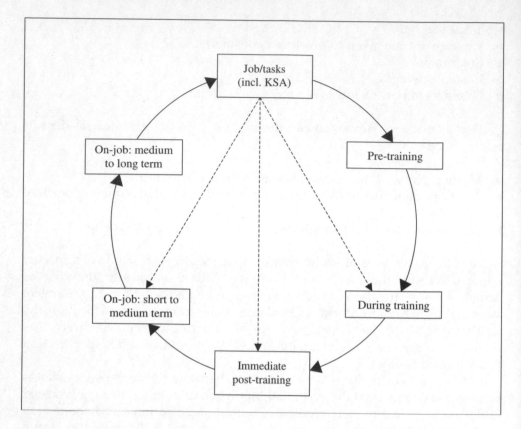

Figure 5.16 Links between job specification and various criterion staging points

sense. The trainees' degree of competence at various stages is judged by how their performance matches these measures and standards. By contrast, norm-referenced measures use the capabilities of other trainees as the standard of comparison as is the case in reporting the results of public examinations. Consequently these kinds of measure and standard usually supply little information about a trainee's specific degree of competence in relation to the task/task elements or KSA in a job specification. The following example illustrates the point:

> Simply knowing that, in a general sense, Frank is a better lathe operator than George, is of little value in organizing and evaluating an improvement programme for George. However, having a clear assessment of George's current performance against absolute criterion measures, e.g. measurement tolerances, etc, would be much more valuable.

From this it can be seen that for training purposes, criterion-referenced measures are infinitely preferable to norm-referenced measures.

Objective and subjective measures An objective criterion is usually expressed in numerical terms like sales figures, production rates, etc. On the other hand, subjective measures rely on the opinions or judgements of an assessor or appraiser regarding the trainee's level of knowledge and skill. At first sight it might appear that objective measures are to be preferred to subjective measures as they would seem to be less prone to contamination and bias. However, the relevance and value of a criterion measure will depend on the purpose for its introduction at certain points in the training cycle. Structured and tutored subjective judgements are often necessary, and more pertinent than objective measures, in assessing how well a trainee has learned certain types of skill such as negotiating, interviewing, etc.

Simulated and actual situations In many off-job training programmes the criteria and the standards in the simulated conditions have to be different from those in the actual working environment. For instance, in relation to criterion measures, training soldiers in small arms proficiency in simulated battlefield conditions would not include as a criterion, for obvious reasons, hits on other trainees or 'volunteers' that might cause death or injury. Similarly, in pilot training actual landings would not be the criterion in the initial phases, rather some index would be developed on the flight deck simulator to indicate safe or unsafe landings.

Even where the criterion in training is the same as in the actual job such as the number of items produced, the standards on the criterion might be lower in the former case. In many situations the trainees would not be expected to reach the same level of performance at the end of training as they would when they had had some experience and were regarded as fully competent.

EVALUATING CRITERIA

Besides being concerned with the standards set on the criteria, the trainer must ensure also that the criteria are adequate in a number of specific ways. They must be relevant, free from contamination, not deficient in any respect and they must be reliable. These requirements have been discussed by Goldstein (1986) and are described briefly below:

Criterion relevance is the degree to which the criteria employed to assess the effectiveness of training during and after the event clearly relate, directly or indirectly, to the relevant knowledge, skills and attitudes, task/task elements and pertinent organizational outcomes, identified through earlier analysis, i.e. job analysis, topic and skills analysis, etc. Figure 5.17 illustrates these relationships:

Thus, for example, the knowledge, skill, attitude and output criteria selected or developed for application during and on completion of training are only pertinent to the extent that they reflect the equivalent components on the tasks

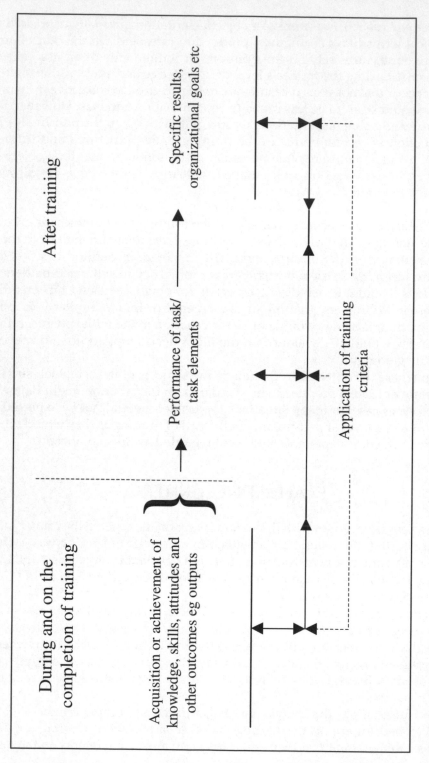

Figure 5.17 Relationships between factors affecting criteria relevance

that need the training treatment. Failure to meet the above conditions of fidelity leads to either criterion deficiency or criterion contamination.

Criterion deficiency is concerned with the extent to which the actual criteria employed at various points 'fall short' of the potentially relevant criteria identified in the training needs assessment. Such a situation may occur for two possible reasons. The training need covered on the training programme, expressed in terms of either knowledge, skill or attitude, is not included in the on-training or on-job criterion construct, or the training need is not included in the training programme at all.

Criterion contamination occurs when extraneous elements or influences are present in the criterion which result in the measure not representing faithfully the factor identified in the training needs analysis. For instance, if a trainee's supervisor knows how well he or she has performed on the training course this may bias, favourably or unfavourably, the supervisor's assessment of the trainee's subsequent on-job performance.

A fundamental requirement of any criterion is reliability. Given the same instrument or means of assessment, *criterion reliability* refers to either how consistent the measure on the criterion is over time, or to the degree of agreement between two or more ostensibly similar methods of assessing the initial position or change on the criterion. For example, in the latter case, poor agreement between two raters making independent judgements of a trainee's performance in a particular skill would indicate low reliability. Low criterion reliability would cast doubt not only on the means of assessment employed but also on the supposed effects of different forms of training treatment or non-treatment.

Training criteria and the methods of assessing a trainee's performance on these criteria will be examined in more depth in Chapter 6 and in Chapter 9. Suffice it to say that criteria must be in the forefront of the trainer's mind from this point onwards because there is a real danger of training 'drift'. It is too easy to allow training curricula to come secondary to, and be attendant on, training methods rather than vice-versa. The danger of succumbing to the flavour of the month, year or decade is only too real for the vulnerable trainer looking to make an impression in an organization that is sceptical about the worth of training.

In this chapter a number of different forms of analysis have been discussed. Each one represents a technique which can help the trainer to examine training needs and training content and subsequently to write training objectives. It is obvious that the likelihood of having to use all of these analyses on one project would be rare indeed. The trainer has to decide upon the most appropriate technique or techniques to obtain the information needed and resist the temptation to over analyse and reach a state of 'analysis paralysis'.

6

Training Objectives

The purpose of a training objective is to state as clearly as possible what trainees are expected to be able to do at the end of their training (or at the end of stages in their training), the conditions under which they will demonstrate their learning and the standards that must be reached to confirm their level of competence. Well-written training objectives can be used as a means to validate and evaluate training, they assist trainers to decide upon method and content of training and they provide trainees with a clear target.

A comparison of the following two examples helps to illustrate the importance of having clear objectives.

1. At the end of training the trainee will be able to saw timber into different lengths.

Working to this objective it is possible that we may conjure up a picture of trainees going forth into lumber forests with chain saws, felling trees and sawing them into suitable lengths for transportation. All of this could well be ideal if the trainees were going to be employed in forestry but if the intention was to train cabinet makers, then the objective has failed in its purpose. The second example might have been more appropriate.

2. Given a tenon saw, mitre block, pencil and ruler, the trainees will be able to cut pieces from a three-metre length of 5 cm x 8 cm timber to any size stated in metres, centimetres and millimetres and to be accurate to within 2 mm.

This is a much clearer guide to what is expected although there is still room for refinement. Example 2 actually allows us to build up an accurate mental picture of the trainees at work.

Before going into detail about the composition, format and presentation of objectives it will be of some benefit to distinguish between different categories of objective used in training.

TRAINING OBJECTIVES

The purpose of training objectives has been explained already; however, the words instructional, learning, behavioural and terminal are often used as prefixes and need to be clarified. The words 'instructional' and 'learning' are alternatives for the word 'training'. The use of the word 'behaviour' is to emphasize the point that the trainees' performance should be described in behavioural terms; that is, described in such a way that an observer can see or has some overt sign to show that they have learned. The words terminal objective are used to indicate that the performance which has been described is what is expected at the end or termination of training and distinguishes between objectives which have to be achieved en route.

Enabling objective

Once a terminal objective has been set it is usually found that it can be broken down into a number of sub-objectives which are called enabling objectives. Achieving the sub-objectives *enables* the trainee to achieve the terminal objective.

Lesson objective

A further breakdown of enabling objectives identifies the learning points which make up the parts of a lesson or training session and are described as lesson objectives.

The example in Figure 6.1 illustrates the points that have been made about training/instructional objectives. It can be seen that terminal, enabling and lesson objectives are arranged in a hierarchy and that all three types of objective can be described as behavioural because they describe the behaviours which trainees have to demonstrate.

This example not only provides the trainer with a clear picture of what trainees are expected to be able to do at the end of their training but it gives an indication of the content of training. However, the information is not complete. There is still a need to know about the conditions in which the tea making will take place and the standard or quality which is expected of the brew.

Terminal objective	Make a pot of tea
Enabling objective	*Identify* and *fill* an electric kettle with cold, fresh water.
Lesson objectives	*Distinguish* the features of a kettle from other kitchen equipment. *Distinguish* between hot and cold water taps. *Operate* a cold water tap. *State* the importance of using fresh water.
Enabling objective	*Boil* a kettle of water.
Lesson objectives	*Identify* and operate an electrical power source. *List* the indicators which show that water has boiled. *State* the safety factors that should be observed when using electricity.
etc.	

Figure 6.1 An example showing terminal, enabling and lesson objectives

STRUCTURE OF OBJECTIVES

The analysis of a complete objective will show that it has three main parts – the performance which trainees are expected to display at the end of their training, the conditions under which they will perform and the standards which they are expected to reach. For ease of use and for easy reference they are usually tabulated in three columns (Figure 6.2).

Performance	Conditions	Standards
Press a pair of trousers	Given: Electric steam iron Ironing board Pair of trousers	Within 10 minutes. Creases to be straight and in correct position. Without damage to fabric.

Figure 6.2 Example of layout of a training objective

Another format is suggested by Romiszowski (1981). He highlights the importance of measuring the criteria or the standards of performance expected by including a column to describe the method of measurement or testing which should be used. In addition, the heading to his columns are statements rather than single words. This gives a flow to the reading of the objective which helps to give it sense (Figure 6.3).

Given the following external conditions	the student will	to the following standard	as measured by the following method

Figure 6.3 Layout of objectives (Romiszowski, 1981)

Occasions will arise when the conditions or standards, or both, are the same for a large number of objectives. For example a bricklayer may use the same tools to learn to build a number of different structures or to apply a variety of building techniques. A safety officer may have to implement safety measures which are all within guidelines or legislation which is documented in a handbook. In both of these cases it could be tiresome, wasteful and confusing if page after page of performance statements are accompanied by repeated descriptions of the same conditions and standards. When this is the case it is often better to state the conditions and standards just once, at the beginning (Figure 6.4).

If the conditions and standards are exactly the same for every performance statement and there are no exceptions to those stated at the beginning, then the conditions and standards columns could be dispensed with completely. This gives the trainer a document which is easier to work with.

A set of objectives is a working tool for the trainer and while they must be clear and accurate in their content, there is some flexibility in their presentation so that those who work from them find them easy to use.

SOURCES OF INFORMATION FOR OBJECTIVES

It can be seen from what has been discussed that a considerable amount of information about jobs, and about the tasks and skills which are contained

---

Gas Central Heating Repair and Maintenance Training

The following Conditions and Standards apply to all objectives except where stated.

Conditions	All training will be conducted in a fully equipped workshop containing the following models of central heating equipment currently being serviced by the Unit: Mark II, Mark IV, Mark IVB, Mark BVI, Mark 2L.
Standards	All maintenance and repair tasks to be carried out following the procedures laid down in the Maintenance Manual G M (Dom).

Performance	Conditions	Standards

Figure 6.4 Alternative form of layout for training objectives

within them, can be gathered from different forms of analysis which will have been undertaken during the previous stages.

The analyses of tasks and skills will have categorized the knowledge, skills and attitudes which the trainee will have to acquire. The breakdown of tasks into sub-tasks and task elements will have indicated the nature of the enabling objectives and lesson objectives which are likely to emerge. Skilled workers and their supervisors will have provided an indication of the standards which are expected and close observation and interviews will have provided full details of the conditions in which the job is performed. Armed with this information the trainer should be able to write detailed and precise objectives.

WRITING PERFORMANCE STATEMENTS

The first step in writing objectives is to identify precisely what the trainee will be expected to do at the end of the training. This is written as a performance statement. Using the information obtained from the analyses of jobs and tasks, three main areas of performance will have been identified – knowledge, skills and attitudes. Behaviour in these three areas can be classified in detail and a listing of appropriate performance verbs can be compiled as a reference and as a form of job aid to help the trainer to compose performance statements.

Knowledge	Memorization	Recall of fact and sources
		Recognition
	Comprehension	Understanding
Skills	Intellectual	Application
		Analysis
		Synthesis
		Evaluation
	Manual	Bodily actions and movements
		Dexterity of hand and eye/hand
		and ear, etc
		Non-verbal behaviour
	Social	Oral and appropriate non-verbal
		behaviour in one-to-one and
		group situations (eg interviews,
		meetings)
Attitudes	Accepting	Respond willingly
	Valuing	Show commitment
	Being receptive	Follow rules and procedures

Figure 6.5 A basic classification of knowledge, skills and attitudes

This will help in the design of training and in the selection of learning strategies. The example in Figure 6.5 illustrates a basic form of such a classification.

More detailed classifications or taxonomies have been developed which have analysed behaviours into what have been described as domains. These are the taxonomies of the cognitive domain (Bloom *et al*, 1954), the affective domain (Krathwohl *et al*, 1964) and the psychomotor domain (Simpson, 1966).

Trainers can draw upon these sources directly, when it is appropriate, or they can use them to develop classifications of their own which are appropriate to the field in which they are working. For example when training is being investigated in a field which involves social skills, a trainer may wish to develop a closely defined set of behaviours relating perhaps to group decision making or to counselling, etc.

The performance statement of an objective should contain a word or a phrase that describes what the trainees are expected to do to demonstrate that they have achieved the objective. For example:

- 'Check the pressure of a tyre'.
- 'Iron a shirt'.
- 'Take and record the body temperature of an adult patient'.

The words 'check', 'iron' and 'take and record' are the action verbs in the performance statements. They indicate clearly how trainees will show what they have learned and it follows that as a test of their learning, trainees could be asked to carry out such actions. In fact, many objectives have this feature that the performance statement itself can be used subsequently as the test item.

However, there are mental activities such as thinking, analysing, etc that are not directly observable and therefore do not lend themselves to performance statements being written as clearly as those described above. To deal with this problem Mager (1973) makes the important distinction between overt and covert performance. Overt performance can be observed directly, e.g. 'Drive a motor car'. Covert performance cannot be observed directly, for example:

- 'Identify bones on a human skeleton'.
- 'Recall the procedure for testing for a gas leak'.
- 'Discriminate between correct and incorrect answers to a test'.

The processes of identifying, recalling and discriminating, which are the main point or intent of their respective objectives or performance statements, function within the individual and therefore an indicator is needed to demonstrate that they are taking place.

The indicator should be included in the performance statement to show what kind of performance is needed. For example:

- 'Identify (by attaching printed labels) bones on a human skeleton'.

The indicator here is the phrase 'by attaching printed labels'. This indicates what overt behaviour the trainees have to demonstrate to show that they are able to 'identify'. Indicators which might be used for the other examples could be:

- 'Recall (by listing in sequence from memory) the procedure for testing a gas leak'.
- 'Discriminate (by ticking correct answers) between correct and incorrect answers to a test'.

On occasions, because the main point or main intent is clearly implied, then only the indicator need be included in the performance statement.

Words which are all too often found in performance statements are 'understand' and 'know'. In such cases, the main point or intent can be obscure, and the questions that need to be asked are 'What does the trainee have to do to demonstrate that they *understand*?' and 'What does the trainee have to do to demonstrate that they *know*?'. Frequently these questions can be answered by the use of words such as 'list', 'state', 'describe' etc.

A performance statement such as, 'Understand the meaning of training', would be clearer if it was written as, 'Define training', or, 'Describe the main stages of the training cycle', depending on what was meant by the word 'understand'.

The performance statement, 'Know how to wire a 13-amp plug', could be interpreted as either, 'Describe how to wire a 13-amp plug', or, 'Wire a 13-amp plug'. The expected outcomes would be quite different depending on the trainer's and the trainee's interpretation.

ESTABLISHING STANDARDS AND DEVELOPING END-OF-TRAINING CRITERIA MEASURES

Having written the performance statement, the next logical step is to decide how it is to be tested. However, trainers can be tempted to ignore this and either come back to it later or place the onus of responsibility for testing on the trainer. It must also be taken into account that in some instances it is not in the organizational culture or perhaps the national culture to test those who have undergone training.

This is often linked with a policy of not reporting on the performance of trainees to their respective departmental heads. When this approach is employed the competence of the trainee has to be taken as an act of faith by everyone concerned and one cannot help but call this approach to question.

During the investigative stages of the process a clear indication of what is expected of the fully competent job holder will have been established with the assistance of supervisors and competent workers. However, it may not be viable to train to such a standard. For example a fully competent and experienced lathe operator may be able to produce items of high quality and in large numbers. It would be wasteful of training time to keep the trainee in training until speed had been built up. It would be more likely that the trainee would be trained to produce items to an acceptable standard in terms of quality and subsequently to develop their skills on-the-job to the standard expected of the experienced worker.

In establishing the criteria, what has to be considered is the minimum acceptable level of performance before the trainee can be allowed to perform the job. This does not suggest that there should be a lowering of standards. If we are training a soldier to operate a mine detector, he would be expected to be 100 per cent accurate before being sent ahead to clear a path for advancing troops.

The criterion measures must be a realistic test of the performance which will indicate that the trainee will be able to transfer successfully the knowledge and skills learned in training to the job situation. Many performance statements indicate very clearly what the test item should be and in some cases can be used, without alteration, as a test question. For example the following performance statements indicate very clearly the test item:

- 'List the benefits of a personal pension policy'.
- 'Discriminate (by placing in two piles) between correctly and incorrectly completed forms'.
- 'Prune a rose bush'.

If criterion measures are not established at this stage there is the possibility that inappropriate tests may be employed. In the example given above, 'Prune a rose bush', one would expect that in the test the trainees would be given a pair of pruning shears and a rose bush which needed to be pruned so that they could demonstrate their skills. If, however, the trainees were given a question in either oral or written form which asked them to 'Describe how to prune a rose bush', there is likely to be some doubt as to whether they might actually be able to do it in practice.

In deciding the criterion measures then, the trainer must consider both the appropriateness of the test and the standard which has to be reached. In many cases the standards will be easy to determine and might include numbers of test items answered correctly, measurements within certain tolerances, time factors, etc. In other cases it will be more difficult to specify and reliance will be placed upon the judgement of the trainers or instructors.

Objectives which relate to interpersonal skills are likely to be measured by the subjective judgements of those involved in the testing and based upon their experience and expectations. When this is the case, one can do little more than to state in the standards column 'To the satisfaction of the trainer-supervisor'. While this may seem something of a hit-and-miss approach, it can be more accurate than might be imagined when those trainers or supervisors have thought out what they are looking for and have agreed some form of checklist of behaviours that they all work to. In fact, studies of inter-rater reliability have shown that a high level of agreement can be achieved with practice.

DEALING WITH ATTITUDES

So far, consideration has been given to objectives which are concerned with knowledge and skills. Objectives which are concerned with attitudes are often found to be more difficult to handle. One of the main reasons for this is that it is difficult to write such an objective within a framework headed performance, conditions and standards. More particularly it is almost impossible, in the short term, to observe and measure whether an attitude has actually changed or developed. What is observed is a behaviour which suggests an attitude and many trainers argue that this is sufficient. For example, if one of the attitudinal objectives for training counter staff in a department store is 'Value all customers as essential to the survival and development of the store', it would be difficult, if not impossible, to measure whether staff did actually have such an attitude.

However, there are a number of aspects of behaviour which could suggest that they do 'value all customers'. These might include helpfulness, courtesy, speedy service, smiling and the employment of other social skills. The trainer, when faced with this kind of situation, often feels that it is something of a dilemma because although staff are demonstrating behaviours which suggest an attitude, underneath they may not have any real concern about customers at all. This should not really be a dilemma; if the customers feel that they are being valued and continue to bring their custom to the store, then in many ways the objective has been achieved. Also, it is believed that when people demonstrate such a behaviour over a period of time, they may find it intrinsically rewarding and, as a result, their attitudes will change to those which the organization desires. Therefore, trainers need to be more concerned with behaviour rather than soul searching to confirm that attitudinal objectives have been achieved.

A further problem with writing objectives for attitudes is that they do not stand alone in the same way as other objectives. Attitude, or the behaviour that reflects attitude, is usually displayed within the context of other objectives. One is not courteous, helpful, caring, etc. in a vacuum. These attitudinal behaviours are related to other performances such as serving a customer, advising a customer on suitability of materials, installing or repairing electrical appliances or receiving a patient. In many ways these behaviours can be seen as standards which are expected within the context of other behaviours even though the assessment of level of competence is likely to be subjective and 'to the satisfaction of the trainer/supervisor'. It has been found that often it is more appropriate to treat attitudinal objectives in this way. The following example of part of an objective indicates how this may be done.

Accounts department training

Performance	**Standard**
Reply to telephone enquiry from a customer relating to an account	Trainee to identify self and department in approved style Give information requested – without error *Trainee to be courteous, helpful and patient in dealing with customer.*

Other aspects of attitudinal development cannot be dealt with as easily as the example given above. In the training of a trainer, for example, one of the objectives may be concerned with the preparation and planning of training sessions or lessons. While the trainee may be able to demonstrate the ability to prepare and to plan, something more may be wanted in attitudinal development, i.e. 'Value the need for thorough preparation and planning'.

In these circumstances one cannot observe the trainee 'valuing' although the process of preparation and planning may be observed. As before, it would be expected, or at least hoped, that in time the trainee would find that preparation and planning has proved to be so important that it would come to be valued. However, while this may be long term and it may be questionable whether it should be listed as an objective, there is a clear need for those who train the trainers to be aware of such objectives. By demonstrating how much they value the need for preparation and planning themselves they can contribute significantly to the attitudes of those whom they are training. In circumstances such as these, there is every reason for listing some categories of attitudinal objectives separately so that the trainers are aware of the attitudes which they may have to display overtly in order to develop the same attitudes in their trainees.

IDENTIFYING THE CONDITIONS

The various forms of analysis which were used to examine tasks and skills will have identified also the conditions in which the jobs are performed. This will provide such information as: the tools, equipment, materials and documents, etc that are used, the physical environment, assistance and supervision given as well as other general working conditions.

If training is to be realistic then consideration has to be given as to how far the conditions of the job should be replicated in training. Obviously, when training is on-job or partially on-job then all or many of the conditions will be replicated. The more realistic that one makes the conditions in training then the more expensive and, possibly, the more time-consuming training becomes. Realism has to be balanced against the critical nature of the performance being trained. There would be no doubt in anyone's mind about the need for investment in complex simulators for the training of airline pilots, particularly for dealing with emergency situations. However, it can be seen that there might not always be a need for telephone networks to train some of the more basic skills in telephone techniques. Some very basic training can be done by just seating two people either side of a screen.

When writing objectives the trainer has to bear in mind the conditions which exist for the job and to decide what the conditions will be for training. It follows that trainers need to be familiar with the job environment either by experience of doing the job or by familiarization visits and attachments.

While replicating the working environment is one important reason for identifying and stating conditions, another reason is linked with testing. When conditions are looked at in detail, it can lead to changing the performance statement completely. The following example illustrates the point. One of the objectives for clerical officers working in an educational environment was stated as:

- 'List the subject passes in other examinations which give exemption from sections of Parts 1, 2 and 3 of the Advanced Certificate'.

The trainees dutifully learned details of subject passes and exemptions upon which they were questioned in exercises and tests during their training. However, upon examining the 'conditions' of their jobs, it was found that they had charts and tables available to which they could refer and advise applicants on their exemptions. Thus the performance statement should have been worded more appropriately along the following lines:

- 'Advise applicants for the Advanced Certificate on exemptions awarded for subject passes in other examinations'.

or

- 'Decide what exemptions should be given to applicants for the Advanced Certificate who have passes in other examinations'.

The conditions statement could then be added

- 'Given: Subject-exemption charts and specimen application forms from applicants'.

This puts quite a different perspective on training for the role of the clerical officer.

Another feature of deciding the conditions for training objectives is uniformity. Not all training takes place in one location. In some large organizations the training may be delivered as courses in geographically dispersed centres or as on-job training. A clear statement of the conditions to be applied in training will ensure greater uniformity. For example, in word-processor training there would be a need to specify what kind of package should be used, the nature of subject matter for dictation or copy typing, the use of technical terms and foreign words, the length of passage, etc.

THE VALUE OF TRAINING OBJECTIVES

From what has been discussed so far it can be seen that there are distinct benefits to be gained from investing time in writing objectives.

- They prevent teaching too much or too little. Too much training is costly and if irrelevant material is included it can be confusing. Too little training results in further performance problems and the cost and trouble of rectifying matters.
- They provide guidelines for course design and are the basis for producing enabling objectives and learning points.

- They clarify for trainers/tutors and for trainees precisely what their goals are in training.
- They provide the basis for measuring the effectiveness of training in terms of the knowledge, skills and attitudes expected of the trainees, the minimum acceptable performance standards and the conditions under which the performance is measured.
- They provide a link between training needs and the training which is delivered so that the training can be validated.
- They provide a first point of reference for any investigation or review of training.

DISSENTING VIEWS ON OBJECTIVES

The time and care invested in writing objectives would seem to be a logical and a common-sense approach to training and few would fail to agree that, at face value, training could only benefit from having specific objectives on which to base the design of training.

Those who were amongst the first to adopt a systematic approach to training found immediate benefits from establishing precise objectives because trainers were able to trim much of the 'dead wood' content from existing training programmes and replace it with programmes that were more streamlined and which cost less. However, it was this same use of objectives that sometimes resulted in the need to extend, enlarge and introduce new training schemes. Ironically, this gave rise to the first objections to the use of objectives. In a number of organizations it was less than popular when the costs of expanding the training programme were balanced against a product which seemingly could not be given a meaningful monetary value.

There were a number of trainers who found the use of a rigorous systematic approach difficult to cope with. In particular attitudes hardened against the writing of objectives. The prescription for writing objectives was seen as unnecessarily rigid in its demands for the outcomes of training to be described in terms of performance, conditions and standards. This has led to accusations that objectives written in this format have made training too cold and clinical and as a consequence this has taken out the human element.

In writing objectives it is expected that the performance that a trainee has to demonstrate at the end of training must be 'observable and measurable'. While this adds to the criticism already introduced, it also suggests that those parts of the training programme that contain general interest, enrichment and educational material should be cut out. To some trainers this means that creative approaches and innovation must be sacrificed for a standard delivery and predictable outcome.

In addition a number of trainers have said that they have had difficulty in composing objectives. One problem is the excessive amount of time spent in trying to find the appropriate word to describe the kind of behaviour the trainee has to demonstrate. Further difficulty is encountered in trying to decide and express how performance should be identified and measured. These problems are increased when trainers try to arrange or force information into columns under the headings of 'Performance', 'Conditions' and 'Standards' when it does not lend itself to this treatment.

There is often so much debate or discussion about how they should be expressed, that the writing of objectives becomes an end in itself. It could be considered that those responsible for the training of trainers are, in part, to blame for this problem by the way in which some exercises on writing objectives are designed and subsequently discussed at a seemingly high academic level.

More specifically, writing performance statements for knowledge-based training seems tedious and pointless for a number of trainers. They feel that there is little more that can be done to describe the performance than to use repeatedly the words 'state' or 'list'.

The value of this is called into question when there is little or no provision in many training programmes for tests which measure whether trainees actually are able to 'state' or 'list' the considerable amount of knowledge that has been directed at them. Therefore, trainers feel it is something of an act of faith, on their part, that the trainees have learned and therefore, not unnaturally, ask 'why bother?'

The problem is more acute when it comes to writing objectives which reflect attitudinal training outcomes. It may be comparatively easy to write performance statements describing attitudinal behaviour, but the problem of measuring whether or not a trainee has developed or changed an attitude is considered to be highly subjective unless trust is placed in the performance observed in such training activities as role-playing. Otherwise it could take a very long time before behaviours could be observed in job performance to judge whether or not the training had been effective. This criticism is equally applicable to objectives that have been written for management development training where it could be many years before there is even an opportunity to observe the kind of management behaviour that hopefully has been developed.

With psychomotor and procedural skills it is usually found to be easier to write objectives because the outcomes are more easily observable and measurable. This probably accounts for the readily and often quoted conclusion that objectives are suitable for skills training but are not practical for other aspects of training or learning.

The practical objections raised above are complemented and supported by criticisms from the academic world about the use of behavioural or instructional objectives in education.

The mechanical or engineering model of training and education, implied by the adoption of the behavioural objectives approach, is considered to be manipulative and contrary to the democratic conception of the individual. This conception sees the individual as having control and choice during, and as a result of, the learning experience. In this context a curriculum based on behavioural objectives is judged to be too narrow and neglectful of personal development. In addition such an approach to training and education is seen as unlikely to produce the flexibility in attitudes and behaviour required by a multi-cultural and technological society.

It is claimed by educationists that the advocates of the use of behavioural objectives tend to downgrade the teaching of theory. Furthermore, when a curriculum is based on behavioural objectives it suggests that training must lead to the attainment of the objectives or nothing has been learned. This implies that the broader educational learning experience is either ignored or takes a subordinate role.

It has been conceded by educationists that behavioural objectives may be relevant to rote learning but not to the acquisition of interpretive skills and the ability to apply knowledge and skills to a new situation. It is felt that creativity and innovation in curriculum development is seriously hampered by too premature a demand for identifying objectives.

Additionally, academic opponents suggest that the apparent emphasis on efficiency implied by the use of behavioural objectives may mean that the fundamental importance of process or experience is ignored or neglected.

A RESPONSE TO THE DISSENTING VIEW

The controversy about the relevance of objectives can be resolved partially by considering the distinctions made by Glaser (1962) between training and education. The first distinction relates to the specificity of the end product. He points out that:

> When the end products of learning can be specified in terms of particular instances of student performance, then instructional procedures can be designed to directly train or build in these behaviours.

On the other hand, if the skill to be learned is highly complex and the relevant performance is difficult to analyse and to specify then the student may be more generally educated by providing a foundation of behaviour which the individual is expected to generalize on or transfer to similar or novel instances.

A second distinction between training and education which Glaser makes is related to minimizing or maximizing individual differences. He suggests that with regard to training, the learning of specific behaviours implies a certain degree of uniformity within the limits set by individual differences. On the other hand education is attempting to increase the variability of individual differences 'by teaching in such a manner that each individual eventually behaves in a way singular to him on the basis of the groundwork of a basic education'.

The distinctions drawn above may help to justify, in a general sense, the process of establishing behavioural objectives in the training sphere. However, there are still a number of more specific arguments in favour of employing objectives in the design of training.

Arguments against objectives seem also to be arguments against planning. Without objectives the co-ordination of activities which form the basis of sound planning in training could be extremely difficult to carry out. In addition, a primary advantage of writing objectives for training is that it explores the underlying assumptions and values being adopted by the trainer.

Setting objectives stimulates clear thinking and helps trainers to communicate in a more precise and unambiguous way with one another. Furthermore, the sequencing of training material and the choice of appropriate instructional media is assisted by the use of training objectives.

In relation to other features of the systematic approach, the process of setting training objectives enables the aims and purpose of particular training activities to be broken down into more manageable elements. As a number of specialists have pointed out, establishing objectives puts training evaluation on a more rational footing. Linked with this is the notion that having specific training objectives forces the trainer to think more realistically rather than in terms of vague hopes and intentions and exalted aspirations. However, the question that still needs to be answered for many trainers is 'how far must we stick to the rigid rules for writing objectives?'

The guidelines which were discussed earlier should not be regarded as 'rules' and there is no need for rigidity in their application.

Objectives are tools of the trainer's trade and if they are unwieldy then they are unusable. It is of no value to try to force objectives into that familiar format of columns headed 'performance', 'conditions' and 'standards' if what is being set out does not lend itself to presentation in that form. It is accepted that there are many instances when such a format is ideal but equally there are procedural and clerical tasks in a wide range of occupations for which the conditions are always the same and the standards are always 'without error'.

As has been shown, in circumstances such as these it is more appropriate, when it is necessary, to state conditions and standards at the beginning and then to set out a list of the objective performance statements.

When standards are governed by procedures and codes of practice as they are stipulated in manuals, standing instructions and other forms of legislation, it has been found sufficient to make reference in a standards column to the appropriate section or page number rather than to slavishly copy out lengthy passages from the text.

When performance statements relate to the use of interpersonal skills and the application of principles of supervision, for example, then sometimes we need to accept the fact that even during training, trainers can disagree with one another about the level of competence achieved by the trainees. There is likely to be further variation in assessment when the former trainee is assessed by a supervisor in the job environment. It is not unusual to see that the standard of performance stated in a set of objectives is 'to the satisfaction of the tutor/ trainer' or something similar to 'to the satisfaction of the supervisor within the norms for that department'. This is felt to be acceptable provided that the performance statement is sufficiently descriptive to give an indication of the behavioural limits. This is not avoiding the issue of accurate and objective measurement but allowing a form of tolerance, albeit fairly broad, in the same way as tolerances are allowed on manual skills tasks.

When the content of training is knowledge based, it is recognized that it may seem to be a pointless task to itemize all of the performance statements using the prefixes 'list' and 'state' or the slightly less precise 'describe' and 'explain' when it is known that there will be little, if any, opportunity to test the trainees. However, all trainers appreciate the need to structure the content of knowledge-based learning and training. Clearly the use of objectives provides the key to this even though we have to accept as an act of faith that the trainees will be able to 'state', 'list', etc.

The use of objectives to determine the outcome of training does not preclude the inclusion of material that supplements or enriches learning. The use of visiting speakers to describe their experiences, provide cautionary tales and give a real-life perspective to the work environment plays an important part. Similar material in text or video form should not be ignored. The fact is that these do not need to have objectives written for them because they have an intrinsic value which cannot be expressed in behavioural terms, but nevertheless make a contribution to the overall learning experience.

It can be seen, and has been experienced by many of us in training, that writing objectives is not always easy and sometimes seems a stumbling block which we could well do without. Those of us who have tried to train without using objectives are more likely to admit that in spite of the difficulty of writing them and of the vagueness that is sometimes born of necessity in expressing them, we cannot design or evaluate our training at a professional level without knowing what we are trying to achieve. Having gone through this kind of experience, the moral to Robert Mager's (1975) much quoted fable of the sea horse has a telling relevance: '. . . if you're not sure where you're going, you're liable to end up some place else – and not even know it'.

7

Learning Principles and Conditions

At the heart of training is the learning process. In choosing or developing instructional methods and media and in arranging training programmes, the trainer must be intimately concerned with the impact that they will have on the ease with which the target population acquires new knowledge and skills. If trainers are going to be able to arrange the training environment in a form which is conducive to learning then they need more than a superficial and a passing acquaintance with the principles and conditions of learning. The purpose of this chapter is to provide, to an extent, for this need. A brief overview and introduction to the topics and issues that will be covered is set out below:

- Sequencing the training material
  An obvious but often neglected consideration when a training programme is being designed is the sequence in which the training material should be covered. The ordering of certain kinds of training content will make a critical difference to the ease of learning. Some sequences of material result in more effective learning than others.
- Readiness of the learner
  A number of factors influence the learner's readiness to learn. Their basic capacity for learning in general and their specific aptitudes or trainability in respect of certain forms of training content undoubtedly will be critical. Equally important will be the trainees' initial and on-going levels of motivation. These may be affected by their needs, previous background and experiences and current emotional and physical states.

- Learning conditions
  The trainer needs to be aware of the ways in which people learn and how conditions of learning can be arranged to aid the learning process. In particular the trainer must know how the organization of the learning material and actions by the trainer and the trainee will influence positively the attainment of different forms of training content. In addition, the conditions that facilitate transfer of learning and prevent or reduce forgetting and skill loss also must be identified.
- Influence of the material to be learned
  Closely linked with learning conditions is the influence that the material to be learned should have on the arrangement and organization of the learning conditions.
- Individual differences
  There are a number of individual differences that have an important impact on the processes of learning. Apart from certain obvious differences such as intelligence, aptitudes, age and previous learning experiences, in recent years other differences have been seen to have an important bearing on the ease of learning. These include personality factors and individual learning styles.

SEQUENCING THE TRAINING MATERIAL

A basic consideration in the design of training is concerned with the sequencing of the subject matter. Appropriate sequencing contributes to the ease and enhancement of learning. The 'laws' of sequence (i.e. progressing from easy to difficult, simple to complex, known to unknown etc) have general application in this area. In addition, ensuring that the learning material follows some logical and rational order also will aid subsequent recall.

However, to identify a suitable sequence in any specific situation may require further careful analyses and observations of performances which distinguish between expert and naive performers, together with empirical testing and consequent revision of sequences. The relevant forms of analyses needed to undertake this kind of exercise have been introduced already in Chapter 5. For example, hierarchical analysis and algorithms should provide information for sequencing procedural tasks. In the cognitive domain (i.e. areas of knowledge, comprehension and intellectual skills), topic analysis should help the trainer to develop learning hierarchies which identify learning prerequisites and hence the sequence in which they need to be learned. An analysis of a complex motor or physical skill may reveal prerequisite part-skills that could or should be learned separately which subsequently must be combined in some 'natural' and rational order.

In the social interpersonal domain, certain basic skills may need to be acquired concurrently, e.g. listening, questioning and complimentary non-verbal behaviour. Accumulative experience and collective wisdom also suggests that the learning of more intimate and sensitive social skills, such as those associated with counselling, should follow rather than precede the acquisition of the foundation or basic skills.

READINESS OF THE LEARNER

The readiness of a trainee to acquire new knowledge and skills can be examined from several different perspectives: intellectual, motivational, emotional, attitudinal or physical. Although these components of readiness will be dealt with separately, in reality they often interact, resulting in either positive or negative consequences for the trainee and for the trainer.

From the intellectual perspective the trainer already should have assessed the trainees' level of prerequisite knowledge and skill, general potential capability or special aptitudes relating to the intended training content. This will have been done through a review of the trainees' educational and occupational background or through the application of diagnostic or psychological tests. For example, engineering trainees might have been expected to demonstrate mechanical and spatial aptitudes to a reasonable level before embarking on their training, whereas for commercial apprentices verbal, clerical and numerical aptitudes might have been seen as more appropriate.

However, intellectually, the trainees bring more to the training situation than simply their general or specific abilities to learn the material presented. Past training and educational experiences may have assisted them to learn how to learn, that is, to acquire learning strategies that enable them to assimilate new subject matter and develop skills more readily.

Several researchers in the training field have investigated how to improve the process of learning. Downs and Perry (1982, 1984) have established short training courses to help trainees to improve their capacity to learn how to learn. In one of their programmes young trainees were introduced to exercises which were designed to improve generally their ability in memorization, in understanding and in doing things.

In another training workshop for supervisors, who were responsible for carrying out training, a checklist of some of the dos and don'ts for improving learning to learn skills was developed and it is reproduced in Figure 7.1 to give a flavour of what Downs and Perry are advocating.

By and large, learners who acquire 'learning to learn skills' become more active learners who are prepared to take a greater responsibility for their learning, who develop habits of learning and concentration and an openness to novel experiences that make them more flexible in their approach to new training challenges. In addition Mumford (1986) has suggested that, in relation to managers, there are a number of specific benefits of learning to learn. These include:

Do	**By**
Show that all your trainees have a contribution to make	Making sure that you take notice of their views
Don't	**By**
Make things too easy	Doing the difficult parts for the trainees
Do	**By**
Make them seek help when they need it	Not rushing in with help too soon
Don't	**By**
Do it for them when they ask for help but encourage them to work it out for themselves	Giving them clues or hints
Do	**By**
Encourage trainees to identify and correct their own mistakes	Providing models and guiding them with questions
Don't	**By**
Make the learning too easy	Breaking it into small parts. Get them to break it up for themselves
Do	**By**
Allow them time to work something out for themselves	Giving them pondering time. If they feel pushed for time, they may become stressed
Don't	**By**
Give unrealistic feedback	Giving undue praise or over critical comment
Do	**By**
Develop the trainees' interest in learning to do things for themselves	Discussing with them how they intend to go about learning something
Don't	**By**
Belittle your trainees' attempts at learning	Laughing at them or comparing them unkindly with others
Do	**By**
Develop the trainees' awareness of how to assess what they have done	Getting them to check their own work and assess it for quality
Don't	**By**
Give tasks which are too easy or too hard	Selecting a task which is inappropriate to their previous experience
Do	**By**
Make your trainees realize that practising is necessary for both consolidating learning and gaining skill	Encouraging them to do things a number of times giving careful attention to any mistakes they make

Figure 7.1 Some dos and don'ts for developing learning skills (Downs and Perry, 1984)

- An increase in the capacity of individuals to learn.
- A reduction in the frustration of being exposed to inefficient learning processes.
- An increase in motivation to learn.
- A recognition that unwillingness to learn from one particular activity cannot be generalized as an unwillingness to learn from anything.
- The reduction of dependence on a tutor.
- The provision of processes which carry through beyond formal programmes into on-the-job learning.

An additional benefit highlighted by Perry and Downs (1985) is that individuals who initially are poor learners can learn to use effectively those strategies employed by better, more efficient learners.

Another feature of the readiness of the learner which is closely linked to learning to learn has been emphasized by Stuart and Holmes (1982) in the context of discussing successful trainer styles. They put forward the view that the trainer has to adjust his or her style, i.e. trainer directive and relationship behaviours, to 'the maturity a learner displays/demonstrates in the context of a particular learning situation'. Learner maturity is defined by them in terms of:

- Capacity to set high but attainable learning goals.
- Willingness and ability to take responsibility for their learning.
- Educational and/or previous experiences.

The latter would be influenced strongly by the methods and approaches adopted and how successful or unsuccessful these activities had been for the individuals concerned. These, in turn, influence their attitudes towards, and expectations of, the forthcoming learning event.

According to Stuart and Holmes if learner maturity is low then a more directive or trainer-centred style might be appropriate. However, as the learner becomes more mature then the trainer directive and relationship behaviours also should be changed (see Figure 7.2).

It can be seen that the learning to learn approach and strategies referred to above are a way of changing the learner situational maturity from low towards moderate and to high levels. This suggests that if a trainer introduces trainees at the outset to some form of learning to learn programme then, for subsequent training tasks, the trainees' learner situational maturity may start at a higher level and the trainer must be sensitive to such a possibility and react accordingly.

Another vital influence that will affect the readiness of trainees to learn is their motivational level on entry to the training programme. Motivation of trainees during the course of a programme will be examined in the next section.

There is abundant anecdotal and research evidence to support the notion that learning is inhibited seriously if a trainee has no desire or is not motivated to

Trainer directive behaviour	Learner situational maturity	Trainer relationship behaviour
Directing, order, tell the way		**Distance**, maintain remoteness
Setting, persuade, 'get on board'	Low	**Recognizing**, acknowledge accord, notice
Guiding, advise, show the way		**Supporting**, prop up, carry the weight
Prompting, incite, prime		**Sustaining**, nourish, keep from falling
Consulting, seek information and advice	Moderate	**Responding**, show sensitivity to
Helping, assist, aid		**Encouraging**, urge, make bold
Releasing, set free, 'make over to'		**Withdrawing**, pull back from, discontinue giving
Resourcing, a stock to be drawn on	High	**Respecting**, having regard/esteem for
Participating, have a share in		**Warmth**, show affection liking for
Collaborating, work in combination with		**Mutuality**, bear the same relations to other

Source: Stuart and Holmes, 1982

Figure 7.2 The qualitative range of trainer directive and relationship behaviour

learn. Motivation can be defined here as that which energizes, directs and sustains behaviour or performance. There are a number of factors that will influence whether or not this 'active, purposive and goal-directed behaviour' is forthcoming. To assist with the identification of the most important of these factors and to aid the general discussion on motivation in the training context, reference will be made to a model of motivation illustrated in Figure 7.3.

The first feature of this model that must concern the trainer relates to the trainees' needs. Such needs can be classified under the following headings:

Physical	● sexual, nutritional
Safety	● support, security
Emotional: individual	● control, independence, achievement, self-confidence, challenge, autonomy, approval

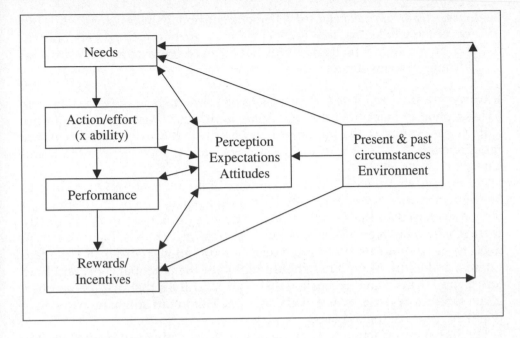

Figure 7.3 Model of motivation

Emotional: social	● acceptance, recognition, respect, status, appreciation, belonging
Intellectual	● curiosity, variety, stimulation
Self-actualization	● self-development, meaning, sense of purpose

In most situations it is very unlikely that the trainer will have to be too concerned with the physical needs of trainees, although nutritional deprivation could prove a problem in some circumstances. The other needs listed may be more or less important depending upon the psychological make-up of individual trainees and, in the case of security, the nature of the training. In addition, trainees may differ as to whether they are likely to be 'perfectly intrinsically motivated', 'perfectly extrinsically motivated' or 'imperfectly intrinsically motivated' (Mawhinney, 1979). McCormick and Ilgen (1985) define these terms as follows:

1. *Perfectly intrinsically motivated* People who really enjoy the activity and will work at it for the whole time period without needing any extrinsic reward to keep at it.
2. *Perfectly extrinsically motivated* Those for whom the task holds no interest and who will work on it only if forced to do so through the promise of extrinsic rewards.

3. *Imperfectly intrinsically motivated* Persons who enjoy the task for a while but not for the whole time that is allocated to it. Therefore, they work only up to a point, after which they will have to receive extrinsic rewards for working on it any longer.

Intrinsic rewards are related to the task to be learned; the trainee sees the task as interesting and meaningful and will gain intrinsic satisfaction from acquiring skill in performing it. On the other hand extrinsic rewards or incentives are independent of the task and include things such as money, promotion and career prospects, etc.

No matter what the circumstances, it would be unusual for any trainee to be 'perfectly intrinsically motivated' or, assuming that there has been some choice exercised in the selection of the target population, to be 'perfectly extrinsically motivated'. Therefore, in most training contexts, the trainer will need to evoke both intrinsic and extrinsic motivation in order to stimulate interest and effort. The trainer should highlight the potential short and long term, and intrinsic and extrinsic rewards or incentives that may be on offer, given satisfactory performance by the trainees. This in turn might help to satisfy the likely needs of the trainees.

The initial introduction to training will have an important bearing on the subsequent perception and attitudes of the trainees in a positive or negative direction and on their expectations of the current training. The trainees' past educational, occupational or instructional experience may have had an adverse effect on their outlook, which the trainer will need to counteract. For example, an unrewarding educational career may affect not only a trainee's attitude towards what he or she thinks they will get out of the training, but may also affect their self-confidence and self-perception. This in turn may create barriers to motivation and consequently to learning.

An approach or procedure which helps to stimulate and sustain motivation is that of informing the trainee, at the beginning of the programme or course, about the training objectives to be achieved and by placing the acquisition of these objectives in a wider context possibly associated with factors that arouse intrinsic or extrinsic motivation. Gagné (1977) points out that the purpose of informing the learner about the objectives is so that they have a clear expectation of what has to be accomplished as a result of the training or learning experience. He feels that subsequently the learners can generate informative feedback matching their performance against what they expect to be acceptable performance. Gagné also suggests that, very often, the best way to explain to learners what standard of performance will be expected of them at the end of their training, is to demonstrate that performance before they begin.

The technique of goal setting, which is related to the approach described above, also may be employed, in some circumstances, to facilitate and enhance the effectiveness of training through the motivational process. Locke and other researchers have demonstrated in non-training settings, through numerous field and laboratory studies, the value of this technique in improving performance, under the following types of condition:

1. That goals must be realistic in the light of an individual's ability to be able to achieve them.
2. That the goal assigned or set for an individual is accepted by him or her.
3. That feedback regarding the degree to which the goal is being met is supplied to the performer at the appropriate juncture.
4. That individuals are given specific challenging goals rather than modest goals or no goals at all or are simply exhorted and encouraged to 'do your best'.

Furthermore Locke and Latham (1984) put forward the view that goal setting works because:

1. Specific goals direct an individual's action more reliably than vague, unclear and general objectives.
2. An individual has a much clearer idea of what is expected of him or her, which can help to mobilize their energies and efforts more efficiently.
3. Individuals are more motivated by hard, challenging goals, provided they have accepted them in the first place.
4. Challenging goals increase an individual's efforts over an extended time period, i.e. it helps to maintain an individual's persistence.

Wexley and Nemeroff (1975) and Nemeroff and Cosentino (1979) have shown that goal setting was applied usefully in furthering the realization of the objectives of a number of management training programmes.

This supports the idea that trainers could employ the goal setting technique in certain training situations, particularly where individual achievement and rates of improvement were being emphasized or where a relatively homogeneous group was required to make uniform progress.

Whatever general approach or specific procedure is used to motivate trainees, it is important for the trainer not to prime the motivational 'pump' too much. For too high a level of arousal or motivation may be counter-productive, particularly if the task to be learned is inherently difficult for the trainees in question. Of course the converse also may be true if the task is too easy. Figure 7.4 is a general view of the learning performance, motivational level and task difficulty.

For difficult tasks, lower motivational levels are likely to lead to higher learning performance, whereas for easy tasks, levels of motivation must be a great deal higher to achieve corresponding performance outcomes. Tasks of intermediate difficulty require levels of motivation that are neither too high nor too low.

Thus stimulating high motivation or 'hyping up' the trainee in the 'run up' to training may interfere with the learning of complex tasks as will high anxiety

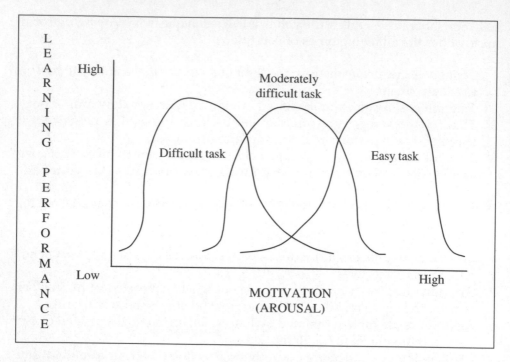

Figure 7.4   The relationship between learning performance, motivational level and task difficulty

and apprehension. These emotions may be experienced by individuals at the beginning of training because of doubts and fears aroused by the memory of previous failures. Also, such feelings may be inadvertently created by the manner in which the trainer prepares the trainees for, and introduces them to, the training event. Clearly, the trainer must appreciate the possible impact that he or she or the trainees' past experiences may have on their attitudes and on feelings towards any forthcoming training event. The trainer's sensitivity, style and approach throughout the training process, but especially in the preliminary phase, can go a long way to alleviate, or at least to lessen, any emotional blockages that might interfere with subsequent learning. If stress and anxiety are due to external influences, e.g. familial, matrimonial, etc, then counselling or postponement of the training for the individual affected may be possible remedies.

So far only intellectual, motivational and emotional components of the readiness of the learner have been discussed. Equally important is their physical readiness. An aspect of this may have been dealt with at the stage when trainees were being selected for the training programme. The personnel specification, which should guide the selection decision, should have set out clearly any essential physical requirements that the trainees had to meet to be regarded as suitable to undertake the training programme. However, there may be additional, more or less temporary, physical conditions, such as ill health, physical injury or fatigue that would either necessitate the trainer excluding an individual or persuading the client to withdraw a candidate from the programme. A further physical factor which the trainer should take into account, with certain target populations, relates to the effect that their circadian rhythms, i.e. 'around the day' changes in body processes, may have on their receptivity and learning performance. This is particularly pertinent with regard to trainees who have been doing shift work just prior to embarking on a programme organized around 'normal' daily attendance. They may require time and some advice on how to adjust and stabilize their circadian rhythms before beginning training (Folkard, 1987). The possible impact of 'time-of-day effects' on training performance will be looked at in the sections 'General Conditions' and 'Individual Differences' which follow.

WAYS OF LEARNING

Essentially in this chapter two questions are being addressed: 'Why do people learn?' and 'How do people learn?'. The latter question is answered partially by considering the physical and mental activities in which human beings engage to bring about relatively permanent changes in their ways of behaving. In line broadly with the views of Bass and Vaughan (1966) it is suggested here that there are basically at least five such activities, which are associated with the human processes of seeing, listening, thinking and motor responses. These are explained briefly below.

Trial and error

This is probably the simplest form of learning. The learner acts or behaves with the intention of achieving some result or end state. Each action that is perceived as leading towards this desired outcome is reinforced and, all things being equal, will be repeated on subsequent occasions. If a particular action or behaviour meets with a lack of success, or even punishing consequences, it is unlikely to be repeated and the learner then 'searches' for an appropriate alternative. By a series of trials, approximations and errors the learner may eventually discover the correct sequence of action.

Perceptual organization

The learner perceives the total stimulus situation – cues, conditions, rewards, etc – and then organizes it or 'maps it out' into a comprehensible or understandable pattern that guides or directs his or her behaviour.

Behaviour modelling

A great deal of human learning is a result of first observing how others have behaved, and have been rewarded or punished in particular situations, and then by attempting to imitate the correct or most appropriate performance or series of behaviours.

Mediation

Language, in oral or written form, is an intermediary or mediational process through which human beings acquire a great deal of what they learn during their lifetime. The communication or language code may not only be in words but also in the form of symbols, diagrams or figures.

Reflection

This way of learning is closely associated with perceptual organization and may, in many cases, follow on from trial and error, behaviour modelling or mediation. It is, as Boot and Boxer (1980) point out, 'a process of thinking back on, reworking, searching for meanings in experience' or, as Boud, Keogh and Walker (1985) suggest, 'an active process of exploration and discovery' which involves 'thinking quietly, mulling over and making sense of experience'.

Training in industry, commerce and the public sector employ all these forms of learning. And what has been learned in a particular context is unlikely to have come about because the trainee was engaged solely in one type of learning.

The above forms of learning may tend to interact and combine to produce changes in knowledge, understanding, skill and attitudes. However, as will be seen later on, certain ways of learning will be more productive depending on the content of what has to be learned and on the inclinations, abilities and past experiences of the trainees.

GENERAL CONDITIONS OF LEARNING

In order to enhance, or in some cases to bring about required changes in knowledge, skill and attitudes, the trainer must engage the trainee in the learning process in an active fashion. Before examining some of the specific actions the trainee and the trainer may need to take in order to fulfil this requirement, attention must be paid to the general conditions of learning within the training situation, that either positively promote, or are conducive to, learning.

Reference has been made already to the criticality of motivational levels in relation to training performance. However, apart from stimulating the trainees' motivation and not to overlook the importance of individual differences, the trainer must also arrange the training environment to maintain sufficient alertness in the trainees throughout. This can be done initially by the trainer supplying the trainees with an overview and a meaningful context in which new learning can be placed. Such a tactic can be effective because it operates both an individual trainee's motivational system and through their thinking/learning processes. Thereafter the trainer must be concerned with maintaining interest in the overall programme and, in particular, stimulating arousal and interest in the trainee during individual training sessions.

With respect to the latter a number of techniques might be used to present the trainees with varied and novel stimulation. For example, during a training session a recurring concern for the trainer is how to maintain group attention for any length of time. Figure 7.5 illustrates the problem.

As many experienced trainers have learned, fall-off in attention can be minimized by employing visual aids, varying pitch, pace and tone of voice, changing physical position, introducing humour and varying the activity of

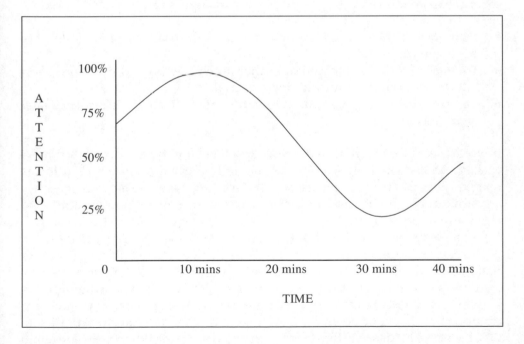

Figure 7.5 Group attention over time (after Mills, 1967)

the groups. In self-study activities such as programmed learning, computer-based training, e-learning or the use of learning packages there is the likelihood of a similar fall-off period. In addition to interacting with the medium of instruction, it is helpful for trainees to have the opportunity to interact with their tutors, other trainees and supervisors to share problems, seek assistance and confirm progress which contributes to increasing their attention level. Furthermore, by continually demonstrating the significance of content through credible and relevant examples the trainer should go some way to maintaining the trainees' interest.

In terms of the overall programme, by sensibly varying the methods and the nature of the content there should be a beneficial effect on the trainees' level of alertness. However, a factor that may qualify the degree of method and content variation necessary to offset mental fatigue and drop in attention is 'the time of the day' phenomenon.

The traditional recommendation that new material should be covered in the morning and early afternoon periods and then consolidated in the afternoon period has been complicated and brought into question by recent research. Certainly, immediate retention generally appears to be better in the earlier part of the day. However, longer term retention (Folkard, 1987) for some tasks may be higher following presentation in the afternoon and evening. There may be several explanations for this seemingly surprising finding.

- Trainers recognize the onset of the mental 'dip' and make greater effort to stimulate trainees.
- Trainees perceive a diminution in their attentiveness and put more effort into concentrating on the training material.
- Certain groups are predisposed towards more effective performance later on in the day.

It would seem that there are 'morning' and 'evening' types. The former wake earlier and become fully operational mentally fairly quickly but tend to tire relatively early in the evening period. The 'evening' types are the converse; they are slow to get into mental action but can stay up much later at night, and remain reasonably alert.

Not to deny the above possibilities, Folkard (1987) nevertheless suggests that with regard to time of day effects in performance research findings on task demands and individual differences make it difficult to recommend the best time for scheduling work over the course of the normal day. Although it is known that task demands affect performance trends, specific recommendations cannot as yet be made about the best time of day to undertake most tasks. In the absence of evidence to the contrary, it would seem that this conclusion could also apply to training. However, where does this leave the trainer on the problem of the timing of learning input? Possibly the most sensible suggestions for the trainer to follow are:

- Irrespective of the nature of the target population, over the course of the day, look to vary the training methods employed
- Build into the training programme 'natural' breaks, rest periods and relaxation 'slots'
- Be keenly aware of the potential problem of input 'overload' particularly with lower ability groups and those who have been out of training and education for some time
- Build in reinforcement strategies.

Apart from taking account of the preceding considerations, the trainer must ensure also that the hygiene factors, both physical and psychological, have no negative effects on the trainees' motivation and training performance. It goes without saying that inadequate physical conditions such as poor lighting, inadequate ventilation and heating and uncomfortable seating can severely hamper or act as a major distraction or barrier to effective learning. In addition, reference has been made already to the importance of the emotional climate that the trainer needs to create at the onset of training.

Another feature of the climate or atmosphere which the trainer should control or influence is the degree of rivalry between the trainees. Although, in some circumstances, healthy competition can have beneficial effects on trainees' performance and progress, it can also be counter-productive and have a detrimental impact both on the trainees' achievements and, probably more critically, on their attitudes towards current and subsequent training events. Of course on occasions, low-key, friendly competition may give certain kinds of training, such as group training, an element of excitement that can be an additional stimulant to the trainees and introduce a form of variety which may give them a 'lift' at a particularly low point in their programme.

Such low points are often unavoidable because of the length of a programme or because of the nature of the training content. However, very careful thought always must be given to the introduction of any form of competition into training. Better that trainees compete against themselves rather than dissipate their energies in competing against one another.

In so many instances it would be more advisable for trainees to build up a co-operative spirit that encourages mutual help and assistance. This would seem to be more in line with meeting the criterion-referenced standards that normally operate in the training context.

PRINCIPLES AND SPECIFIC CONDITIONS SUPPORTING LEARNING

Organization of the learning material: whole versus part learning

Besides considering how the training material should best be sequenced the trainer must also think carefully about another important organizing issue, namely whether or not to cover what has to be learned as a whole or in parts. For instance when the task has several elements, should they be learned all at once or should the trainee be taught the elements separately, before combining them into the whole? The answer to this question seems to be 'it depends'. Baldwin and Ford (1988) in their literature review suggest that the whole method is more advantageous when the learner has high intelligence, when practice on the task is distributed rather than massed (see below) and when the learning material is high in task organization but low in task complexity (task organization refers to the degree to which sub-tasks or task elements are interrelated). Goldstein (1986) deviates to an extent from the views of Baldwin and Ford. Interpreting the examination of the literature on whole versus part learning by Naylor (1962) and Blum and Naylor (1968) the following training principles are supported:

> When a task has relatively high organization, an increase in task complexity leads to whole methods being more efficient than part methods, and when a task has low organization, an increase in task complexity leads to part methods being more efficient.

Goldstein emphasizes the importance of analysing the task in order to determine whether it can be split up easily into coherent parts. In addition, he suggests that the analysis may indicate that a form of progression learning could be usefully adopted. There are a number of options that can be used:

Progressive part, where the first two parts of the task are practised in isolation and are then practised together. The third part is practised in isolation and then added to the first two parts and so on.
e.g. A, B, A+B, C, A+B+C etc

Repetitive part, sometimes known as cumulative part, where the first part of the task is practised in isolation and then the second and subsequent parts added.
e.g. A, A+B, A+B+C etc

Isolated part, where some of the parts of the task are practised in isolation before the whole task is practised.

e.g. A, C, E, A+B+C+D+E etc

Retrogressive part, where the last part of the task is practised in isolation, then the last and the penultimate part, and so on until the whole task has been learnt. e.g. C, B, A, A+B+C

Actions by the trainer

Depending upon the nature of the training content, the characteristics of the target population, the training methods employed, etc the trainer will need to use one or a combination of the following to ensure that the trainees learn effectively:

Setting sub-goals

In line with the principles and technique of goal setting described earlier the trainer can reinforce and support the trainees' on-going attitudes and motivation towards the training programme by setting or agreeing with them a series of sub-goals. This process of progressive goal setting will enable the trainer to monitor closely their achievement and, to an extent, individualize the organization of the training.

Directing attention

On occasions the trainer will need to draw the trainees' attention to certain distinctive features of what has to be learned. They may do this through verbal, pictorial, auditory or other means. The trainer must be familiar therefore with the various ways in which 'to give selective emphasis to stimulus presentations for learning' (Gagné, 1977).

Humour

The employment of humour by the trainer can be an effective means of stimulating and maintaining the trainees' level of arousal and attention and consequently can have a positive effect on their learning performance. Humour can operate in several ways to bring about this outcome:

- Humorous anecdotes may dramatically illustrate and reinforce specific learning points.
- Amusing actions, comments, etc, whether stemming from the trainer or from the trainees, can help to prevent stress and thus create a more relaxed

atmosphere. This may be conducive to learning as it can put the trainees in a more receptive frame of mind and make it easier for them to receive new information and feedback.

- Humour can lead to improved communication within a trainee group and between trainer and trainees, both of which can enhance morale and stimulate creative problem-solving.
- Introducing humorous exercises, which may or may not be directly related to the learning content, can generate the trainees' energy, particularly at points in the programme where there may be an inevitable and unavoidable 'dip'.
- Fundamentally, humour can make the learning experience enjoyable for trainees; they'll want to be there and will be motivated to learn.

However, a word of warning needs to be struck at this point. Although humour can facilitate, it can also detract from learning. It would have to be introduced into a training programme in a skilful, judicial and timely manner.

Pictures and demonstrations

An old Chinese proverb, now often quoted by trainers, serves to highlight the value of pictures and demonstrations:

I hear and I forget
I see and I remember
I do and I understand.

Pictures and demonstrations can provide trainees with a mental plan or template which will help them to remember the sequence of actions or steps involved in procedural, physical or manual skills. In addition, as Gagné points out, pictures in particular can aid the learning of manual skills by drawing the trainees' attention to the external cues that control motor responses.

Human modelling

Closely associated with demonstrations is the provision, by the trainer, of a human model. For human modelling to be effective the model used must:

- Appeal to, and have credibility for, the trainee.
- Demonstrate the desired course or choice of action.
- Be seen to be rewarded in some way for the carrying out of the desired course or choice of action.

Verbal instruction

Language is a meditational process which can be employed in the training and instructional contexts in a number of ways:

- 'to provide cues for procedural steps. . . can operate to increase the distinctiveness of external cues' (Gagné, 1977). These will assist the learner to recall the material or instruction to be learned.
- To communicate background information, ideas, etc that provide the meaningful context in which to fit any new learning.
- To explain concepts, rules, principles and theories that provide the necessary foundation for acquiring intellectual, social and manual skills.
- To be the essential concomitant to other learning principles and conditions.

Guidance, prompting and cueing

Guidance involves either showing trainees the right answer or style of behaving or compelling them to make only appropriate responses. This approach has been referred to as 'error free' training because the trainer tries to ensure, by various means, that errors do not occur during learning. Stammers and Patrick (1975) describe four types of guidance:

- *Physical restriction* A physical device restricts movement within certain acceptable limits, e.g. golf harness.
- *Forced response* The required movement of limbs is initiated and directed by an external force, e.g. physical rehabilitation exercises to retrain limbs.
- *Visual guidance* The trainee is shown the appropriate movements to execute or a path to follow.
- *Verbal guidance* The general nature of the task and relevant actions are described and the trainee can be alerted to when mistakes seem imminent.

A certain amount of guidance early in training is conducive to learning particularly with complex tasks. Probably this is because if errors are allowed to occur in this phase they are likely to be repeated and then a proportion of subsequent learning time has to be devoted to unlearning those early mistakes.

Bass and Vaughan (1966) emphasize that proper guidance helps to eradicate incorrect responses before they have a chance to become ingrained. Preventing errors occurring in circumstances where the occurrence of errors early in training might lead to serious safety problems or damage to equipment, is another benefit of effective guidance. However, Bass and Vaughan also point out that the degree of guidance required depends on the nature of the task or skill to be learned. Interestingly, they feel that for some complex skills the learner should not be 'protected' from committing errors as more may be learned from making mistakes than from making correct responses. Protecting the trainee, through the over-use of guidance, may prove counter-productive in several other ways. If the trainee uses guidance as a prop, rather than an aid, then learning performance consequently may be retarded. In addition, too much guidance may create boredom in the trainee by not giving him or her sufficient autonomy and independence.

In the view of Stammers and Patrick, guidance as a learning condition or tactic is applied usually to manual skills, whereas prompting is more applicable to learning verbal and perceptual tasks. In verbal learning the trainee has to associate stimulus and response terms, e.g. the merchandise and the relevant floor in a department store. After some initial exposure to the stimulus – response pairing – the trainee may be required to state the response after being 'prompted' by the stimulus. Alternatively, part of the response can be presented in order to encourage the learner; for example the prompter in a play normally only gives the first word or phrase of the 'lost' sentence. Skilful questioning of the trainee may serve as a form of prompting leading to the correct response or action. As with guidance, prompting appears to be particularly effective in the initial phase of learning.

Finally, trainers can sometimes accelerate a trainee's learning by highlighting or providing easily identifiable and easily remembered cues which 'trigger' the correct response or sequence of actions. In some types of social skills training the trainees' attention can be directed towards auditory and visual cues such as facial expressions, tone of voice, etc that will assist them to interpret verbal information and to act appropriately.

Learning strategies

Patrick (1992) discusses how the trainee's learning and retention can be improved by the trainer developing appropriate orienting tasks: 'thus activities engaged in by the trainee such as summarising, questioning, notetaking, re-reading, reviewing and following the instructions of the trainer are examples of orienting tasks designed to nudge the trainee to develop appropriate learning strategies'. There follow three well-known orienting tasks highlighted by Patrick:

Questions can be included at various points in the training to stimulate the trainee to process and remember the new material more efficiently. An alternative to the trainer generating the questions would be for the trainees to be encouraged to think up their own questions.

Analogies may be employed by trainers to help trainees to bridge the gap between the new learning and what they already know. However, as Patrick points out, there is a risk of picking an inappropriate analogy and therefore the analogy should be chosen so that '. . . it maximises the similarities between the new and old task, situation, idea, etc'.

Mnemonics are widely used as aids to remember procedures and specific information. The essence of mnemonics is to get trainees to associate familiar facts or images with what has to be learned. For example, the initial letter of each activity or element of knowledge to be learned could be used to form a familiar word or phrase, which then acts as a memory jogger by providing an annotation of ideas. In some circumstances it may be useful to let the trainees make up their own mnemonics to reinforce learning.

Feedback, knowledge of results and reinforcement

Trainees need to know how well they are performing at all stages in their training, if they are going to learn effectively and improve their performance. Improvement in performance can be attributed to the motivational and informational functions of knowledge of results (Goldstein, 1986). The latter is satisfied through extrinsic and intrinsic feedback. Extrinsic feedback comes from sources external to the actual task being performed, e.g. from the trainer, other trainees or by mechanical devices. This type of feedback may focus on how well a trainee performs a particular task, i.e. on the process, or on the outcome or the results achieved. Intrinsic feedback refers to cues within the task or job itself. For instance in learning to play a musical instrument the learner will hear, see and feel how well he or she is performing. Effective training is partially about using extrinsic feedback to focus the trainee's attention on the intrinsic cues. Furthermore, as Stammers and Patrick suggest, it may be advisable to withdraw the extrinsic feedback at some point during practice in order to force the trainee to utilize the intrinsic feedback of the task.

Apart from the relationship between internal and external feedback two other important issues for the trainer to be concerned with are the specificity and amount of feedback that should be provided to the trainee. Too much specific feedback in the early stages of training may not necessarily lead to anticipated improvements in performance. The trainee may become 'overloaded' with detailed information which only serves to confuse and, as Jinks (1979) emphasizes, over-informing a trainee about failure is liable to have an adverse effect on motivation. However, as the trainee gains increased competence on a task, full and specific feedback is likely to be more effective.

The general recommendation on feedback for training would seem to be to give the trainee a modicum of feedback early on, increase the amount and specificity as the trainee increases in competence and then withdraw it gradually as the skills to be learned become more established before finally excluding it altogether. Of course the trainer must realize that feedback should be designed to fit the task, the training programme and the capabilities of trainees.

If informational feedback is clearly linked to sub-goals, it will go some way towards satisfying a trainee's motivational needs. The trainer must also appreciate that in many situations for a trainee to wish to continue to learn, some form of emotional reward, e.g. 'well done', should follow effective performance of parts, or the whole, of the task. Again, as with informational feedback, this form of reinforcement must not be overdone otherwise the trainer's sincerity may be brought into question or the trainee may become over-reliant on the trainer's emotional support, which may have an adverse effect on the trainee's confidence and consequently their performance when such support is withdrawn.

Russell (1994) differentiates between feedback and debrief. Feedback is seen as letting trainees know what has reached the standard and what has not, so that plans can be agreed on what further work needs to be done. Debriefing is seen as a process of reviewing trainees' judgements and considering the merits of their decisions with those of alternatives. It is used in situations where there is no right or wrong way of doing things but where different approaches may be taken.

Among Russell's guidelines for giving feedback, he suggests that it should be:

- *Participative.* In most cases, trainees have some idea of how they have performed and do not like to be told what they already know. It is of benefit to get them to contribute to the feedback by asking them how they feel that they have performed. This can be taken forward as an objective review of what has been achieved and what action can be taken to develop it.
- *Objective.* It should relate exactly to what happened. That is, what people said or what they did and what the trainer has recorded. It should not be based on generalizations such as 'You didn't always. . .' or 'I felt that. . .'
- *Balanced.* There should be a balance of the positive as well as the negative aspects of the trainee's performance. It is not recommended that balance should be achieved by praise alternated with criticism. The trainer should also consider what capacity the trainee has for receiving feedback. Some can take very little feedback before they begin to forget the points that have been made, and may also become dispirited very quickly by negative feedback. At the other end of the scale, some trainees are like sponges and can absorb any amount of comment.
- *Hierarchical.* It has been noted already that individuals' capacity for feedback varies. Therefore, it is advisable to deal with the most important points first; that is, those things that were done best and those that, given attention, would make the greatest improvement to performance. If feedback is given chronologically, it could be that the trainee has reached saturation point before all of the key points have been covered.
- *Comparable.* Performance should be comparable with the criteria that have been set for achieving the task and/or the previous performance of the trainee on that particular task.
- *Understandable.* The level of language that the trainer uses should be understandable to the trainee. Jargon should be limited, or checks made to

ensure that it is understood. When training has included a considerable amount of technical or specialist language it should not be assumed that all of it has been learnt.

- *Sufficient.* It is important that sufficient time is allowed for feedback if it is to be of any value. Trainees are likely to have put a great amount of time and effort into their work, and will expect more than a superficial review of what they have achieved or failed to achieve.
- *Actionable.* Any guidelines for improvement agreed between the trainee and the trainer should be capable of being put into practice. There is no value in agreeing that the trainee's confidence will improve if he or she chairs meetings if he/she is never likely to have that opportunity.

Debriefing is a more open and possibly wider ranging discussion than that used to give feedback, because in the tasks being learnt the emphasis is on different ways of doing things. That is not to say that such tasks are void of things that have to be done in a specific way. For example in training for selection interviewing there are specific guidelines relating to legislation that have to be followed to the letter, but such skills as establishing rapport, encouraging people to be expansive in their replies and the use of questioning techniques can be open for discussion.

Russell suggests that debriefing should address the following questions:

- What was the task?
- What were the criteria for success?
- To what extent was the task achieved?
- How was the task approached?
- What helped to achieve the task?
- What hindered the achievement of the task?
- How could the task have been achieved more effectively?
- What must be done to improve performance?

In certain circumstances a trainee also may require on-going emotional reinforcement. Praise from the trainer for sub-goal achievement or reassurance when progress is depressingly slow or non-existent may be necessary and important on occasions.

Trainee activities

It is trite, but nevertheless true, to say that ultimately it is the trainee who does the learning. Trainers can only facilitate this process by their actions and by establishing the physical, social and psychological conditions conducive to learning. Trainees also have to be actively involved and participate in the learning process. Several of the important activities trainees themselves must engage in, under the influence and direction of the trainer, in order to acquire new knowledge, skills and attitudes are detailed below:

Practice and rehearsal

'Practice makes perfect' is a well-supported adage. However, sheer repetition of the elements making up a skill is not sufficient to bring about improvement and retention. Two critical conditions need to be present, if practice is going to 'make perfect'. Firstly, there is a desire on the part of the trainee to achieve an improvement in performance and secondly on-going and/or terminal (i.e. at the end of a practice period) feedback is provided to the learner.

Similarly for rehearsal to be an effective means of ensuring the retention of verbal material it must involve active retrieval and recall by the trainee, with confirmation of the degree of accuracy following soon afterwards.

Bass and Vaughan (1966) give the reasons why this form of activity is so important in verbal learning:

- It requires active participation by the learner and this helps to maintain attention and interest.
- Active recall gives the learner an opportunity to practise on the material.
- Knowledge of results regarding accuracy indicates to the learner what he or she does or does not know which will help them direct and distribute subsequent effort and time.

Imagining and reflection

There is research evidence available to substantiate the view that motor-skill learning can be enhanced by the trainee engaging in mental practice. This procedure would entail the trainee observing a demonstration of the skill, having some initial experience of it and then being encouraged to imagine the relevant movements, etc. Decker (1982) also has demonstrated improvements in the social skills needed to handle coaching situations and employee complaints after trainees had been directed to mentally rehearse such skills.

Reflection, as a form of mental rehearsal, may lead the trainee to 'reveal' or raise pertinent questions about the training content; the answer to these questions, given either by the trainer or by other means, may then accelerate subsequent learning.

Distribution of practice

Consideration will need to be given as to whether practice should be 'massed' (i.e. all at once) or 'distributed' (i.e. spread over several training sessions).

Unfortunately, research into this issue provides the trainer with no universal, conclusive guidelines. However, the following should be borne in mind:

- In learning manual skills, distributed practice is usually more effective than massed practice both in terms of acquisition and retention.
- The optimum time interval between practice sessions and the length of the session itself will depend on the trainee's age, personality, previous learning experience, etc; and the nature of the task or skill to be learned. If the interval between practice sessions is too long then forgetting becomes a problem and relearning or a 'warm-up' period may be necessary with a consequent extension of overall learning time. On the other hand, if the rest interval is too short then trainees may suffer boredom and mental or physical fatigue because of insufficient recovery time.
- With verbal material, massed practice can be superior to spaced practice for acquisition but inferior for retention.
- The less meaningful that the material is to be learned, the more difficult it is to learn it in a massed session as opposed to a series of sessions.
- Baldwin and Ford (1988), referring to Holding (1965), suggest that 'there is also evidence that difficult and complex tasks result in higher performance when massed practice sessions are given first, followed by briefer sessions with more frequent rest intervals'.

Discovery learning and exploration

In discovery learning the trainees work through a problem, task or situation with little or no involvement by the trainer. This method of learning is designed to enable learners to formulate their own understanding of a subject by solving a carefully designed sequence of problems. Trainees would need to be 'prepared' for discovery learning by developing a number of prerequisite skills, concepts and rules. Besides discovering higher-order principles through the activities involved in this method, trainees may also 'pick up' transferable strategies of learning to learn.

Sometimes a less formal means of discovery can be of benefit to the trainees. If they are simply allowed to explore the training situation and 'play with' the equipment, then safety considerations permitting, greater interest may be generated resulting in more inquisitiveness and ultimately wider learning.

It should be obvious that the actions and activities of trainers and trainees respectively do not or, in some cases, cannot operate independently. In some situations it is sensible for the trainer actions to work in tandem. For instance to maintain attention and motivation, feedback and guidance are often interspersed. In addition, certain trainer actions and trainee activities are inextricably linked as has been seen already with practice and feedback. The trainer's skill, or art, is to apply the principles and conditions best suited to particular knowledge, skill and attitude requirements, bearing in mind time pressures, priorities, resources and characteristics of the target population. The influence of the latter on this decision will be looked at in more depth later.

Learning curves and plateaux

If training is to be adaptive and managed flexibly then it is important for the trainer to monitor carefully the progress of individual trainees over an appropriate period of time. Where it is practicable to do so, the construction of learning curves could be of major assistance in this endeavour. Learning curves are a way of describing the changes in performance brought about by training and take the form of a graph tracing the improvement, or otherwise, of trainees during the course of the training programme.

The general benefits of learning curves are:

- They provide diagnostic information that may help the trainer to determine the effectiveness of the training tactics and methods employed (group learning curves can be constructed by averaging the individual performance of trainees at various points in time).
- They can be used to give feedback to the trainee. (In some circumstances it may be feasible for the trainees to trace their own learning curves; this linked to the setting of sub-goals can serve as an effective motivational technique.)
- They can alert the trainer to difficulties being experienced by the trainees as indicated by slow progress or no progress being made.

However, in relation to the last point the shape of the learning curve may have certain implications for the action that the trainer needs to take. Bass and Vaughan (1966) draw attention to three shapes that occur regularly and lead to different trainer actions. Figure 7.6 illustrates a typical negatively accelerated learning curve.

The shape of this curve indicates rapid early progress followed by relatively marginal or minor improvements as the trainee begins to acquire increased competence. Several reasons have been put forward to explain the development of this pattern of performance:

- The task to be learned is reasonably easy and therefore dramatic initial progress is possible.
- The trainee's previous learning experience enables him or her to organize the new material in a meaningful way fairly quickly.
- The trainee may be highly motivated to start with but then begins to lose interest, particularly if the task is simple and straightforward.

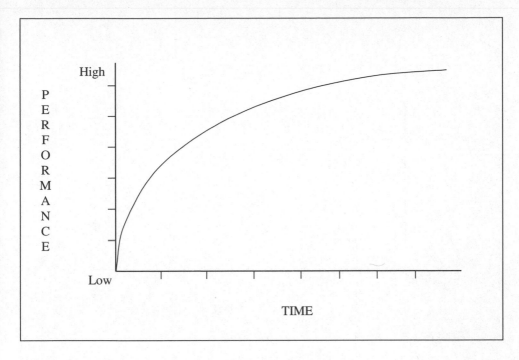

Figure 7.6   Negatively accelerated learning curve

● The basic task is essentially easy to learn and, *at the beginning*, a high quality outcome is not required.

In order to combat the effects of these influences the trainer may need to pay greater attention to the trainee towards the back end of the training either by supplying more accurate and more specific feedback or by being more encouraging in order to 'lift' the trainee's motivation or by introducing temporarily some stimulating alternative activity so that the trainee may return to the main task refreshed.

The second curve (Figure 7.7) is the converse of the first. This type of curve is usually associated with very difficult and complex training material and, where the trainee does not have the requisite experiential or educational background or special aptitudes to 'pick it up' quickly. Not surprisingly, the trainees' motivation also may be fairly low in the initial stages which further serves to depress their performance. In these circumstances the trainer probably will need to give more guidance and encouragement early on.

Another familiar and characteristic shape observed in some learning curves is shown in Figure 7.8.

The period in the learning process when no obvious progress is being made is referred to as the *learning plateau*; it is normally only a temporary levelling

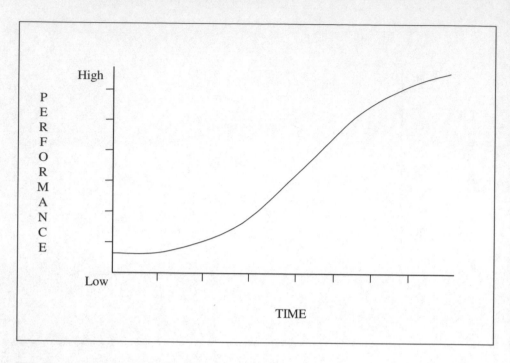

Figure 7.7 Positively accelerated learning curve

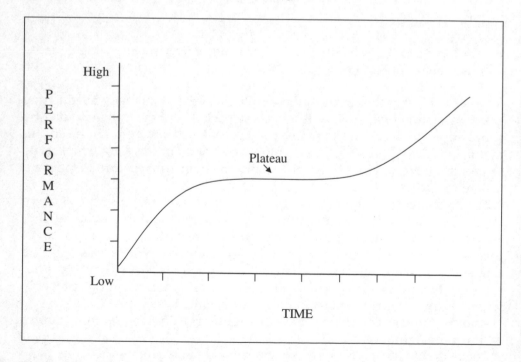

Figure 7.8 The learning plateau

off in performance. There are a number of explanations for the occurrence of this type of phenomenon which in outline are as follows:

1. One explanation has been called 'The Hierarchy of Habit Hypothesis', which presents the notion that certain skills are made up of a series of habits 'positioned' in the form of a hierarchy. Habits high up on the hierarchy are more complex than those lower down. However, the learning of complex habits is dependent on the trainee first having acquired the less complex ones. The plateau occurs when the trainees have mastered lower order habits and are making the transition from these to higher habits.
2. A complex task comprises several simple tasks or parts. As the learner tackles each task or part, he or she meets and eventually overcomes new problems. These gradually give way to easy and accelerated learning.
3. For a variety of reasons such as boredom, fatigue, etc motivation falls away at several points during the course of learning.
4. Incorrect responses or bad habits are being eliminated and while this is happening no new learning can take place.

Kenny and Reid (1986), referring to the work of Fleishman and Hempel (1955), suggest another reason why the plateau might occur which is closely related to the first two reasons given above. Specific abilities may vary in their degree of importance as competence in a skill increases. Initial progress in learning may be dependent on one ability; however, in order to improve the trainees have to concentrate on another, now more relevant, ability which has yet to be developed.

It goes without saying that the trainer must be alert to or have advance warning about the onset of the learning plateau, and make every attempt to ascertain the cause(s) for its occurrence and then introduce appropriate alterations to the training conditions on the current or future programmes. In relation to the explanations for learning plateaux, there are a number of possible training modifications that might be made:

- *Explanations 1 and 2* The trainer should examine the viability of changing the whole versus part learning regime.
- *Explanation 3* Introducing some form of incentive or changing the trainees' activity for a short period may be sufficient to move them through the plateau.
- *Explanation 4* Earlier introduction of more accurate and detailed feedback might ensure quicker elimination of errors and incorrect responses.

A number of fundamental lessons for trainers are underlined by an examination of the foregoing discussion on learning curves and plateaux. They must be observant, analytical, patient and sensitive, not cast their programmes in stone and, above all, be prepared to substantially modify or vary the principles and conditions of learning that they employ initially to meet unanticipated changing circumstances.

Forgetting, skill loss and transfer of training

The trainer is particularly interested in three effects resulting from the trainee's learning experience and these are related to the following questions:

- How effectively did the trainee learn initially?
- How well was this learning retained over an extended period?
- How easily did the learning 'transfer' from the training situation to the work situation?

So far, this chapter has concentrated on the principles and conditions of learning relating to the first of these questions. The other two questions have been addressed only indirectly and now need to be considered in more depth.

Retention and forgetting

Forgetting or failing to retain all that was originally learned is a common enough human experience. In some circumstances this could have serious or even disastrous consequences. It is often vital to ensure that the skills and knowledge learned in training are retained and made full use of back on the job. This may be difficult to achieve if there is little or no opportunity to practise the skill or to employ the knowledge in that context. However, there are a number of suggestions or procedures that the trainer may be able to introduce which could prevent or minimize the retention problem and these are outlined below:

- Introduce a job aid during the training programme; subsequently this can act as a form of aide memoire after training. (A job aid is any form of printed document kept in the place of work which can be used as a memory jogger or as a procedural guide for a difficult, complex or infrequently performed task.)
- Train according to a spaced rather than a massed practice regime.
- Train to produce over-learning in the trainee; that is, train to a level of performance above that which is strictly necessary to achieve the training objectives.
- Encourage the trainees to engage in mental practice or rehearsal in the work location.

- Make the training material as meaningful as possible by linking it with the trainees' previous knowledge and experience and by organizing and sequencing it to make initial learning easier.
- Ensure that the general conduct of the training programme motivates the trainees, stimulates their interests and is not an experience that they would rather forget or that is simply unmemorable.

Transfer of training

Transfer of training is an issue, sometimes a problem, closely associated with forgetting and skill loss. It occurs whenever the existence of a previously established habit or skill has an influence on the acquisition, performance or re-learning of another habit or skill.

In the training context positive transfer will have taken place if the trainee is able to apply on the job what has been learned in training with relative ease or is able to learn a new task more quickly as a result of earlier training on another task. Conversely negative transfer arises when performance on the job or on the new task is decelerated or hindered by what knowledge and skills have been acquired. Changing from a conventionally geared car to an automatic illustrates potential transfer problems. In this situation a number of skills learned on the conventional vehicle are likely to transfer positively to the automatic vehicle, such as steering, general road sense, etc, whereas to begin with gear changing and foot controls might be awkward to apply and not synchronize particularly well because of negative transfer.

Two sets of ideas or theories have been put forward to explain the transfer phenomenon and these have different implications for training. The theories have been referred to as the identical-elements theory and the transfer-through-principles theory. Figure 7.9 helps to explain and illustrate these two theories.

The identical-elements theory claims that the nature of the transfer that takes place will depend on the degree to which there are common or identical stimulus and response elements in the training and work situations.

If the stimulus conditions (ST/SW) and response requirements (RT/RW) in the environments of training and work are very similar, then there should be high positive transfer. Some forms of on-the-job training come close to fulfilling this kind of specification and this is the reason, no doubt, why this form of training can prove to be very effective. The opposite case, where the stimulus conditions and response requirements are totally dissimilar, would normally lead to no transfer at all. This kind of training scenario is highly improbable and, should it occur, would naturally raise very serious questions about the competence of the trainer or whoever undertook the training analyses and programme design. Similar reservations about the trainer might be appropriate in the case of negative transfer; this is likely to occur where the stimulus situations are much the same or similar but the response requirements are

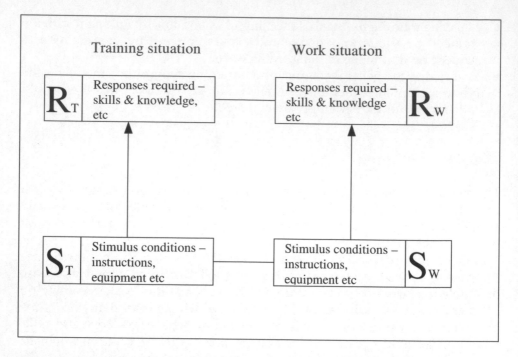

Figure 7.9   The identical-elements theory and the transfer-through-principles theory

different. The displays or equipment used in training may be or may look similar to what is used in the work situation. However, minor modifications or subtle alterations which have not been noted by, or communicated to, the trainer could have changed the response requirements to a significant degree. The trainees' on-the-job work performance will be affected directly. The work of others also may be disrupted and time may be wasted while the trainee learns new and more relevant responses.

Finally, what happens when ST and SW are dissimilar but RT and RW are the same? The answer to this question would seem to be – it depends. If ST and SW are quite different then no transfer should take place, because the trainee will not associate SW with RW which is identical to RT and therefore will not respond appropriately when SW occurs. However, as ST and SW move closer together then provided there are common critical elements in these conditions positive transfer should result.

Approaching the transfer problem from the standpoint of the identical-elements theory would seem to be appropriate where the task conditions and requirements are predictable and can be defined clearly and specifically. The 'trick' for the trainer is to be able to identify the critical elements in the stimulus conditions and response requirements through a close examination of the work and, where feasible, introduce them into the training programme environment. This may not be as straightforward as it seems at first sight. For as Baldwin and Ford (1988) highlight, it may be a problem to identify what exactly has to be made the same or identical in the training environment to match the work environment in order to promote learning, retention and transfer. They suggest that there are two aspects of the notion of similarity – *physical fidelity*, i.e. the extent to which the training conditions (task, equipment, surroundings, etc) are similar to the work environment, and *psychological fidelity*, i.e. the degree to which the trainee attaches similar meanings to what is introduced in the training environment and what exists in the work context. In the opinion of Baldwin and Ford these concepts and their relative significance in different training contexts have been overlooked in the industrial training literature.

A second approach to the transfer issue emphasizes the importance of the trainee learning conceptual or behavioural principles that can be generalized and transferred to a set of varied, though circumscribed, situations. For example, in training in counselling skills trainees would be encouraged to learn skills enabling them to perform flexibly and adaptively towards their clients rather than acquire a set of behaviours and attitudes which might be applied only rigidly and in a limited number of circumstances. This theory seems to pay less attention to physical fidelity and to be more concerned with psychological fidelity. To fall in line with these ideas, training programmes would also focus on helping trainees to acquire 'perceptions for sensitive discrimination of their environment' (Bass and Vaughan, 1966). However, it should not be assumed that these theories are incompatible; it might be wiser to think of their application as following a 'horses for courses' philosophy. At one extreme, where the work environment seems to prescribe unvarying task conditions and requirements, then a training programme based on the identical-elements theory might be appropriate. On the other hand if it is not possible to anticipate fully or to predict the stimulus conditions and if the response requirements vary, then the training situation may need to reflect a transfer through the principles approach.

Although there are still a number of issues to be tackled and settled regarding transfer of training, several broad recommendations can be made to trainers about how to facilitate this process:

- Where it is feasible to do so make the training situation similar to the work situation in terms of stimulus conditions and response requirements.
- Where it is appropriate draw out in the training environment general principles and strategies and show their application through varied examples.
- Give trainees ample opportunity to practise and rehearse the task or skill to the point of over-learning.
- Introduce the trainees to a variety of contexts or stimulus conditions in which to learn and practise or exercise the relevant skill and knowledge.

This should enable them to generalize more easily to the work situation what they have learned in training.

- Ensure that the critical features of the stimulus conditions in work are drawn to the attention of the trainee during training and distinguished clearly from likely competing stimulus conditions existing in the work context.
- Avoid putting trainees through rote-learning sessions as this tends to discourage transfer.
- Try to make the training material meaningful by locating 'the individual items of skill or knowledge. . . in a rich network of related items' (Annett and Sparrow, 1985).
- If possible and relevant introduce discovery learning and learning-to-learn sessions into the training programme.
- Stimulate motivation and show the value of the training to the work setting; the trainers' motivation to succeed in training, strongly influenced by their perception of its value, may carry over to the job which, in turn, will have a positive impact on transfer.
- In the post-training situation set goals for or with the trainees and give pertinent and timely feedback.
- Attempt to create a climate in the organization that is conducive to positive transfer; establish good liaison and communication links with trainees and their managers in order to involve them in the transfer process, discussions on their expectations and on how to maintain the trainees' skill, knowledge and attitudes in the work setting.

The application of the learning principles, strategies and tactics already covered will hopefully ensure, at a minimum, that a trainee is moved from a situation of unconscious or conscious incompetence through to conscious competence. However, the transfer process is enhanced if the trainee goes beyond this to the stage of unconscious competence or automaticity. Automaticity means the ability of a trainee to perform the required skill, or aspects of the required skill, without conscious awareness. For example, the highly competent car driver has a number of routines that he or she can carry out automatically that then 'frees up' his or her cognitive capacity to deal with unusual road or traffic conditions, emergencies or the unexpected. The National Research Council (1991) makes the claim that 'The more automatic the skill, the greater the chance that the skill will be retained over non-use periods without refresher training or rehearsals.' In order to achieve this more resources (time, manpower and so on) may have to be devoted to the training period. In many circumstances such increased initial investment would make both economic and psychological sense.

Baldwin and Ford (1988) make two other suggestions to assist transfer namely 'buddy systems' and 'booster sessions'. Buddy systems involve two trainees being paired off to work together post-training and to give one another mutual support, provide advice and be alert for signs of relapse in themselves and the buddy. Booster sessions are basically an extension of the original training with trainer and trainee meeting face-to-face for some kind of revision input period.

Principles, conditions and material to be learned

The principles, conditions and features of learning which have been covered so far are not all equally relevant to the kinds of material that could be included in a training session. Figure 7.10 sets out those which generally are most applicable to the different categories of training objective listed in Chapter 6.

Gagné and Briggs (1979) describe a more complex and more detailed scheme for linking learning categories and conditions that would further assist trainers in their efforts to design and develop training programmes. However, irrespective of what scheme is employed, it is vital for trainers to appreciate this critical point; the programmes they establish, in order to realize particular types of training objective, must take clear account of and incorporate the learning principles and conditions that relate to those objectives. The relevant principles and conditions must be an integral part of the methods chosen or designed to achieve the stated objectives.

Individual differences

A number of the principles and conditions of learning outlined above provide trainers with some general guidelines to assist them in the planning and design of training programmes and events. However, the trainer must appreciate that not all target populations react or respond uniformly to these principles and conditions. In reality there can be significant differences within and between training groups which requires some flexibility in their introduction and application.

Naturally, it is not possible for the trainer to make allowances for every individual who has to be trained. Initially, far too much time would have to be spent measuring and testing people in order to identify all their differences, similarities and idiosyncracies. To match training to the trainees' individual characteristics would need such an enormous requirement for resources that the whole exercise would be impossible or unrealistic to carry out. Nevertheless, it is important to have some knowledge of individual differences for two very good reasons. Firstly, it may help to explain why certain individuals are not behaving or responding as might be expected (i.e. in a similar way to others in the group). Secondly, it could offer an opportunity to deal with trainees on an individual, sub-group or group basis when something is known about their styles and preferences. Four important factors that illustrate the link between individual differences, learning principles and conditions, and training programme design are age, level of intelligence and ability, background and emotional disposition, and learning style.

Training objective	Learning principles and conditions
Knowledge:	
Memorization	Meaningful context Accurate and immediate feedback Prompting Rehearsal (retrieval) Distributed practice
Comprehension	Verbal introduction Meaningful context Rehearsal and feedback Reflection Distributed practice (reviews)
Skills:	
Intellectual	Verbal introductions Demonstration Guidance, cueing and feedback Practice – whole/part regime Discovery learning Reflection
Manual	Demonstration Practice – distributed Feedback, guidance and cueing Explanation Over-learning
Social	Verbal introductions Human model Practice Feedback, guidance and cueing Imagining and reflection
Attitudes:	Observation of human model reinforcement (action taken)

Figure 7.10   Training objectives, learning principles and conditions

Age

Physical and mental abilities deteriorate with age. In relation to the latter, basic abilities such as numerical aptitude and intelligence decline from the early twenties. There is also an impairment in people's short-term memory, and their capacity to process information and ignore irrelevant task details diminishes as they get older. For example, we do not find many stock exchange and commodity dealers or air traffic controllers in the upper age groups. Another feature of the older person's performance in a learning situation that has a significance for training, is the fact that if he or she makes a mistake early in training then eliminating it becomes more difficult. Generally speaking, the older individual learns more slowly and has more difficulty 'grasping' new material than his younger counterpart. However, all is not 'doom and gloom', a number of suggestions have emerged from studies of older trainees on how to modify training programmes to compensate for some of the difficulties they experience. A summary of these suggestions has been presented by Newsham (1969) and is reproduced at Figure 7.11.

The theory of adult learning – andragogy – developed by Knowles, Holton and Swanson (1998) also bears on the question of what considerations need to be borne in mind when training the older individual. The andragogical model is based on a number of assumptions clearly different from those that underpin the child-centred pedagogical model, and these assumptions are set out below:

- *The need to know*. Adults need to know the reasons for learning something before carrying out the learning. And it is important that trainers engage learners in a collaborative exercise to answer three questions: What is going to be learnt? Why they should learn? How is learning going to be conducted? Furthermore organisations can raise the awareness of individuals of the 'need to know' through a variety of methods including work appraisal systems, development centres and job rotation.
- *The learner's self-concept*. In Knowles's opinion adults develop a self-concept of independence, by being responsible for making their own decisions and being self-directed. Actions by the trainer that imply a dependent relationship can in many learning situations lead to a withdrawal by the learner. To avoid this Knowles suggests that educators and trainers devise learning experiences that encourage adult trainees to become self-directed learners.
- *The role of the learner's experience*. Adults come to a training event with a multitude of past experiences, which create a wider range of individual differences than is normally found among younger trainees. The positive consequences of this are that in a number of training situations the learner's experiences can supply the learning resources. Experiential learning techniques such as simulation exercises and case studies exploit this resource. On the down side, the past experience of the adult trainees may generate habits, biases and prejudices that close their minds to new ways of thinking and behaving. The trainer must be aware of this possibility, and institute methods that will help trainees to analyse this negativism and to consider new possibilities.

Difficulties increase with age	Suggestions as to how the training could be suitably adapted for the older learner
When tasks involve the need for short-term memory	<ul><li>Avoid verbal learning and the need for conscious memorizing. This may often be accomplished by making use of 'cues' which guide the trainee.</li><li>When possible, use a method which involves learning a task as a whole. If it has to be learned in part, these parts should be learned in cumulative stages (a, a + b, a + b + c, and so on).</li><li>Ensure consolidation of learning before passing on to the next task or to the next part of the same task (importance of self-testing and checking).</li></ul>
When there is 'interference' from other activities or from other learning	<ul><li>Restrict the range of activities covered in the course.</li><li>Employ longer learning sessions than is customary for younger trainees (i.e. not necessarily a longer overall time, but longer periods without interruption).</li><li>To provide variety, change the method of teaching rather than the content of the course. A change of subject matter may lead to confusion between the subjects.</li></ul>
When there is need to translate information from one medium to another	<ul><li>Avoid the use of visual aids which necessitate a change of logic or a change in the plan of presentation.</li><li>If simulators or training devices are to be used, then they must be designed to enable learning to be directly related to practice.</li></ul>
When learning is abstract or unrelated to realities	<ul><li>Present new knowledge only as a solution to a problem which is already appreciated.</li></ul>
When there is need to 'unlearn' something for which the older learner has a predilection	<ul><li>Ensure 'correct' learning in the first place. This can be accomplished by designing the training around tasks of graduated difficulty.</li></ul>
When tasks are 'paced'	<ul><li>Allow the older learner to proceed at his own pace.</li><li>Allow him to structure his own programme within certain defined limits.</li><li>Aim at his beating his own targets rather than those of others.</li></ul>
As tasks become more complex	<ul><li>Allow for learning by easy stages of increasing complexity.</li></ul>

When the trainee lacks confidence	• Use written instructions.
	• Avoid the use of production material too soon in the course.
	• Provide longer induction periods. Introduce the trainee very gradually both to new machinery and to new jobs.
	• Stagger the intake of trainees.
	• If possible, recruit groups of workmates.
	• Avoid formal tests.
	• Don't give formal time limits for the completion of the course.
When learning becomes mentally passive	• Use an open situation which admits discovery learning.
	• Employ meaningful material and tasks which are sufficiently challenging to an adult.
	• Avoid a blackboard and classroom situation or conditions in which trainees may in earlier years have experienced a sense of failure.

Figure 7.11 Problems of learning for the adult (Newsham, 1969)

Reprinted from *The Challenge of Change to the Adult Trainee* with permission of The Stationery Office.

- *Readiness to learn.* Knowles claims, 'Adults become ready to learn those things they need to know and be able to do in order to cope effectively with their real-life situations.' The development phases through which individuals move during the course of their careers are often the appropriate points to introduce development activities, as they are then in an amenable frame of mind to learn. In addition an individual's readiness to learn can be stimulated proactively through development procedures such as career counselling, mentoring and secondments.
- *Orientation to learning.* Adults are oriented to learn when confronted with real-life situations or problems. However, it is critical that they perceive the learning they have to undertake as enabling them to perform effectively the tasks making up these situations or problems.
- *Motivation.* Although factors such as money and career prospects may, in a number of situations, act as effective external motivators, intrinsic motivation provided by job satisfaction, interest and meaningfulness are likely to be more powerful influences on an individual's performance.

Finally, it should not be assumed that there is a standard or 'clone'-like older person. In terms of mental capacity, evidence is available to support the notion of there being a greater disparity in intelligence and intellectual ability amongst older people than in the younger age group. It would seem that the rate of decline in measured intelligence is greatest amongst those whose scores were low to begin with and the decline is slowest for those who had high scores originally. Furthermore, the degree to which a person has exercised and stimulated his or her intellect over the years through further study and intellectual interests and pursuits also will affect the rate of decline. Some of the training suggestions, e.g. allowing the older trainee to proceed at his or her own pace, could be moderated in the light of these findings.

Levels of intelligence and ability

Most groups or individuals who have to be taught a particular skill or task are selected using criteria, e.g. educational level, which places them in roughly the same range of intellectual ability. What ability or intelligence range the trainees fit into should have a bearing on the principles and tactics the trainer employs on their training programme, for instance:

- Trainees in the lower ability range usually prefer to progress from concrete examples to general principles whereas those of a higher ability or those who have had a more academic education, possibly are more inclined to work in the reverse direction.
- Depending on the complexity of the task, higher intelligence groups can cope with learning a task as a whole; individuals of lower intelligence manage better using the cumulative part method, i.e. A, then A + B, then A + B + C, etc.
- Unstructured training situations might be unsuitable for individuals of low ability because they 'may be more easily distracted by irrelevant information leading to an inefficient strategy. . . This would suggest that guidance training would be initially beneficial for such trainees' (Stammers and Patrick, 1975).

Background and emotional disposition

In addition to what was covered in a previous section, the trainees' general motivational readiness could depend, amongst other things, on their cultural or educational background or emotional disposition. Because of their background, some trainees may perceive their trainers in a particular way, possibly as the fount of all wisdom. This undoubted misapprehension is very likely to make them reluctant to question or challenge different ideas or to enter into a discussion. In these circumstances the trainer will need to exercise patience and tact to 'bring the trainees out' so that they might benefit from a more open learning climate.

An individual's emotional state or disposition may influence the how and what of learning. Anxiety, fear of failure and lack of confidence are the kinds of emotion experienced by some trainees that can adversely affect their motivation and willingness to learn. In order to counteract these barriers the trainer may need to: modify the pace and style of the programme; set more easily attainable goals for certain individuals; and counsel those trainees who feel inadequate or experience difficulties. Of course, individuals who are over-confident, arrogant or unwilling to face up to the fact that they have learning difficulties also may need some form of individual counselling.

Learning style

Increased attention has been given to the concept of individual learning styles when considering learning strategies. This idea refers to the fact that individuals differ in their propensity or inclination to learn from different activities or approaches. Some people prefer practical exercises at an early stage of training and will be prepared to learn by their mistakes, whilst others like to receive demonstrations and explanations first before reflecting on the content and assessing its relevance and importance to their own circumstances. Again, others are more inclined to theoretical, abstract discussion, to establish a thought process and method for action, whilst some individuals prefer to be given information or taught skills that they feel can be transferred to their work environment.

The work of Kolb and colleagues (1974, 1984) in the United States has been particularly influential in furthering our understanding of the importance of learning styles. In the United Kingdom, Honey and Mumford (1986) examined the implications of managerial learning styles for management training and development and identified and defined four basic styles:

Activists Enjoy the here and now, dominated by immediate experiences, tend to revel in the short-term crisis, firefighting. They tend to thrive on the challenge of new experiences, but are relatively bored with implementation and longer-term consolidation. They are the life and soul of the managerial party.

Reflectors Like to stand back and ponder on experiences and observe them from different perspectives. They collect data and analyse it before coming to any conclusions. They like to consider all possible angles and implications before making a move so they tend to be cautious. They actually enjoy observing other people in action and often take a back seat at meetings.

Theorists Are keen on basic assumptions, principles, theories, models and systems thinking. They prize rationality and logic. They tend to be detached, analytical, and are unhappy with subjective or ambiguous experiences. They like to assemble disparate facts into coherent theories. They like to make things tidy and fit them into rational schemes.

Pragmatists Positively search out new ideas and take the first opportunity to experiment with applications. The sort of people who return from management courses brimming with new ideas that they want to try out in practice. They respond to problems and opportunities 'as a challenge' (the Activists probably would not recognize them as problems and opportunities).

An individual's profile of learning preference based on these styles can be assessed by questionnaire and Honey and Mumford suggest a number of activities that can be used to promote the learning of those with specific preferences:

Activists learn best from activities where:

- There are new or novel experiences, exercises and problems from which to learn.
- They can involve themselves in short 'here and now' activities such as business games, competitive teamwork tasks, role-playing exercises and, where it is appropriate, to have a go.
- There is excitement and drama, things are in rapid flux and chop and change with a range of varied activities to cope with.
- They are thrown in at the deep end to tackle a difficult task.
- They are involved with other people in solving problems as a part of a team and by bouncing ideas off them.

Activists learn least from, and may react against, activities where:

- They are in a passive role, i.e. reading, watching, listening to lectures.
- They are required to observe and not get involved.
- They are required to assimilate, analyse and interpret 'messy' data.
- They are given theoretical explanations.
- They must practise an activity over and over again.
- They have precise instructions to follow with little room to manoeuvre.

Reflectors learn best from activities where:

- They are allowed to watch and/or think over activities.
- They are able to stand back from things and listen or observe, i.e. observing a group at work, watching a video, etc.
- They are allowed to think before acting, 'look before they leap', i.e. given adequate time to prepare.
- They have the opportunity to review what has happened and what they have learned.
- They can exchange ideas, views, etc with other people in a risk-free atmosphere.

Reflectors learn least from, and may react against, activities where:

- They are 'forced' into the limelight, i.e. role play in front of onlookers.
- They are 'thrown' into situations without warning and which require action without preparation.
- They are given cut and dried instructions of how things should be done.
- They are moved on rapidly from one activity to another and are worried about time pressures.
- They are required to make short cuts or do a superficial job in the interests of expediency.

Theorists learn best from activities where:

- What they are being offered is part of a system, model or theory.
- They are intellectually stretched, i.e. being tested in a tutorial session, and have an opportunity to question and probe basic methodology, assumptions or logic.
- They are in structured situations with a clear purpose.
- They are offered interesting ideas and concepts even though these are not immediately relevant.
- They are required to understand and participate in complex situations.

Theorists learn least from, and may react against, activities where:

- They are pitchforked into an activity having no apparent purpose.
- They have to participate in situations emphasizing emotions and feelings.
- They are involved in unstructured activities in which ambiguity and uncertainty is high.
- They are asked to act or decide without a basis in policy or principle.
- They find the subject matter platitudinous, shallow or superficial.

Pragmatists learn best from activities where:

- They can see an obvious link between the subject matter and the job.
- They are introduced to ideas or techniques for doing things that have obvious practical advantages and have high face validity.
- They have a chance to try out and practise techniques with coaching/ feedback from a credible expert.
- They are given opportunities to implement what they have learnt.
- They can concentrate on practical issues, i.e. drawing up action plans with an obvious end product.

Pragmatists learn least from, and may react against, activities where:

● The timing content is not perceived to be related to an immediate need they recognize or have practical relevance and benefit.
● There is no practice or clear guidelines on how to do it.
● Trainees or the content itself seem divorced from reality, i.e. in an ivory tower.
● They feel that people are going around in circles and not getting anywhere fast enough.
● There is no apparent reward to be gained from the training permitted or there are political, managerial or personal obstacles to implementation.

Although Honey and Mumford's ideas on learning styles appear, on the surface at least, to resemble those of Kolb (1984), to whom they recognize an important debt, several points of difference can be detected between them. In Kolb's view acquiring new knowledge, skills and attitudes is a process of 'confrontation among four modes of experiential learning'. These four modes which are concrete experience (CE), reflective observation (RO), abstract conceptualization (AC) and active experimentation (AE) make up a cyclical process of learning (Figure 7.12).

Kolb argues that for learners to be fully effective they need to acquire abilities related to these four modes of learning:

Concrete experience abilities (CE) – Learners must have the capacity to involve themselves fully in new experiences in an unprejudiced way.
Reflective observation abilities (RO) – Learners must be able to observe, and to reflect on their experience from different angles or viewpoints.
Abstract conceptualization abilities (AC) – Learners must be able to incorporate their observations into valid and rationally based theories.
Active experimentation abilities (AE) – The theories learners develop must enable them to make decisions and to be able to solve problems.

In Kolb's opinion the learning process can be reduced to two primary bipolar dimensions, incorporating the four learning modes outlined above. One of these dimensions is described by concrete experience at one pole and abstract conceptualization at the other, whereas the polar opposites of the other dimensions are active experimentation and reflective observation. Learning consists of moving in varying degrees between these opposite modes. Kolb suggests that individuals' choices of experience will influence which modes of learning are emphasized and which learning strategy or strategies they develop. Learning strategies involve combinations of basic learning modes, i.e. CE/RO, RO/AC, AE/CE/RO, etc. Kolb suggests that it is the combination of all four of these elementary learning forms that produces the highest level of learning. In Kolb's schema the learning styles that he has identified relate to pair combinations of the basic learning modes or abilities:

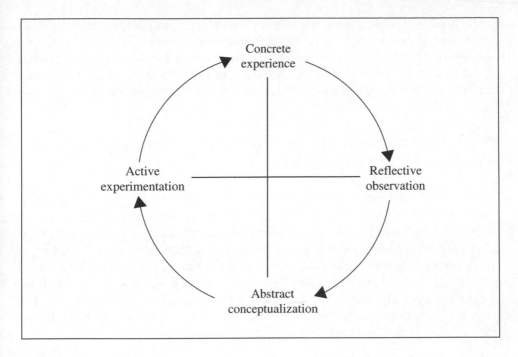

Figure 7.12   The learning cycle – Kolb

- *Convergent style* – the individual emphasizes the learning abilities of abstract conceptualization and active experimentation and shows strength in the practical application of ideas and problem solving.
- *Divergent style* – concrete experience and reflective observation abilities characterize individuals showing this style. Being imaginative and seeing things from many perspectives would describe people in this category.
- *Assimilation style* – the learning abilities of abstract conceptualization and reflective observation are dominant in a person adopting this style. Inductive reasoning and the ability to encompass disparate observations into an integrated framework are particular strengths of individuals displaying this style.
- *Accommodative style* – emphasis is placed on concrete experience and active experimentation abilities. The person adopting this style gets things done and gets involved in new experiences. Intuition and trial-and-error rather than theory are the basis for problem solving.

Kolb does not conceive learning styles as fixed personality traits but rather as adaptive orientations influenced by an individual's basic psychological make-up or type, educational specialization, career, present job and the specific task or problem the person is currently tackling.

The foregoing discussion emphasizes that Honey and Mumford, and Kolb attach a great deal of importance to learning from experience. However, Caple and Martin (1994) find that there are a number of criticisms and questions that could be raised and observations made about their ideas, which may have implications for the usefulness of these ideas in a training context:

What is meant precisely by 'experience' in Honey and Mumford's and Kolb's models?

Fundamentally, Honey and Mumford and their adherents argue that learning from experience is critical to effective learning. But what they mean by experience and what constitutes experience, is not clear or is assumed. Kolb (1984) is a little clearer on this point. He suggests that experiential learning is 'the process whereby knowledge is created through the transformation of experience. . . the learner is directly in touch with the reality being studied, rather than purely thinking about the encounter or only considering the possibility of "doing something with it"'. However, even this extended definition of experiential learning begs a number of questions:

- Are some forms of experience more valuable or useful to learn from than others and, if so, which?
- What precisely can we learn from experience?
- Are skills, knowledge and changed behaviours/attitudes all equally acquirable experientially?
- Can activities that would commonly be associated with Reflector or Theorist learning styles – e.g. observing a process or event or reading a stimulating book – be regarded as a significant experience, as defined by Kolb, or does the experience have to be concrete?

These questions are not semantic cavilling but are fundamental to any consideration of the virtues of learning from experience. After all, if we are not clear about what experience is, or what we can learn from it, why should we choose experience as a means of meeting our learning objectives?

How accurate is the learning cycle in describing how people actually learn from experience?

Earlier on in this chapter it was suggested that individuals may learn through five basic activities: trial and error, perceptual organization, behaviour modelling, mediation and reflection.

These ways of learning are likely to be employed in differing combinations for a great deal of what we learn, including learning through experience.

In contrast, Honey (1984) has a more mechanistic view, observing that he has always accepted the notion that learning from experience is a four-stage process:

1. Having an experience
2. Reviewing the experience
3. Reaching conclusions from the experience
4. Planning the next steps

Again, the sequence implied by this statement and the integrity of the learning cycle as commonly depicted must be questioned. If experience is literally the starting-point, then this assumes that experience just happens to an individual when often, in reality, he or she chooses to have experiences on the basis of anticipation and conceptualization, e.g. they may decide to expose themselves to certain activities/circumstances which they believe may be beneficial to them in some way.

Even in those learning situations, such as sensitivity training, where trainees are directly in touch with 'here and now' experience, there is a reliance upon the observations and reflections of facilitators, who are themselves steeped in particular theoretical approaches.

A more valid way of representing a learning cycle incorporating experience therefore might be as shown in Figure 7.13.

This cycle reflects more accurately, for instance, how scientific knowledge is actually acquired. For, as Chalmers (1982) has argued, in this context, beginning an enquiry with data collection or experimentation undirected by theory would constitute a 'naive inductivist approach to the acquisition of knowledge'. By the same token, it is contended here that learning from experience is 'theory' dependent.

Another quote from Kolb might be instructive at this point: 'It is in this interplay between expectation and experience that learning occurs.' This clearly implies the important role played by reflection and theory in the expectation phase, thus contradicting the immutable cycle of experiential learning set out by Honey.

To counter some of the above objections, it is sometimes argued that learners could enter the cycle at any point and, provided that all four stages were gone through, effective learning would ensue.

If this is so, however, a number of further questions arise.

Why argue, as Honey does above, for the primacy of experience as the motor of learning? Is learning likely to be less or more effective if reflection or conceptualization is the starting point? How is it possible, anyway, to start from a pragmatist mode, i.e. 'Planning the next steps'?

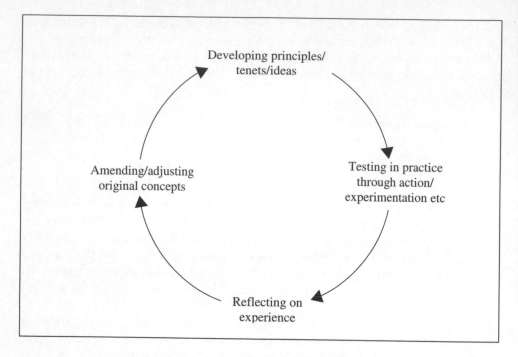

Figure 7.13   A learning cycle incorporating experience

It may also be true that, with some learning, it would be positively harmful to begin from an 'activist', having an experience standpoint. We would hope, for instance, that the training of surgeons would preclude the application of an activist mode until after a very substantial amount of observation, review, theorizing and planning had preceded it! Again, this brings out the issue of what specifically are the objectives of experiential learning?

To what extent do situational features/influences on individuals' abilities determine the appropriateness of learning from experience?

Although learning situations may be flexible or diverse, in the sense that they may be approached through differential learning styles, it may, or should be, the interpretation of the learning situation that dictates the form of action that is experienced. In other words, some reflection/theorizing may need to be undertaken before the action experience. Furthermore, it is possible that the situations which learners imagine they are facing (including time constraints, perception of complexity etc) will influence the learning style they initially employ. Experiential learning, in this sense, results essentially from a trans-

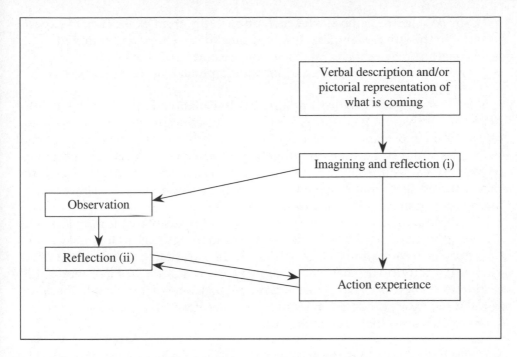

Figure 7.14 Verbal description and/or pictorial representation of what is coming

action between the individual and the situation. An illustration of this form of transactional learning is set out in Figure 7.14.

The perception of our ability, or our actual inability, to do or learn things will also have an impact on our adherence to the learning cycle. Thus, if an individual is intellectually unable to grasp and/or apply a given concept or lacks, for example, the small motor capabilities required to attain certain manual skills, he or she will fail to learn, however purposefully the learning cycle is adhered to.

Indeed, a conscious application of the learning cycle by a trainee using a learning log (Honey and Mumford's tool for recording experiences) might be counter-productive, i.e. a misinterpretation of an experience may result in the wrong conclusions being drawn and flawed future actions being planned.

How realistic and meaningful are the learning style preferences depicted by Honey and Mumford?

Honey and Mumford attempt to describe the learning styles and activities commensurate with those who have marked preferences for any one stage of the cycle. With some imagination it is possible to visualize:

- *Extreme activists* as those who rush animatedly from experience to experience in the spirit of enquiry, trying things that are new and different.
- *Extreme reflectors* capable of dispassionate and insular analysis.
- *Extreme theorists* characterized by lofty conceptualizing and logical reasoning.

It is far less easy to visualize a pragmatist in isolation. How plausible is it to depict an individual who learns simply by applying practical skills heedless of previous experiences, and who has no fundamental knowledge of the principles and theories underpinning the performance of a task? The pragmatist, *in extremis,* would surely be no more than a robot. Suffice to say, therefore, that it would seem that pragmatism can only be said to be the application of learning. It cannot constitute a learning style in itself.

This raises a quite fundamental question: what is meant by the term learning style? Is it, as Dixon (1982) suggests, '. . . the unique way each individual gathers or processes information'? Or is it an attitude towards, or value placed on, a particular activity? Honey and Mumford do not seem to have made this distinction very clear. The activist and pragmatist styles come close to the latter and the reflector or theorist styles to the former version of learning styles.

Other questions that need to be addressed include:

- To what extent does the individual's level of intelligence or cognitive complexity influence the learning style he or she prefers?
- To what degree are people flexible in terms of learning styles across situations? Are learning situations more or less diverse in respect of the opportunity they provide for different modes of learning? Talbot (1985) points out 'We believe that such information about individuals and situations can be used both to increase a person's flexibility and help him choose situations in which his strengths are relevant.'
- How valid is the idea that the highest level of learning requires the combination of all four elementary learning modes? Over what time period, in relation to a specific learning situation, would these modes need to come into operation? How important is the sequence in which they come into effect?

Without denying the validity of or anticipating the answers to these questions trainers nevertheless would benefit in a number of ways from being able to gauge, in a reasonably objective way, for example through questionnaire responses, trainees' dominant styles. Some of the possible benefits are:

- It would help trainers to design programmes that fit in with the predominant and main subordinate styles of the trainees.
- It would assist trainers to understand better the relationship they were trying to create with the trainees.
- If the results of the questionnaire were 'fedback' to the trainees it could help them to appreciate the difficulties they might experience with the

training methods that out of necessity have to be employed on the programme.
- It would identify for trainers those individuals who may need special attention because their learning style differs from the norm or majority of the group.
- It could allow trainers to put into perspective the trainees' observations and comments about the training content and methods.

However, even without such structured questionnaire data, trainers can often make a general assessment or prediction of trainees' styles on the basis of their educational or occupational background. For example, salesmen working in a dynamic marketing environment are very likely to differ, both in temperament and learning styles, from personnel administering stable bureaucratic structures and systems thus necessitating different training activities. Where the group is or appears to be heterogeneous in terms of learning styles the trainer will have to be flexible and may have to adopt a 'trainer for all seasons' approach and try to cater for individual needs in the context of the overall aim of the programme and its specific objectives.

On occasions the training content may 'match' the dominant style of the group, e.g. new graduates being presented with conceptual material. This is not always going to be the case and the trainer will have to give careful thought to initial explanations and exercises on the programme. Alternatively the trainer may give consideration to how the less prominent styles of the trainees can be developed through preliminary or pre-programme activities.

Honey and Mumford put forward several interesting ideas on the kinds of action that may help to develop learning styles. In a way this notion is akin to the learning to learn strategy which was referred to earlier. The ability to use all four styles is advantageous for trainees because for instance, as Kenny and Reid (1986) point out, reflection and conceptualization can assist transfer of learning to new situations. No doubt, in other circumstances, being comfortable with an action-based approach would also be of advantage to the learners. To sum up the topic of learning styles a particular quotation from Kenny and Reid would seem highly appropriate:

It is important for the trainer to realize that he has a natural learning/teaching style, and that in choosing appropriate techniques he should consider the trainees' preferred or desired learning style, as well as his own, in so far as it is practicable to do so.

CONCLUSION

Before leaving the subject of learning it would be as well to sound a note of caution. A number of the principles and conditions of learning outlined in this chapter have been investigated and validated mainly in experimental and nonworking settings and their general application must be approached, therefore, with care and intelligence. For as Baldwin and Ford (1988) emphasize operationalizing these principles in controlled experimental settings is relatively straightforward; it becomes more problematic on complex organizational training programmes. Therefore, within the general guidelines trainers must find out what works best in particular circumstances with certain types of training material and target populations rather than assume that the guidelines can be applied in a mechanistic and unthinking manner.

8

The Training Programme: Selection, Design and Delivery

The selection, design and delivery of the training programme can be under-taken only when a well-written set of objectives has been produced. These objectives serve three main purposes within the context of the selection, design and delivery of training. They state what has to be achieved by the end of training, they provide a sequence or order in which the training should take place and they give an indicator of what kinds of strategy and tactic should be used. Strategies and tactics are the general and the specific methods which the trainer uses to ensure that the most effective form of learning is employed, e.g. strategy – learner-centred, tactic – programmed learning. However, the trainer does not have a completely free hand in the choice of methodology. There are a number of factors which influence choice and these include learning principles, target population and a number of possible constraints. The interaction of these factors with the design process is illustrated in Figure 8.1.

CONSTRAINTS

Always, there are a number of constraints at the back of the trainer's mind that influence decisions about the design of training. Some constraints will have been imposed upon, negotiated or agreed by the trainer when the terms of reference were drawn up. As the training project continues and at the stage of selecting and designing training, further negotiation and discussion is likely

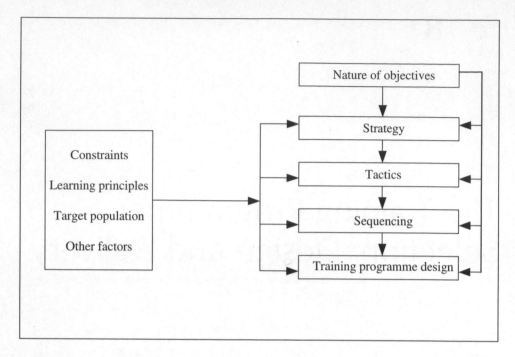

Figure 8.1 Diagram to show interaction of factors that influence the design of training

to take place. One of the greatest constraints that has to be contended with is time. Trainers are usually expected to react quickly to meet the needs of the client and, after the initial investigation, time has to be considered in a number of ways. There is the consideration of time in terms of how soon the programme has to be launched and how much time there is to design training and to prepare the materials for it. There is the balance of the length of time that people can be spared for training and the length of time that is needed to achieve the objectives. Very often there is a backlog of personnel who need to be trained before the programme takes on its expected pattern of frequency which means that deadlines will need to be set for clearing the backlog.

When the constraints of time are such that it is difficult to fit everything in, trainers should expect to go back to their clients to discuss and ask for decisions about which objectives should be omitted so that no one has unrealistic expectations of the outcomes of the training. For example it may have to be realized that because time is so limited, a trainee may be able only to 'state' how something is done rather than actually 'do it'.

Time constraints are usually linked closely with accommodation, facilities and their availability. Organizations vary in their allocation of dedicated space for training. Some organizations have staff colleges and training centres while others find it more cost-effective to use conference centres and hotels as the venues for their training. In some cases on-job training has been found the most appropriate strategy for training and therefore accommodation becomes less of a problem. There are circumstances when a shared dedicated space is provided for meetings, conferences, presentations and training for which there is a 'booking' system which may not allow anyone to book further than a certain number of weeks in advance or where there is a 'pecking order' in which training does not come very high. The availability or non-availability of accommodation has an influence on tactics which the trainer may wish to use. For example, computer-based training may need permanently dedicated space and the use of syndicate exercises is likely to call for a number of syndicate rooms.

Included with the consideration given to accommodation are the furnishings and equipment which influence how rooms can be set up and what visual aids can and cannot be used. These factors are particularly relevant and worth checking when training is being run in hotels or other locations with which the trainer may not be familiar.

All forms of training have to be paid for either directly or indirectly and budgetary considerations are further constraints with which the trainer has to contend. It would depend on how individual organizations cost their training as to what items should be included in the training budget. However, everything has to be paid for in some way and the costings which could affect budgetary constraints might include the salaries of trainers and the opportunity costs of the trainees, notional or real costs of accommodation including heating and light, travel, catering, training material such as capital expenditure on new equipment, etc.

Those trainers who have been involved closely with the delivery of courses will know the importance of good administration and will be able to anticipate the kind of administrative support that is needed for managing teaching and learning strategies. Those who administer training need to liaise very closely with the trainers themselves and devise effective systems. Lack of adequate administrative support in terms of staffing level and expertise can cause problems such as joining instructions being sent out late, teaching material not being printed, pre-course work not received by students, etc. It is important to confirm that the administrative system has capacity to take on additional or different responsibilities when new training initiatives are introduced.

In common with other parts of the organization, the training department is not immune to 'political' constraints. The introduction of a training programme as well as its content and methodology can be the subject of 'political' scrutiny. For example, the inclusion of a discussion period which might provide the opportunity for trainees to comment on the management style, organization, administration, etc of their respective departments could result in intervention at a senior level to remove the discussion period. Another example could relate to the title given to a course or learning programme where the description 'teamworking' may be more acceptable politically than the title 'supervisory skills'.

TARGET POPULATION

The term 'target population' refers in general to all those to whom the training will be given. However, close scrutiny needs to be made of the profile of the target population before any training decisions can be made or any design work begun. The numbers who need training and their geographical distribution can impact on the strategies that might be used especially when number and distribution are linked with financial constraints. It could be that taking the training to the trainees is more cost-effective than bringing the trainees to a central location.

Age and experience are two closely related factors that affect the decision-making and design processes. The features of learning preferences of the older worker have been discussed already in Chapter 7. It was seen how older workers have a preference for working from the concrete to the abstract; this can influence the sequencing of events in a training session. Similarly, it would be non-productive to design training sessions which need to draw on experience when the trainees have little or no experience upon which to draw.

The abilities and aptitudes of the target population are also variables which need to be taken into account to ensure that the training is pitched at the right level and that, as far as is possible, no one is left bewildered by the training content nor wondering when they are going to be told something that they don't already know.

The best that most trainers are likely to achieve is a broad picture of the target population which is sufficient for planning in the initial stages but there are other specific features of the target population which it is useful for trainers to know about when the training event gets nearer. Often these can be identified through some form of pre-training administrative procedure. Some trainees may have disabilities which have to be accounted for and while it is likely to be impractical to restructure the training for everyone, thought can be given to making alternative arrangements when appropriate. It is not unknown in the training field for visually-impaired people to sit through videos and large numbers of overhead projector transparencies.

STRATEGIES AND LEARNING TACTICS

Ideally, before thinking about strategies and tactics, the trainer should give consideration to the availability and skill level of those who are going to be involved in the delivery of the training. However, even though the trainer may work sequentially through all the stages which make up a systematic approach, it is impossible to prevent thoughts about strategies and tactics coming into mind at a comparatively early stage in the process. Therefore, it is felt to be more valuable to discuss strategies and tactics first so that the skills which the deliverers of training need to exercise can be put into perspective.

A number of classifications have been used to distinguish between different strategies all of which have some areas of commonality. Strategies have been categorized as centralized and decentralized, as trainer-centred and learner-centred, as on-job and off-job training, etc. There has been a considerable emphasis placed on the learner and on learning skills and therefore it is appropriate to review strategies within the context of the learner-based:trainer-based classification.

Trainer-centred strategy is best described in terms of the course. It is structured by the trainer who leads the learners or trainees through a series of lessons, exercises, activities and experiences towards the achievement of a set of objectives. The pace, tactics, sequence, etc of the training is decided and controlled by the trainer. Learner-centred strategy places the onus of responsibility for learning upon the trainee. The trainee is involved much more in the pace-setting, sequencing, choice of materials and general management of the learning with the trainer operating more as a resource or a manager of resources upon whom the trainee is able to draw.

Both strategies have their respective strengths and weaknesses. Trainer-centred strategy reflects the traditional approach with which everyone feels comfortable. Line managers and senior management have something to relate to when decisions on strategy have to be made. Trainers find it easier to plan, administer and control the learning using tactics and material which have proved to be successful. Trainees often value a well-structured programme which directs their learning and provides them with the opportunity of mixing with their peers, sharing experiences and using others as a yardstick against which to measure their own progress.

One of the disadvantages of trainer-centred strategy is that the learner is moved along at a pace which is often dictated by timetable constraints if all objectives are to be taught. This could result in some trainees not being able to learn the material as well or to the level which is expected. In addition, a trainer-centred strategy, as its title suggests, is reliant upon the skills of the trainer. The trainer has to be not only technically competent but skilled in making decisions about pace, content, tactics, etc and in using interpersonal skills to motivate, give feedback, counsel, etc. Trainer skills will be examined in some detail later; however, it is clear that poor trainers can quickly negate the advantages of a trainer-centred strategy.

The term 'learner-centred' does not mean that the responsibility for training is taken away from the trainer. One of the advantages of a learner-centred strategy is that the trainer is responsible for and controls training albeit by adopting a different role which is likely to include managing resources, acting as a facilitator, etc. The emphasis on the learner is expressed in terms of pace, sequence, choice of materials and more direct contact with the trainer when the trainee feels in need of advice, information or feedback.

In the same way that a trainer-centred strategy makes demands on the skills of the trainer, the learner-centred strategy relies considerably on the motivation, disposition and skill of the learner to adapt to a learning situation which may be unfamiliar and seemingly unstructured. Not everyone is able to pace their own learning. Additionally, there is a substantial amount of work involved in the setting up, management and up-dating of the resource materials that are needed to support this kind of strategy. The trainer has to change roles and may not like nor be able to adapt to a new role.

The strategy that is chosen will depend very much on what is being trained, knowledge of the target population and the constraints which the training designer has to work to. It could be that both strategies are used as part of the training plan, for example trainees may undertake some form of learner-centred training such as working through a learning package as a prerequisite to attending a course. Also, constraints such as time and availability of trainees may lead to members of the same target population being trained by the use of different strategies.

Having decided upon the appropriate strategy, the trainer is in a position to select the most appropriate methods or tactics with which to apply the strategy. As with the strategies, the tactics have their relative advantages and disadvantages which the trainer needs to bear in mind at this stage of the design process.

TACTICS

The lecture

A talk or presentation usually supported by visual aids in which information about practices, procedures, policies, etc are described and explained to the audience. There is little or no participation by the trainees until they are invited to ask questions which is usually at the end.

Advantages

- The trainer has complete control over content and sequence in which the material is presented.
- Large numbers of trainees can be catered for.
- More material can be presented in the time available than by many other methods.

Disadvantages

- Not a method which can be used to teach skills.
- Lack of interaction between trainer and trainees.
- Difficult to hold trainees' attention due to lack of participation.
- Skill demand on presenter very high.

The demonstration

An illustration by live performance of a task, skill or procedure accompanied by an explanation by the trainer or an assistant. Usually, it is part of or a follow-up to a lesson or training session to provide a model for trainees before they are called upon to practise themselves.

Advantages

- Comparatively easy to attract and retain interest of trainees.
- Reinforces correct procedures by providing a model.
- Shows relationship between different activities within a task.
- Speed can be adapted to suit pace/level of group.

Disadvantages

- Needs careful preparation by demonstrators to ensure correct model is shown.
- Can be time-consuming to obtain materials, set up and dismantle if dedicated space is not available.
- May have to be repeated a number of times if student numbers are large or if task is intricate and can be seen by only small numbers at a time.

The lesson

The most used and most versatile tactic which the trainer has. It can be used for teaching both facts and skills. The structure of the lesson allows for a high level of interaction between trainer and trainee through question and answer, practice and the giving of feedback.

Advantages

- Flexible and adequate so that it can incorporate other tactics.

- Lesson can be adapted in terms of content, pace and level of approach depending on experience and ability of trainees.
- Ideal medium for teaching skills.
- High level of trainee participation.
- High level of interaction between trainer and trainees.
- Opportunity for trainer to assess performance of trainees.
- Lesson format makes it comparatively easy for new or inexperienced trainers to deliver.

Disadvantage

- Size of group must be limited to allow for participation.

Simulation/Role-playing

The presentation of job and task activities which as near as is practicable replicate the essential features of the real situation. Trainees are required to use equipment, solve problems, follow procedures and to practise as if they were performing the job for real. A number of activities can be included in this category:

- In-tray (basket) exercises present the trainee with an in-tray containing letters, diary notes, reports, etc which have to be actioned. The exercise can be enhanced and made more testing by the inclusion of telephone calls, interruptions, visitors, hastily called meetings, etc. Usually trainees work individually on the same in-tray material but exercises can be devised in which trainees have different material which require them to interact with one another.
- Interpersonal exercises in which the trainees practise in scenarios that require the use of interpersonal skills. This might include dealing with disciplinary matters, dealing with customer and employee complaints both face-to-face and by telephone, conducting various forms of interview, running meetings, etc. Trainees and trainers can become involved in acting out the parts.
- Case studies present problem situations for the trainees to devise a solution either working individually or as syndicated groups. The solution can be presented in either written form or as a presentation.
- Management games are played to a set of rules within the framework of a business scenario. The trainees act out the roles of key personnel in the same or different organizations to achieve the objectives of their function.
- Simulation exercises are based on the application of skills to machinery and equipment. They are best used when access to the real equipment is

difficult and when the consequences of error could be costly or a danger to life, e.g. flight simulators, driving simulator, etc.

Advantages

- Introduces an element of realism.
- Involves high level of activity which arouses interest and motivates trainee.
- Can draw upon the experience of the trainees.
- Can be used as a measure of level of competence of trainees.
- Involves high level of activity for trainees.
- Can include activities involving critical decision making without danger.

Disadvantages

- Preparation and conduct of exercises is time-consuming.
- Can be very expensive depending on what resources are required and the level of fidelity which is needed.
- In-tray and case study material could need constant up-dating.
- Interpersonal skills exercises could be threatening to inexperienced or inadequately prepared trainees and some exercises could be spoiled by 'over-enthusiastic' trainees over-playing their roles.
- High level of skill required by trainer to direct, manage and control the exercises.

The tutorial (coaching)

Structured training which is conducted on a one-to-one basis between trainer and trainee. The training could be on-job or off-job. In on-job situations the trainer could be a job holder who demonstrates, explains and guides the trainee through the activities and procedures which make up a job or task. It can be used for remedial training and for developmental training. Developmental training could include a programme for potential managers or be built into a succession plan.

Advantages

- Individual needs can be met in terms of pace and content.
- Constant interaction between trainer and trainee.
- Constant feedback for trainee.
- Job continues to function while training takes place.

Disadvantages

- Time spent in preparation and training of one person is the same as for training a group.
- On-job training could be subject to interruption due to operational priorities.
- Sequence of training activities could be influenced by work on hand and not delivered in best sequence for learning.
- Trainer must be technically competent as well as skilled in coaching techniques, diagnostic skills and remedial methods.
- Trainer and trainee must be compatible as a working pair.

The discussion

A group activity usually led by the trainer in which the participants examine suggestions, attitudes, ideas, solutions to problems, etc. Best used in support of other tactics and to reinforce main points drawn out of other sessions.

Advantages

- Opportunity for individuals to express opinions and to listen to the views of others.
- High level of participation by trainees.
- Experience and knowledge of trainees can be drawn out.

Disadvantages

- Can be time-consuming if not properly structured.
- Can be a non-event if participants are not prepared or are lacking in knowledge and experience.
- Considerable skill required by trainer to shape the direction of discussion, to control the participants and to manage time so that the objective is achieved.
- To be effective, no more than twelve should be allowed to participate.

The syndicate exercise

This tactic can be used to give trainees the opportunity to work in small groups, to put into practice or apply what they have learnt, or to draw upon existing knowledge to draw up lists of ideas and thoughts on a particular topic. This could include the use of problem-solving exercises, case studies and such tasks as listing ideas and drawing up guidelines. The exercise is concluded with a plenary session to discuss the outcomes.

Advantages

- Achieves activity.
- Provides an opportunity to exchange thoughts and ideas.
- Can encourage creativity.
- Encourages teamwork.
- Provides a challenge.
- Can cover more ground by setting different tasks to each group.

Disadvantages

- Trainer could lose some control.
- Can be time-consuming especially at the plenary stage.
- Exercises need to be carefully structured.
- Demanding on trainer to monitor activity of groups.

Learning packages

A collection of learning materials which could include directed reading, activities, case studies, sound and video recordings, assignments, assessment exercises, etc. Usually used by individual trainee as a form of distance learning.

Advantages

- Self-pacing and trainees may begin at any time.
- Contents of package can be made attractive which assists motivation.
- Can make provision for those who wish to study topics in greater depth through further and additional reading and activity.
- Can be used with a widely dispersed target population.

Disadvantages

- Trainees can feel 'cut off' without reference to others working on the same material or to a tutor.
- Assessing assignments and exercises can be difficult and time-consuming.
- Cannot be used effectively and safely for skills training.
- Administrative, updating and monitoring activities could be time-consuming and costly.

Learning journals

Whilst it cannot be regarded as a tactic used directly by the trainer, encouraging the use of a learning journal or log has proved to be an effective way of tracking personal development through the tactics described above but more specifically placing an emphasis on unstructured, informal activities. Journal entries relate to the nature of the learning event, what was learned and how the learning will be put to use in the future.

Advantages

- Encourages self-development.
- Records what has been learnt and put into practice.
- Records achievement.
- Helps learners to analyse and reflect upon what they have learned.
- Helps to match personal development objectives to business needs.
- Can be used during appraisal to assess development and to identify new training and development needs.

Disadvantages

- Commitment needed to maintain a complete record.
- Skill and self-confidence needed to be able to analyse and record learning experiences.
- Difficult to bring oneself to record negative experiences.
- Hard to complete when things are going well or when nothing of any significance has occurred.
- Can be difficult to identify how feelings and thoughts relate to actions and vice-versa.

Computer-based training and online learning

There is no doubt that the major innovations in training delivery over the last 25 years have involved the use of computers and/or telecommunications. The packages and strategies that have become available employing these technologies provide a wide range of learning opportunities to meet different needs. At one end of the range there is the knowledge-based package, which provides learners with information in a structured, logical sequence that they can work through in their own time. Such packages may be supplemented by other information sources such as libraries, archives and databases, available on the World Wide Web.

CD ROM technology employing multimedia allows for a more interactive facility to be used to develop intellectual or technical skills and, in some circumstances, lay the foundation for the improvement of certain kinds of social skills. Some computer-based learning systems allow for individualized instruction by diagnosing the trainee's current level of expertise and then 'designing' a programme to meet the individual's particular needs. The programmes described above are usually self-paced and do not rely, or not to any great extent, on tutor support.

On the other hand, moving to similar programmes online may involve the trainee in regular interaction with a designated tutor. Online learning also opens up the possibility of group interaction and collaboration being part of the learning experience. This approach involves a group of trainees and a tutor linked by computer, exchanging ideas and opinions and discussing the subject matter being studied and/or individual responses to training exercises. These exchanges can be timed synchronously or asynchronously or in some suitable combination of the two. The notion of computer-mediated conferencing involving e-moderators, also known as online tutors, is fully explored by Salmon (2000).

Finally, at the other end of the range, computer technology has enabled virtual reality training to be created. In this form of training the trainee is faced with situations, in three-dimensional space, similar to those experienced in the workplace, and objects can be seen, touched and moved around. As Goldstein and Ford (2002) point out, virtual reality training 'capitalizes on visual learning and experiential engagement very similar to the transfer context without the physical space requirements of full-scale training simulators'.

The advantages and disadvantages of these various approaches are outlined below. However, it should be appreciated that they apply in varying degrees to any particular approach and may seem contradictory.

Advantages

- Learners may begin at any time and learning is self-paced.
- Maximum involvement in responding to stimuli presented on the screen.
- Consistent presentation of material using attractive design features.
- Material structured so that it is presented in digestible chunks.
- Progress can be monitored.
- It can be a cost-effective way of providing training.
- Up-to-date material can be made more quickly available to the learner.
- It can cater for large numbers studying at the same time.
- Views and ideas about subject matter can be exchanged with others.
- Rapport can be developed with other learners.
- There is an opportunity to communicate with the tutor in private.

Disadvantages

- It could initially be costly if capital expenditure is needed for equipment.
- If large numbers are involved, administration could be difficult.
- Aversion to this form of learning; frustration with or dislike of this way of working.
- Isolation from other learners and tutor; lack of visual contact with other participants.
- Non-verbal reactions cannot be expressed or picked up.
- Working relationships and ground rules for participation difficult to establish.
- High level of demand on the tutor to co-ordinate and involve everyone.

Although we do not deny the above disadvantages, the new technologies have certainly opened up new learning possibilities and opportunities. However, as Goldstein and Ford (2002) emphasize, 'Technology by itself will not and cannot become the Holy Grail of the training field.' In many situations blended learning programmes, which combine an appropriate mix of learning tactics, should be designed in order to meet the requirements of individual learners. Furthermore all the stages of the systematic approach to training need to be accorded the necessary attention to ensure learning is achieved efficiently and effectively.

Both the general conditions of learning and the principles and the specific conditions supporting learning that were covered in Chapter 7 have general applicability to the tactics described above. However, in relation to the training of groups, there are one or two additional considerations that need to be taken into account. For example, it is critical for the trainer to establish rapport with the group. Leigh (1996) points out, 'One of the essential ingredients for training success is the ability to develop rapport or understanding with those being trained.' He points out that rapport can be generated and maintained through:

- *The personal approach.* It is important for trainees to feel they are being treated as individuals and their contribution is valued. Therefore a trainer should give recognition to individuals who contribute within a group context.
- *Encouragement.* Trainees must feel able to make mistakes and, within certain limits, take risks without fear of being ridiculed. If the trainer adopts a negative and critical attitude it will not encourage the trainee, and his or her confidence will be adversely affected. In addition it may have a knock-on effect on other trainees by discouraging them from experimenting and moving outside their 'comfort zones'. This is likely to be to the detriment of their overall learning and development.
- *Involving people.* Some degree of participation by trainees in the training process is likely to be more effective than passivity. The trainer should therefore build into the training programme opportunities for the trainees to be actively involved in their learning.

- *Providing enthusiasm.* If a trainer shows a lack of enthusiasm for the subject matter or for the process of training it will 'rub off' on the trainees. Furthermore the trainer's enthusiasm is also likely to help to maintain the trainees' motivation during any difficult or boring phases of the training programme.
- *Creating understanding.* It is important for the trainer to employ language that is comprehensible to the group; it should not be too complicated, beyond the limits of the group's vocabulary, or replete with jargon or unfamiliar technical terms.
- *Empathizing with the group.* The trainer should appreciate and understand the problems and difficulties the trainees may be experiencing, but without becoming so involved that he or she loses his/her objectivity.

Besides developing rapport, and in order to encourage learning within the group, the trainer also needs to exercise the process skill of facilitation. A fuller discussion of this is included in Chapter 11. In a similar vein to Leigh, Stewart (1996) emphasizes the importance of establishing and maintaining an appropriate climate in the group. To further this aim he recommends the use of icebreakers, contract setting exercises and facilitating behaviours.

REINFORCEMENT AND TRANSFER TACTICS

A concern which is shared by all trainers is the trainees' retention of knowledge and skills not only during training but after training when they apply that knowledge and skill to a job in a live working context. Training, in most cases, takes place over a comparatively short period and sometimes it is very intensive. At the end of courses, trainees often volunteer the opinion that they would have liked to have spent more time on a number of activities; the opinion that less time was needed is an uncommon event. With what is known about the decay of skill when it is not used and the loss of knowledge when it is not put to use, the trainer needs to consider the tactics that can be employed so that time and effort invested by both trainer and trainee are not wasted.

Briefing and debriefing

Before undertaking any form of training, trainees should be briefed by their line managers about the training they are about to undertake. This should include its general objectives, its methodology and structure, the reason why the trainee is doing it and how the trainee will put the training into use on completion. The debriefing confirms the use that will be made of the training, may make provision for additional or remedial training and examines the reaction of trainees so that information can be passed back to the trainer.

A thorough briefing ensures that trainees are motivated and prepared to begin their training programmes and avoids the trainer being placed in the unfair position of having to take on the responsibilities of the line manager. It is unfortunate that many trainers report that they are often placed in the position of having to take on such responsibilities and try to motivate those who are unconvinced of the value of their training. However, line managers do not always have sufficient information to brief their staff effectively and the trainer can help in this respect by preparing a set of briefing notes which will assist them.

Tests, exercises and practice

These types of activity include written and oral tests of knowledge, exercises and case studies which test the use of procedures and intellectual skills, and practice to develop manual skills. The aim is not only to check that trainees have learned but to reinforce the learning so that it can be retained and taken back to the workplace. Most people learn more by doing than by listening and observing. The reinforcement of correct answers, responses and performance increases the probability of recall of information and retention of skill. Some trainees do not react well to 'testing' and it is sometimes appropriate to use the terms 'reinforcement exercise' or 'check' or 'quiz'. When objective tests, particularly multiple choice, are used considerable time and skill is needed in their design.

Handouts

These are summaries of the main points covered during training sessions. Trainees should be encouraged to make their own notes as an aid to concentration and so that they will have a reference to the key learning points of the training. However, unless the trainer is able to check notes there is no guarantee that everyone will have complete and factually correct material. The handout overcomes these problems and although there are claims that they are not read, it has been found that well constructed and well presented handouts are read and when appropriate they are used as job aids.

Some handouts are produced in the form of a worksheet. This is a document that includes key headings and some detail, but leaves space for the trainee to complete the detail as the session progresses. This involvement can help to focus attention but has to be balanced against the possibility that it could be a distraction.

Job aids

The learning of procedural tasks is assisted by the use of checklists and algorithms or decision charts. These can be used during training and taken away to use in the job situation. The use of good design techniques, including the use of colour and laminated materials to give them a longer life, provide trainees with a useful tool which can be put to good use.

It is important to discuss the job aid with line managers and supervisors to ensure that they are not at variance with operational practice.

Refresher courses

After training has been completed it is very difficult to introduce refresher courses because of the constraints imposed by budget and time, etc. However, jobs change, not all skills are exercised frequently and the job holders may not get the kind of feedback they need to maintain or develop their skill levels. The refresher course is a short training period which serves to remind job holders of the main content of their training. It is particularly useful for attitudinal development and could be presented in the form of study days and workshops.

SELECTING THE STRATEGY AND TACTICS

It is possible that existing courses within the organization and those run by outside bodies make provision for achieving the training objectives in part or in whole. Ideally, the trainer should have reviews and reports written by former trainees on such courses, if they have been used in the past, which will contribute to the decision making. More frequently, the way forward is the need to design training which will be delivered within the organization.

The selection of the strategy and the tactics for internal programmes is often based on some form of compromise. The constraints, the target population and principles of learning all have an influence on courses designed internally and before going into detailed planning the trainer has to balance out these factors. For example, looking back to the principles of learning in Chapter 7, when the learning involves the acquisition of a skill then the trainee must practise in order to learn. Practice sessions can be time-consuming and time constraints could be restrictive.

The proper design of training involves much more than drawing up a programme for a week's training. Such programmes are often constrained by coffee and lunch breaks which are usually written in first and around which the training activities are written. This also involves shortening or lengthening some sessions to fit into these pre-arranged breaks.

The planning format shown in Figure 8.2 is an illustration of the process that the trainer needs to go through in designing a course. Trainers can adapt the headings to suit their own needs and those shown here are not intended to be exhaustive. One might want to include a column for costs, for example if a video or any specialist equipment needs to be bought. However, it is suggested that all of the columns across as far as the final selection of strategy and tactics should be used in order to avoid undertaking unnecessary work.

The first three columns list the objectives; classify them in terms of Knowledge and Skills, and identify the learning principles involved. It is then possible to list a range of alternative strategies and tactics which can be used to estimate how much time would be needed for each. The trainer is seldom given unlimited time to devote to a training programme; time constraints are usually placed on the programme from the outset. By using the design matrix it is possible to calculate the maximum and minimum amount of time that would be needed depending on which strategies are used. In the example shown, the maximum amount of time needed would be 14 hours and 15 minutes and the minimum would be 8 hours and 45 minutes, together with approximately an hour and a half of pre-course reading.

It is also worth noting that administration, course introduction and conclusion are included in the matrix as these are often overlooked. The assumption is also made that those attending the course would be able to manage the pre-course reading. For the purposes of illustration the training is being designed for six participants on each course and the time constraint is that twelve hours have been made available for training. In deciding the way forward, it is vital to keep the practical session intact so that the participants will be able to practise their skills. It is also important to try to keep those strategies which will give variety to the programme, such as discussion, syndicate exercise and role play. In our example, we have chosen to meet the knowledge-based objectives by using job guides and pre-course reading. If it is important to confirm that the pre-course work has been done, then we should, perhaps, include a session for testing on our matrix.

If the time constraint only allows for one day or six hours' training, which is below the absolute minimum needed, then the trainer should not try to achieve the impossible but go back to the 'client', show them the matrix and ask which objectives they would like to leave out. On the other hand, the trainer can advise the client that some of the skills objectives could be turned into knowledge-based ones. However, although the trainees would be able to list or state what they have done, it is unlikely that they would be able to perform those tasks. In most cases a time plan on the matrix helps to gain the co-operation of the client.

Once the strategies have been decided the trainer can consider in more depth the detailed content of the sessions. It can be seen that much time could be wasted in preparing material for sessions which subsequently might not be used. Time and effort can be saved by taking stock of what resource material exists already that can be used or adapted for the programme being designed.

For every strategy or tactic there needs to be a session plan. While there should be some guidelines as to the content of a session, those trainers who deliver the sessions should do their own planning. For example, in addition to the objective(s), it is useful for the trainer to have a list of the ideas or views that might come out of a discussion, key points that would be expected to emerge from a syndicate exercise, core information that should be included in an input session, anecdotal material to enrich the subject matter, and facts that might be included in the introduction to a session. However, trainers must be allowed to sequence the material and manage it in their own way, and deliver it in their own style rather than be given a 'script'.

An agreed 'house style' for the presentation of material gives a professional image, when for example the same handouts, exercise briefs and projected images are used across a range of courses. This task is made easier when a well-organized resource centre has been established. This does not necessarily mean having a dedicated room. A tidy cupboard or filing cabinet which has an adequate index is often sufficient. However, the temptation to develop the programme around existing material rather than to be selective and use only that which is appropriate and meets the need should be avoided. When the trainer has support from others, tasks can be allocated and deadlines set for the production of the material.

As has been mentioned already, other columns could be added to the matrix to meet the needs of the trainer. Figure 8.2 is an illustration of a short course in which the objectives have been arranged in sequence. For a longer and perhaps a more complex programme, it would be useful to have a column in which to sequence the objectives.

It will always be difficult to balance activities so that the most appropriate tactics are used at the best point in the training and so that learning principles are applied correctly. There will always be an element of compromise. However, the trainer should aim to ensure that the trainees' level of motivation and interest remain high by using a variety of tactics and by taking account of how people learn and the best times for learning new material. The notorious 'graveyard' session after lunch can be used to good effect if the programme is well planned.

An alternative, but complementary approach to training course design has been developed by Anderson. Using Kolb's learning cycle as a framework he suggests a four-stage process model, which charts the progress of learning through the essential process stages of concepts, techniques, application and transfer (CTAT). Figure 8.3 summarizes the essential features of the CTAT model.

Anderson believes, applied flexibly and without being unduly rigid, that completion of all four stages of the model is essential to close the learning loop. He also suggests that each of the stages requires the use of different training methods and the application of a complex mix of training skills by tutors if all four stages of the learning process are to be realized successfully.

Objectives	K/S	Strategy/Tactic Alternatives	Time	Selected Strategy	Material Available	Material Needed	Allocation of Tasks	Deadline	Notes
1. *Deal with incoming mail*									
• State the procedure for receiving incoming mail	K	Lesson Reading (on course) Reading (off course) Job guide	30 mins 20 mins (20 mins) Nil						
• Open and distribute incoming mail	S	Practical lesson Job guide	45 mins Nil	✓		Job guide to be prepared	Alastair	14 Mar	
• Redirect mail	S	Practical lesson Job guide	20 mins Nil	✓					
2. *Deal with outgoing mail*									
• State the importance of ensuring outgoing mail is correctly addressed	K	Lesson Discussion Reading (on course) Reading (off course)	15 mins 30 mins 20 mins (20 mins)	✓	Tutor notes from Secretarial Course	Adapt tutors notes for pre-course reading	Julie	7 Mar	
• State the importance of ensuring correct postage is paid	K	Lesson Reading (on course) Reading (off course)	15 mins 10 mins (10 mins)	✓		Compose passage for pre-course reading	Julie	21 Mar	
• State the importance of keeping a postage book	K								
• Calculate postage payable on outgoing items	S	Practical lesson Job guide	45 mins Nil	✓	Table of postal charges	Tutor notes Practical exercises	Julie	28 Mar	
• Operate a postal franking machine	S	Practical lesson	50 mins		Manufacturer's and Post Office Operator's Guide	Tutor notes Practical exercises (Access to frank-ing machine)	Julie	9 Apr	
• Maintain Postage Book	S	Practical lesson Job guide	40 mins Nil			Tutor notes Vu Foil Practical exercises handout	Julie	9 April	

Figure 8.2 Example of a format for planning a training programme

	K/S	Method	Time	✓	Resources	Action	Person	Date
3. Receive visitors								
• State the procedure for receiving expected and unexpected visitors	K	Lesson Reading (on course) Reading (off course)	20 mins 15 mins (15 mins)	✓	Tutor notes from Secretarial Course	Adapt tutor notes	Karen Mathew	9 Apr
• Receive an expected visitor	S	Role-play	(6 students × 30 mins) 3 hours	✓	Some role-play exercises from Secretarial Course	Check and adapt role-play exercises Write new role play exercises Check video available	Karen Mathew	9 Apr
• Receive an unexpected visitor	S							
• State the importance of having an effective security system	K	Lesson Discussion Reading (on course) Reading (off course) Computer-based training (on/off course)	30 mins 45 mins 20 mins (20 mins) (30 mins)	✓	Tutor notes from Induction Course Vu Foils	Prepare tutor's guide for discussion Handout	Karen Mathew	9 Apr
4. Deal with incoming telephone calls								
• State the importance of good telephone technique	K	Lesson Discussion Video & discussion	20 mins 30 mins 45 mins	✓	Video Telephone Techniques	Tutor notes Handout Ensure video available	Alastair	9 Apr
• Operate a 10-line telephone exchange system	S	Practical lesson/ Role-play	(6 students × 10 mins) 60 mins	✓	Manufacturer's Guide	Tutor notes Handout – Job guide Access to telephone training equipment		
• Take messages	S	Practical lesson	60 mins					
• List strategies for dealing with confused or offensive callers	K	Discussion Syndicate exercise	30 mins 45 mins	✓		Tutor notes Exercise brief Check 'break out' room available	Alastair	9 Apr

Figure 8.2 *Continued*

Objectives	K/S	Strategy/Tactic Alternatives	Time	Selected Strategy	Material Available	Material Needed	Allocation of Tasks	Deadline	Notes
• Take appropriate action to deal with confused or offensive callers	S	Role-play	(6 students × 15 mins) 1 hr 30 mins	✓	2 Role-play exercises from Supervisors' Course	Check video available	Alastair	9 Apr	
Administration	–	–	10 mins			Joining instructions Guidance on pre-course work Tutor notes	Sandra	9 Apr	
Course introduction	–	–	10 mins						
Course conclusion	–	–	15 mins						
		Maximum time	14 hrs 15 mins						
		Minimum time	8 hrs 45 mins + 1 hr 25 mins						
		Time available	12 hrs (2 days)						

Figure 8.2 *Continued*

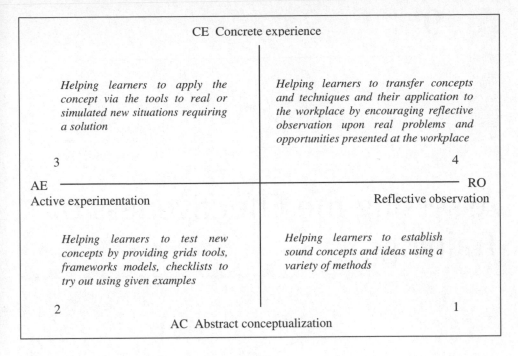

Figure 8.3 CTAT course design model

Although Anderson accepts the validity of the learning cycle of Kolb *et al* he recognizes the importance of beginning many learning experiences in the Reflective Observation/Abstract Conceptualization quadrant. This view accords with those of training theorists/researchers such as Fitts (1962), Adams (1987) and Anderson (1987) whose work is reported extensively by Patrick (1992).

9

Assessing the Effectiveness of Training

The final logical stage in the training process is to find out how effective the training has been. There are few who would disagree with this and yet practice tends to suggest that in many organizations validation of training is either ignored or it is approached in an unconvincing or an unprofessional manner. In some organizations, it has been claimed that validation is too costly, it doesn't really prove anything or it isn't really applicable because training cannot be valued in financial terms. Some trainers have reflected a defensive approach to validation because they have felt that it invites criticism and apportions blame when training has not been as successful as it might have been. However, if training is to enjoy the high profile which it should have, then thorough validation of its activities is vital so that, along with other departments, the training department can demonstrate its worth.

In most diagrammatical representations of a training system, validation is shown as two discrete parts of the process which are described as internal validation and external validation. In practice they are intimately linked and most trainers see them as a single function because one is dependent upon, or has little value without, the other.

Internal validation is concerned with assessing whether a training activity has achieved its objectives, in other words, 'did the trainees learn what they were taught?' External validation aims to find out if the former trainees have applied what they have learned in training to the job context and whether they are able to perform to the level expected of them after training.

Another term which is used in the process of assessing the effectiveness of training is evaluation. For many trainers, evaluation has taken on more vague connotations but generally it is seen as the process of attempting to assess the total value of training – that is the cost benefits, and general outcomes which benefit the organization as well as the value of the improved performance of those who have undertaken training.

The close relationship of the activities of internal validation, external validation and evaluation suggests the need for an integrated approach to assessing the effectiveness of training. Suggested steps or levels within such an approach, which reflect the work of Hamblin (1974) and of Kirkpatrick (1967), are:

- Reaction: how the students and the trainers reacted to the training; their feelings about the structure and content of the training and the methods employed.
- Learning: the principles, facts and techniques learned by the students.
- Job behaviour and performance: the changes in job behaviour and perform-ance resulting from the training or how learning at the previous level has been applied by students.
- Organization: the tangible results of training in terms of organizational improvements and change.

A further level could be added or developed from the organization level. It would relate to the impact which training has on the organization's climate or attitude to training, the general health of training and its possible expansion within the organization and the kind of learning environment which the organization fosters.

REACTION LEVEL

The reaction level as it is described by Hamblin and by Kirkpatrick relates to how the students or trainees reacted to their training, in other words, how much they liked it.

These reactions reflect the trainees' opinions in four main areas:

- The knowledge and skills content of training as it is expressed in the training objectives.
- The training methods or tactics used in the training and the trainers who delivered it.
- The general learning conditions and environment in which the training took place.
- The degree to which the attitudinal objectives of the training programme have been achieved.

In addition, there is a likelihood that some indicators will be given of the trainees' attitude to learning in general and their willingness to undertake further training. Naturally, what information is obtained depends upon what is asked for and how the questions are asked.

This has often manifested itself as the so-called 'happy sheet' which is issued at the end of a course or a training session usually when there is little time left and when the trainees are anxious to be on their way. It consists of a number of questions with response boxes in which the trainees are invited to place ticks to record their level of satisfaction with various aspects of the training. Additionally, there may be spaces for the trainees to record their suggestions and general observations; however, this opportunity is not often taken because it may delay the trainees' departure. The completed sheets are sometimes given no more than a superficial 'analysis' by the trainers who are probably used to getting the same kind of response each time they present the training. When asked about their validation procedures a number of trainers have responded almost apologetically that they have little regard for its value.

Reactions begin from the moment that the trainees learn that they are to be involved in a training event, including the style and content of the briefing they receive from their line managers. The joining instructions and the details of any work that they have to do in preparation can affect their motivation and readiness to learn, and the attitude that they develop towards the event. Attitudes can be affected further by reception arrangements, the appearance of the venue and other 'hygiene' factors.

These reactions continue when trainees start their training and therefore provision needs to be made to gather data from the outset rather than leaving it until the end of training. Many of the questions asked on the so-called 'happy sheet' do seek useful information and could be used more effectively as part of a more structured approach. Before considering such an approach, it is worth mentioning the sources of informal feedback which the trainer can make use of.

In general conversation during a coffee or lunch break or at any break during training, the trainees frequently will offer comment or ask questions which give the trainer an indication of their reactions. Parts of conversation which may be overheard or comments made by one trainee to another may also alert the trainer to the trainees' likes and dislikes or their difficulties.

A slightly more formal opportunity to gauge reaction presents itself when the training programme includes feedback sessions and tutorials or when there is a need to give feedback and counselling to individual trainees. When the trainers establish a good rapport with the trainees, there is no shortage of feedback at the reaction level to which trainers can respond to meet the needs of their trainees sooner rather than at the end of training when it is too late.

A structured approach to gauging the reaction of the trainees involves the use of a learning journal. Basically, the aim of the journal is for the trainees to record on a daily or sessional basis their reactions to what they have learned.

However, the journal is a flexible instrument and can incorporate other measures which relate to training content and trainer performance. The journal should begin by asking the trainees to write down their expectations of the training which they are about to undertake. If the training is in the form of a course, the expectations of trainees can be shared as part of the course opening procedure.

From this the trainer should be able to gain a clear picture of the trainees' level of preparedness and commitment together with the effectiveness of their pre-course briefing which will, without doubt, affect their initial reactions.

The journal then provides space for the trainees to record their reactions to each day or session of the training. This can be reviewed at the beginning of each day or each new session when one or two trainees can be invited to contribute their reactions to the remainder of the group.

The final section of the journal is completed at the end of training when time should be allowed for the trainees to look back to their original expectations and re-examine them in the light of the training they have received. Their comments may then be shared in some form of open forum. The journal should be retained by the trainees and can be used subsequently during the debrief by their line managers.

Trainees can be asked to fill in other validation documents concurrently which provide the trainers with data on their own performance and on the training content. The precise nature of questions that are asked will depend on the criteria which are chosen by which to measure the effectiveness of the training. This might include the trainees' reaction to the relevance of the training objectives to the jobs for which they are being trained, the value of the training to them as individuals, the time spent on different topics, how much material was new, the effectiveness of visual aids, the presentation skills of the trainer etc.

The concept of using a learning journal can be extended beyond the more formalized setting of a course to record learning from any source. This might include all forms of open learning, experiences from the workplace, reading professional journals and books, attending conferences and exhibitions, and, in fact, anything which contributes to an individual's learning and development. Subsequently, the journal could be used as part of an appraisal process or included in a portfolio for those who are working towards vocational qualifications. An illustration of how this may be done is at Appendix 3.

So far attention has been given to the reaction of trainees but they are not the only ones who have reactions worthy of note. The trainers or tutors also have reactions which provide useful information about the training and the trainees who participated. Many tutors, particularly those working as members of a team, conduct their own debriefing sessions on a daily basis or at the end of a course or period of training after the trainees have left.

Their discussions are likely to include the balance of the programme, activities and periods of instruction which may need to be changed, a reaction to new or restructured sessions that have been run for the first time, reaction to the attainment and attitude of the trainees and reflection on their own performance. It is not often that the outcomes of these discussions are placed on record and therefore much valuable information is lost. Although it may seem just another time-consuming chore, a written tutor's review places on record information about training which can be used for a number of purposes. These include the following:

- Statistical analysis of the number of courses or training sessions which have been run, numbers of trainees who have been trained, status of trainees, pass/fail rates, etc. These details can be used for annual returns, establishment reviews, job evaluation, space planning, annual programme planning, inspections, etc.
- Details of how the courses or training sessions have developed in terms of changes to training objectives, content, methodology, etc to record how the training department has reacted to changing needs.
- Recommendations and reaction of trainers relating to revision and innovation which they wish to draw to the attention of the training manager.
- Reactions of trainers to the overall performance of trainees and, when appropriate, the performance of individuals so that feedback can be given to line managers when it is considered to be important.
- Reactions obtained from students about their training to stimulate ideas about developing the training programme.
- Notes on general and specific administrative points to ensure that the training is resourced and administered properly.
- A permanent record of the historical development of the courses or training sessions to assist new trainers to 'read their way in', to explain the rationale behind change, to provide background information on initiatives and pilot schemes for trainers who are researching or planning change.

The actual structure of the review will depend very much on the nature of the training but without being rigid it is always useful to have a standardized format.

The following headings could be considered for reviewing courses and adapted for other forms of training.

Title

This would include the title of the course, the dates on which it took place, the course number, the venue, for whom the course was presented (if by special arrangement, etc).

Background

There may not be many occasions when it is necessary to include this section. It could include details about why the course was introduced (if it is a new one), reasons for any substantial changes in terms of length, content, approach, etc.

Introduction

Any introductory comments about target population, the trainers who were involved, location of course if different from usual venue, etc.

Course programme

This section may not be included very often. It should be used when the course programme or content has been changed in some way.

Course review

This is the section which should contain all of the tutor's comments, observations and recommendations about the course, tasks which need to be done, etc. In addition an overview can be given of the trainees as a group and, if and when appropriate, mention can be made of individuals.

Trainee reaction

This section records general comments, suggestions, recommendations and observations made by the trainees.

Administration

Observations or recommendations can be recorded here about accommodation, travel, expenses, food, joining instructions, etc.

Action

It is useful to have an action column down the right-hand side of the page to indicate or to allocate areas of responsibility.

It would be expected that for courses which are long standing and presented frequently that reviews would be fairly short. Appendix 4 gives an example of a more lengthy review which illustrates the content described above.

LEARNING LEVEL

The learning level of validation is directed at measuring trainees' performance in terms of their knowledge, skills and attitudes against the criteria which were set for the period during which they are in training and the immediate post-training period. The criteria used at this stage and the standards set are not necessarily the same as those which might be used when assessing an experienced worker. For example, the period of training may concentrate on accuracy and subsequently speed will be built up whilst performing the job. The standards expected of the trainee and the method of assessment should have been considered during the design of the training stage and therefore should be included in the training objectives.

To many trainers, this stage of measurement means an end-of-course test or assessment. However, to make optimum use of training, measurements of competence should be continuous so that the trainee can receive regular feedback and so that trainers can introduce remedial strategies and further practice when it is appropriate.

Measuring acquisition of knowledge

All jobs require the job holder to possess a body of knowledge which will be drawn upon and applied in different ways and at different times during the performance of the job. The nature of the application of this knowledge will have been categorized when the performance statements were written for the training objectives and the expected behaviour of the trainees will have been described using prefixes such as 'define', 'state', 'list', 'calculate', 'describe', etc. These words suggest to the trainer that short, open questions can be used as a measure of learning. For example,

- 'Define the term validation'
- 'List the features and benefits of a current bank account'
- 'Calculate the arithmetical mean of the following sets of data. . .'

The answers to questions such as these are not likely to vary to any great extent. They can be marked easily and quickly and there is little possibility of there being any significant variance between the marking of different trainers.

When a less precise question is asked the trainee is given the implicit invitation to write more expansively. For example,

- 'Describe how different design features influence the valuation of a property'

In cases like this, the answers are likely to vary more than they would with the short answers and an element of subjectivity on the part of the trainer is almost certain to affect the marking. In such circumstances, the trainers need to agree upon a checklist of points which they would expect to find in the complete answer. In some cases, critical points may have to be identified the omission of which might affect whether the trainee passes or fails that item. Trainers usually have to pilot their checklists and monitor their application over a number of trials before final agreement is reached.

It follows that the more general the question is and the longer the answer, the greater become the problems of reliability and consistency which suggests that the essay-type question would be inappropriate in the context of measuring training.

In addition to using short open questions, a greater level of objectivity can be achieved by using objective tests. As the term suggests, the aim of this type of test is to remove the subjectivity of the assessor. Objective test items can take a number of forms.

Multiple-choice questions

These consist of a stem and a number of alternative responses. The stem takes the form of a direct question or an incomplete statement. The alternative responses are made up of a correct or clearly best response and three or four plausible distractors. For example,

Stem	The capital of Australia is
	or
	Which of the following is the capital of Australia?
Alternative responses	a. Melbourne ☐
	b. Sydney ☐
	c. Canberra ☐
	d. Adelaide ☐

The following conventions guide the design of multiple-choice questions:

- They should request significant information.
- They should clearly formulate a problem.
- They should not contain irrelevant material.
- They should include as much as possible in the stem.
- They should be plausible to all students.
- They should have only one correct or clearly best response.
- They should have positive stems.
- They should use 'none of these' or 'all of these' sparingly.
- They should be free from extraneous clues and not use as responses:

textbook phrases or lengthy sentences
key words from the stem
all opposites to the correct response
overlapping responses
grammatically different responses
- They should have correct responses randomly distributed.
- They should have each item independent of the other.

True/false questions

These consist of a single statement which the trainee has to judge as true or false. For example,

	True	False
In the United States of America cars should drive on the right-hand side of the road.		

The statements used should relate to a single idea. It would not be a good item if the statement was 'In the United States of America cars should drive on the right-hand side of the road and at no more than 50 mph'. In circumstances like this, having a correct answer to one part of the statement automatically provides an answer to the other part. It can be seen that further complications would be met if one part of the statement were correct and the other incorrect.

Completion/deletion questions

These consist of a single statement which contains either a blank or blanks which the trainee has to complete by inserting the correct word or words, or one or two alternative words from which the trainee has to delete those which do not relate to the correct answer. For example,

- Complete the following statement:
    A thermometer measures _____.
- Delete the words in brackets which do not apply:
    A tachometer measures (road speed/engine speed)

The words which are omitted or offered for deletion should be words which are indicators of learning, for example it would be inappropriate to leave out the word 'measures' in the completion item above.
   The blanks should be placed towards the end of the statement to assist continuity and the item constructed in such a way that only one answer is

possible. When it is found that a sufficient number of plausible distractors cannot be found for multiple-choice items, the questions can usually be presented as true/false or completion/deletion items.

Matching pairs

The trainee is presented with two lists of words or words and illustrations. Each item in one list can be paired with an item from the second list which the trainee has to identify. For example,

Study the two lists printed below. Column A is a list of countries. Column B is a list of capital cities. Match each country with its capital city by writing the number of the country in the box alongside its capital city.

A	B	
1. Belgium	Copenhagen	☐
2. Holland	Vienna	☐
3. Sweden	Brussels	☐
4. Denmark	Helsinki	☐
5. Norway	Stockholm	☐
6. Finland		
7. Austria		

One list has more items than the other so that the chance of finding the correct answer by the process of elimination is reduced.

Other objective test items can be devised from the ideas presented here. Questions could ask trainees to categorize items by writing them under a number of given headings, etc. A complete test does not necessarily have to be made up of items of the same type. When a range of different items is used it is advisable to group together items of the same type, e.g. a section of multiple choice, a section of true/false, etc. This helps to avoid confusion and repeating the instructions and examples of how to answer the different types of item.

The data collected from the administration of these assessment items can be used for other purposes in addition to confirming the acquisition of knowledge on the part of the trainees. Multiple-choice items lend themselves to detailed item analysis which will help to identify how easy or how difficult each item was to answer (facility value), how well each item discriminates between the better and the poorer performers (index of discrimination), how effective the distractors are and how comparable tests are in terms of reliability. The statistical techniques used in this kind of analysis are to be found in most standard texts on descriptive statistics.

Measuring the acquisition of skills

It was seen earlier when training objectives were being discussed (Chapter 6) that skills could be categorized as intellectual, manual and social. The measurement of trainee competence in these skills should take the form of a practical test or exercise. The appropriateness of the measure selected is of great importance if the achievement of training objective is to be confirmed. For example, if the objective states that at the end of training the trainee will be able to 'Strip, clean and assemble a domestic gas central-heating boiler' it would be totally inappropriate to give a written test of competence asking the trainee to 'Describe the sequence of operations. . .' The trainee would need access to a boiler and to demonstrate that he could meet the requirements of the training objective. Similarly, the measurement of intellectual skills and social skills would need to be set in an appropriate context. It follows that measuring the acquisition of skills will involve considerable use of sample materials, equipment, tools, simulation of physical conditions and role-playing, etc. From this it can be seen that the trainer has to contend with a number of problems in setting up practical tests:

- The equipment could be expensive, could take up a considerable amount of space, could be highly sensitive and easily damaged.
- Time has to be allowed within the programme for testing.
- Additional staff may be needed to assess performance.
- It may be difficult to prevent trainees from observing the efforts of their fellow course members.
- There is a danger of subjectivity affecting the assessment of the trainer.
- Paper-based tests, i.e. in-tray/in-basket exercise, may need continuous updating.

Many of these potential problems should have been identified and catered for during the design of the training. Again, the training objectives would have been the indicators of what would be required. The area for more detailed consideration here is trying to achieve greater reliability and reducing subjectivity in the assessment. In most cases this can be done by the use of some sort of checklist. The format of the checklist and the amount of detail which it contains will depend entirely on the nature of the skill which is being assessed. The successful application of some manual skills may only need to be assessed on the completion of the exercise whereas others may have to be assessed throughout to ensure that actions are performed in the correct sequence and in the right way.

For example if the skill was for a groundsman to measure out and mark a football pitch it would be only necessary to see the completed exercise and assess it on its accuracy of measurement and the straightness and clarity of the lines within the tolerances stated in the training objectives. However, if the skill being assessed was changing the wheel on a motor car which involves the

Marking scheme Changing a wheel on a motor car			
Serial	Sub-Task	Yes	No
1	Stop car on hard, level surface		
2	Apply handbrake	*	
3	Switch off engine	*	
4	Position warning triangle approx 20 metres to rear of car	*	
5	Remove spare wheel and tools		
6	Place jack in position at nearest jacking point to wheel to be changed		
7	Remove hub cap		
8	Loosen wheel nuts		
9	Jack up wheel to approx 3 cm above the ground		
10	Remove wheel nuts – top one last (and place in hub cap)		
11	Remove wheel		
12	Place spare wheel in position		
13	Replace wheel nuts – top one first	*	
14	Tighten all nuts diagonally	*	
15	Lower jack so that wheel rests on ground		
16	Tighten all nuts fully	*	
17	Replace hub cap		
18	Return tools, warning triangle and replaced wheel to stowage compartment		
NB	Items indicated * are critical and all must be performed correctly to pass the test		

Figure 9.1 Example of a marking scheme for a practical test

performance of a number of actions in sequence then a checklist something like that in Figure 9.1 would be needed.

The assessment of the application of interpersonal skills becomes a much more complex affair when it comes to objectivity. In the assessment of inter-personal skills there may not only be a need to confirm that certain things are done but to quantify how well they are done. For example in selection inter-viewing an assessor would probably need to confirm that the interviewer asked appropriate probing questions but it is quite likely that the style or manner of asking questions would have to be taken into account as well. This means that checklists would have to be more sophisticated and are likely to include indicators of quality of performance. For example, the checklist could contain a number of statements arranged on a bi-polar scale against which the trainee is assessed. This type of scale takes the following kind of format.

	1	2	3	4	5	6	
Listened actively using many verbal and non-verbal cues to encourage subject to continue							Hardly listened at all. Easily distracted. Gave no overt signs of interest
Asked clear, relevant probing questions which drew out significant information							Asked rambling, confused questions, which yielded no significant information OR Failed to ask questions

The range of the scale used for assessment will depend on what is being measured, the need for precision and the level of agreement which assessors are able to achieve in their scores. The broader the scale, the more likely it is that scores will vary, for example the position can arise where two assessors observe the same performance and identify the same skill elements but rate the performance differently on the scale. When this kind of situation is likely to affect the assessment of trainees to the extent of giving an unreliable overall grade or a ranking, the scale can be reduced or more indicators can be used. The example given above could be developed along the following lines:

Identified and used every opportunity to ask probing questions	Identified and made use of a number of opportunities to ask probing questions	Identified and used one or two opportunities to ask probing questions	Failed to identify opportunities and to ask probing questions
Asked clear, unambiguous questions	Asked questions which generally were clear and unambiguous but needed occasional clarification	Asked questions which needed frequent clarification	Asked rambling confused questions most of which needed clarification or rephrasing

From this illustration it can be seen that a checklist of this sort could prove to be a lengthy and an unwieldy document. Before developing such an instrument, those involved in making the assessment need to agree the criteria for the measurement and the wording of the indicators. The instrument would then need to be piloted. In the case of interviewing it would be useful at the pilot stage to use a number of video-recorded interviews which the assessors could view and assess together so that their own level of agreement could be measured.

Measuring changes in attitudes

This is probably the most difficult area in which to measure change or development. In the assessment of the acquisition of knowledge and skills, the actions of the trainees are, in the main, observable and measurable. However, attitudes cannot be assessed in the same way. The behaviour which a trainee displays may not reflect the attitude which is held. For example, if the attitude which was being assessed was to 'Value the importance of good customer relations', an assessor may observe a behaviour which reflects the holding of that attitude but it doesn't necessarily mean that the 'performer' actually holds it.

The observed behaviour might include politeness, an apology, a smile, a 'thank you', use of the customer's name, etc but the trainee may not care at all about customer relations and is merely going through a drill which is expected in such circumstances. Many trainers believe that it doesn't matter what is felt so long as the behaviour is appropriate. Others believe that repetition of the behaviour will eventually bring about a change of attitude.

For those who are interested only in behaviour then the assessment can be made using similar checklists to those which are used for assessing skills. When it is felt that a measurement of attitude and attitude change is important, there are a number of techniques that might help. Basically, these techniques attempt to assess the strength of a particular attitude at the beginning of training and reassess it at the end or at some time after completion of training. This can be achieved by the use of some sort of semantic differential scale. For example, a group of trainees attending an instructional techniques course could be assessed in respect of their attitude towards a number of activities by rating them on a scale before training begins. For example,

Preparation and planning   Important |—|—|—|—| Unimportant

Learning theory   Relevant |—|—|—|—| Irrelevant

The same measure could be used again at the end of training to see if there has been a change in their attitude and subsequently some time after training to see whether the attitude has been retained, has become stronger or has weakened.

JOB BEHAVIOUR AND PERFORMANCE LEVEL

At this level the assessment of the effectiveness of training moves from the training context into the work environment. The trainer is naturally going to be concerned with how well the training experience has enabled the trainee to perform certain duties, tasks and responsibilities to the required standards. In other words, to what extent and how effectively have the knowledge, skills and attitudes acquired through training transferred to the job. In addition, the trainer is likely to want answers to the following complementary kinds of question:

- Have all the training needs of the job holders been satisfied?
- What factors have facilitated or prevented training transfer?
- Were the methods and procedures employed on the training programme entirely suitable?
- What additional learning, if any, took place on the training programme that was not covered by the formal training objectives?
- Was all the training content relevant or was any of it redundant?
- Could any of the training content have been learned more effectively on the job?
- To what extent can job performance or changes in job performance be attributed to the influence of the training programme or other influences?

Answers to these questions should help the trainer to confirm the adequacy or otherwise of training programmes by identifying the reasons for past and current successes, failures and errors of omission and commission. However, in order to undertake this assessment in an effective manner, the trainer will have to address a number of further questions, issues and concerns:

What specifically should the assessment cover?

This should be dictated mainly by the objectives of the training programme and by the particular questions the trainer wishes to answer. The training objectives will sometimes indicate the criteria and standards against which the trainees' post-training job performance should be judged. However, as high-lighted earlier, on occasions, the trainer may need to discuss or negotiate with the client these on-job criteria and standards, which may differ from those used at the reaction and learning levels, before carrying through the training programme. The agreed job and performance objectives established through this process should be expressed in terms of the behaviours, actions and results expected of the trainees on their return from the training event.

When should the assessment take place?

To a large extent this should depend on the nature of the job or position in question and the time required for sufficient relevant information on the trainees' on-the-job performance to become available. In theory, this suggests that it might be appropriate to conduct a series of evaluations spread over the post-training period to measure the emerging performance of trainees as it relates to the different agreed objectives. However, in practice this is likely to be extremely unrealistic. Gaining the co-operation of the various relevant parties for such an extended exercise might prove difficult for such obvious reasons as its disruptive effect, time, etc. Furthermore, as Campbell (1987) suggests 'If more than a normal settling in period elapses before the graduate and supervisor are contacted it becomes difficult to discriminate between knowledge and skills acquired in training and those acquired on the job.' The trainer will, no doubt, in many circumstances, need to strike some kind of balance and compromise. The necessary judgement, as to when to conduct the follow-up assessment, should be made easier if the trainer is very familiar with the make-up of the job and the circumstances in which it is performed.

Who should be involved in the assessment?

The two obvious candidates are the trainee and trainee's immediate line manager. In most cases the latter should have frequent enough direct or indirect contact with the trainee to make an informed and reliable judgement about their work performance and related matters. Peers, subordinates, clients and other organizational contacts may also be in a position to make valid appraisals of the trainee's post-training performance and give answers to some of the trainer's enquiries. However, it may not be possible, for practical, business, ethical or political reasons, to get such individuals to participate. Whoever is involved must have sufficient knowledge and skill, gained through training, experience and integrity to be able to make an assessment in an unbiased and rational way.

At the learning level the performance of all trainees would have, or should have, been checked against the training objectives. However, it may not be possible to include every trainee in the assessment study at the job behaviour and performance level, particularly when a substantial number of trainees have been through the training programme over a relatively short period. In these circumstances, therefore, it will be very important to adhere to the sampling principles set out in Appendix 2 when selecting those who will be included in the study.

What methods and techniques of assessment are available?

The trainer could employ, separately or in combination, a number of methods and techniques to cover the questions and issues of interest at this level; the main ones are outlined below (several of these techniques or methods have been mentioned already in relation to job and training needs analysis and are described in Appendix 1 together with their main advantages and disadvantages):

Questionnaire

The questionnaire can be employed to help the trainer to answer most of the questions of interest that were highlighted at the beginning of this section. Usually, it is recommended that this document be kept brief and simple as short questionnaires are more likely to produce higher response rates and maintain subsequent 'consumer' interest. However, a potential disadvantage of short questionnaires is the limited detail and, sometimes, ambiguous information supplied. The trainer can combat this problem to a certain extent by careful design and thorough piloting of the questionnaire. A detailed pilot study may not be feasible in some circumstances especially when only small numbers of trainees are involved.

The follow-up interview

A follow-up interview or series of interviews with the appropriate parties using trained interviewers and structured interview pro formas can be used to obtain details not captured through the questionnaire. As Bramley (1986) points out this is particularly important if attention is being directed to:

- Re-appraising training needs that had been identified earlier.
- Exploring the degree of transfer of training.
- Examining the effectiveness of certain training or instructional methods and techniques.

Action planning

An action plan consists of a list of prioritized statements drawn up by the trainee at the end of a training programme. It indicates what actions or skills he or she is committed to implement and by when, on returning to or starting back at work. This type of procedure not only facilitates transfer of training but can be an invaluable aid to subsequent job and performance related evaluation of the training. In particular the action plan could be the basis for the design of the follow-up questionnaire or interview schedule. The trainer would be interested in ensuring these documents covered:

- How much of the action plan had been implemented.
- What skills had been put into practice.
- What had been 'sidelined' and why.

Obviously, if the trainees' action plans did not include most, if not all, of the important training objectives then serious questions would have to be raised about the adequacy of the preceding training needs analysis and any other analyses that may have been undertaken.

Critical incident

This technique is essentially a procedure for collecting observed work incidents or behaviours that have proved to be extremely important or critical to job performance, i.e. which make the difference between success or failure in a job. In order to qualify as a critical incident two criteria have to be met:

- The incident has to be observed or experienced at first hand by the person reporting it.
- The consequences of the critical incident must be so clear cut as to leave no doubts regarding its effects.

The incidents should be collected through interview or group discussion. Participants usually complete a specially designed questionnaire before taking part in the interview or group discussion.

After collecting together a number of incidents the trainer should then relate them to the relevant training and job objectives. Comparing the nature of the incidents against the performance requirements and standards contained in these objectives should yield evaluative data regarding the effectiveness of the training programme. Two possible sets of factors might explain why incidents cannot be categorized as suggested above. In the case of uncategorized negative incidents new training needs may be revealed whereas the occurrence of positive incidents that cannot be categorized may indicate that job holders have already acquired the necessary skills in another setting or by means other than the formal training programme under review.

Performance appraisal and self-appraisal

Performance appraisal systems are a means of identifying training needs and, by the same token, can be used to ascertain whether or not the actual or potential job performance gap, giving rise to such needs, has been closed. This evaluative data can be collected in the normal course of regular staff appraisal or a special appraisal exercise could be mounted at an appropriate point after the training programme. The former possibility is probably the most acceptable to line managers, who would carry out the appraisal, because it is likely to be the least disruptive procedure. It goes without saying that for performance appraisal systems to be of any value at the job behaviour and performance level, the performance dimensions and scales employed must be clearly defined. The critical incident technique can be extended to assist in the design and development of appraisal schemes meeting these requirements (Latham and Wexley, 1981).

Self-appraisal by the job holder, which is often an integral part of some appraisal systems, also can provide the trainer with information about post-training competence and transferability.

Direct observation

Direct observation of the trainees in their workplace carrying out job activities is sometimes the only realistic way of determining the influence of training on their job performance. The observer would record the trainees' performance on some activity or behaviour analysis schedule or pro forma. Comparisons could then be made between the results of this analysis and the activity or behaviour patterns previously assessed as being effective. This technique can be difficult to apply on jobs that have a long activity cycle or that are made up of an irregular and unpredictable sequence of activities. In addition, the presence of the observer may have an effect on the enactment of certain forms of behaviour which might lead to incorrect conclusions being drawn.

Examination of output and results

For some positions there are indices of performance, which can be expressed in numeric form, that give a clear indication of the quantity and quality of the work produced. These indices would be examined subsequent to training to determine whether the trainees were achieving the expected level of output and results. Careful attention would have to be paid to the period over which the examination or analysis was undertaken and to the trainees' work environment in case influences other than the trainees' ability were affecting their output and result. Of course, this should be a consideration whatever method or technique is adopted in the follow-up study.

Decision criteria

In any particular post-training situation a number of alternative methods, techniques and strategies may be available. Bramley and Newby (1984) suggest several criteria that the trainer should bear in mind when deciding the techniques and the depth and extent of the strategy to employ:

- Importance: The benefits of training. The costs and consequences of failing to check on its effectiveness will determine importance.
- Frequency: The modification and improvement of frequently occurring training programmes would necessitate some form of on-going monitoring. This would not be a consideration in a one-off programme. However, as Bramley and Newby point out, if the programme is addressing a critical organizational problem then this might take precedence over the frequency criteria.
- Cost: No doubt if the cost of the follow-up or evaluation study outweighs the cost of the original programme, serious questions would be raised.
- Utility: The results of the study should satisfy the information needs of all the parties concerned, e.g. trainers, organizational decision makers, etc.
- Feasibility: Realism, political defensibility and administrative convenience should guide the choice of technique(s) and the design strategy.
- Ethics: Legal and ethical considerations, as they impinge on those affected, must always be in the forefront of the trainer's mind.
- Technical soundness: The study should aim to be accurate and honest.

Certainty about the validity of training

Reference has been made already to the possibility of post-training changes in the trainees' job behaviour and performance being due to factors other than the training programme. For example, simply being exposed to the work, or receiving effective on-job instruction and guidance or experiencing changes in the work environment and organization may be more influential than what was learned on the programme. Ideally, the trainer would like to be convinced that training brought about required changes in the job behaviour and performance of the trained group and that, over the same time period, these changes did not also occur in untrained groups.

If the trainer is restricted to looking solely, albeit objectively and systematically, at the trained group's post-training performance then some doubts about the validity of the training programme must always remain. Even with pre- and post-training assessments of the trainees' work performance having been carried out and showing positive change and improvement there is still no surety on this matter. This is because either the pre-training assessment may have 'sensitized' the trainees and they may have learned from this experience or the influences referred to above may be operating. Basically, by focusing only on the trained group there is not the necessary control of these other influences when considering the results of the post-training nor a clear delineation of the causal links. In order to introduce more scientific rigour into these post-training assessment procedures, several arrangements have been suggested in the academic literature involving control groups, i.e. groups who are similar in all relevant respects to the trained group apart from not having done the training programme. Some of these arrangements are detailed below:

Control group design	Comments and observation
1. *Group A* Pre-training ... Training ... Post-training assessment assessment *Group B* (Control) Pre-training ... No training ... Post-training assessment assessment	As with the other arrangements described, it would be necessary in this arrangement, in order to minimize contamination, for the trainer to try to operate a parallel time scale for both groups. The trainer should also attempt to ensure Group B undertook no special activity in the 'no training' period that might have an impact on their subsequent work perform-ance, which was being compared with Group A. Despite these precautions, this design cannot overcome the possibility of the pre-training assessment affecting the result of post-training assessment, which is particularly important when examining Group B's results.

2. *Group A*
 	
Training ... Post-training
       assessment
 	
   Group B (Control)
 	
No Training ... Post-training (A)
       assessment
	Although this design combats the possible effects of pre-training assessment, there is no means of measuring the gain that might be attributable to training.

Control group design	Comments and observation
3. *Group A*	This design, referred to as the Solomon Four Group Design, combines 1 and 2 and offers the greatest degree of control over non-training factors.
Pre-training ... Training ... Post-training assessment assessment	
Group B	It is very unlikely that the trainer will ever be able to run four groups on a parallel time scale. However, where a large number of similar groups go through the same programme, over an extended time period, it may be possible for the trainer to organize a variant of this design; a notion that would also apply to designs 1 and 2.
Pre-training ... No training ... Post-training assessment (A & C) assessment	
Group C	
No assessment ... Training ... Post-training assessment	
Group D	

No assessment .... Post-training
       (A & C)
       assessment	

The control group arrangements describe how, in theory, account can be taken of the possible effects of non-training factors and influences. In reality this is likely to be impracticable as the trainer will rarely have the opportunity or the luxury of being able to command resources to organize such arrangements. Given the lack of control groups the trainer will have to do as well as circumstances allow; adhering to the recommendations listed below should help to pinpoint the role training has played, as opposed to other influences and factors, in bringing about the required levels of job behaviour and performance:

● Establish clearly and specifically defined training objectives.
● Set objectives, where possible at all levels of evaluation.
● Use standardized, well piloted structured interview, observation, questionnaire, performance or results schedules.
● Choose a representative sample of the original target population to take part in the follow-up study.
● Use appropriate 'others' in addition to the trainee and his immediate superior, where feasible, in the study.
● Educate or instruct all those making comments and observations on the trainees' post-training performance in the principles of sound, reliable and valid assessment. Introducing the assessors to the performance model and

questions in relation to causal analysis might be instructive for them in this respect.

- Take cognizance of the performance model and causal analysis questions in Chapter 5 when reviewing data obtained through the follow-up study.
- 'Evaluate systematically and at as many levels as practicable in order to obtain the total picture' (Kenny and Reid, 1986).

ORGANIZATION LEVEL

The effects and value of training now need to be viewed from a wider and longer-term perspective. The basic question to be addressed is: What organizational improvements and results has training brought about or determined? A question more easily posed than answered.

The difficulties of establishing unambiguous cause-and-effect linkages outlined in the previous section are even more pertinent and applicable at the organizational level. However, despite these problems the trainer must still be prepared to give some consideration to the impact of training at this higher level and over an extended time period. An outline of the consequences of training in terms of organizational effectiveness and value for money can be built up from the views and ideas of Bramley (1986), Cameron (1980) and Newby (1985). Organizational effectiveness from this standpoint can be analysed in several ways:

Goals/targets achieved

These goals and targets might be expressed in terms of the following kinds of indices: units produced, improvements in productivity, documents processed, items sold, turnover, error and reject rates, wastage rates, accident rates, profit operating or running costs, overtime, etc.

Resource acquisition

The ability of the organization to acquire resources from the external environment will be an important determinant of its present and future viability. These resources could include: new materials, specialist and trained manpower, new customers and markets, finance, etc.

Satisfying clients and constituents

Indicators of the extent to which the expectations of internal and external clients and constituents have been satisfied may come from: customer complaints, consumer survey, meeting order deadlines, goods returned, internal attitude surveys and audits, etc.

Internal processes

How well internal processes operate may be as important an indicator of an organization's health and ultimate effectiveness as other measures. Signs and symptoms of this may come from: staff attitudes and morale, levels of conflict, absenteeism, turnover, transfer requests, grievances, disciplinary actions, group working, speed of reorganization and change, quality, level and extent of internal communication.

A number of the methods and techniques of assessment introduced in the section on job behaviour and performance level can also be employed at the organizational level; particularly questionnaire and interview surveys and examination of output and results. The data from these sources would have to be aggregated over time and maybe, in some circumstances, over other categories of personnel, in addition to the trainees.

Cost benefit and cost effectiveness analysis

For many, trying to value training in monetary terms is a forlorn enterprise. In their view it would be impossible or extremely difficult to isolate training costs and attach a monetary value to training results and effects. Without denying the inevitable obstacles some attempt should be made, where it is even marginally feasible, to produce a 'bottom line'. Training must be seen to be subject to the same kind of discipline as other functions in the organization. Cost benefit and cost effectiveness analyses are techniques or approaches designed to examine training from this financial viewpoint.

Newby (1985) defines these terms as follows:

- Cost benefit analysis (CBA): any analysis where both costs and benefits of training can be expressed in monetary terms.
- Cost effectiveness analysis (CEA): will be employed for analyses where the costs can be specified but the training outcomes, though identifiable, may not be priceable.

In CBA, Newby suggests that the 'costable inputs' should include: fixed and working capital, administrative and staff costs associated with the training function, costs of providing training personnel, training development costs, cost arising from participants attending the training programme, etc. On the output side these may be priceable results or outcomes linked to: reduced training costs and higher output resulting from reduced training time to reach mastery, improved quality of output, improvement in sales, greater resource utilization, etc.

In simple terms, CBA involves comparing anticipated or actual costs against the worth of anticipated or actual outcomes. The relevant outcomes should stem directly or indirectly from the training objectives and the analysis of criteria. Newby points out that the time span within which the costs and benefits should be calculated and other technical decisions are a matter for discussion between the accounting department of the training organization and the training function.

Cost effectiveness analysis can cost the inputs but is unable to value the outcomes in monetary terms. However, as indicated under organizational effectiveness, it may be possible to quantify some of the outcomes. This form of analysis may enable the trainer to make valid comparisons: between the costs of training programmes intending to produce or having the same learning effects; between the learning outcomes of programmes incurring the same costs or having the same budgets; and by monitoring over a period of time whether the costs and learning outcomes of a programme vary, possibly necessitating some re-evaluation of its usefulness.

Undoubtedly, trainers would face problems and difficulties in undertaking an assessment of the effect and value of a number of forms of training at the organizational level. In considering and planning such an exercise, they should bear in mind the recommendations listed at the end of the previous section and in particular the exhortation of Kenny and Reid (1986).

Warr (2002) describes an evaluation framework which has been developed from and which enlarges upon Kirkpatrick's model, which he feels may not go far enough. It covers the areas of Context evaluation, Input evaluation, Reaction evaluation, Outcome evaluation and Process evaluation (CIROOOP).

- *Context evaluation* focuses on the context of current and future requirements to achieve strategic goals for the organization and behavioural goals for individuals. It assesses whether training solutions are the most appropriate way of solving problems or whether there are other options such as changing systems, changing procedures or changing staff. This is reflected in the filtering process described by the authors on page 41.
- *Input evaluation* reviews the learning strategies to determine their effectiveness in terms of cost and their appropriateness for the nature of the learning.
- *Reaction evaluation* is the same as the reaction level described by Kirkpatrick.
- *Outcome evaluation* covers three stages of outcome – the immediate outcome, the intermediate outcome and the longer term outcomes. These stages are the levels of learning, behaviour and results in the Kirkpatrick model.
- *Process evaluation* examines how the training was conducted and considers training facilities, trainee–trainer relationships, the training context, its sequencing and its timing etc.

CONCLUSION

The implications for the trainer of carrying through evaluation and assessment of training at the four levels, especially at the job behaviour/performance and organization levels, seems formidable at first sight. However, there are at least three very sound reasons why the trainer should make every effort to do so:

- Reliable and specific informational feedback will help the trainer to improve the design, organization and implementation of current and future training programmes.
- By being able to demonstrate the effectiveness of training, the trainer should find it easier to negotiate and bargain for resources in the organization's political arena.
- The credibility of the training function will be enhanced over time, if as a result of evaluation its products can be made even more worthwhile for the consumer, and this in turn should create more positive attitudes in the organization towards learning, training, education and development.

Warr sees evaluation as more than the final stage of a systems or systematic approach to training. He sees it as an on-going and superordinate function, a concept which is developed in greater detail in this book in Chapter 10 on the training audit.

10

Auditing Training

In the earlier editions of this book the notion of auditing the training system focused mainly on the training programme, course or event. A number of authors, Adamson and Caple (1996), Applegarth (1991), Bramley and Hullah (1987) and Murphy and Swanson (1988), suggest that this is too narrow an interpretation of such a concept.

They consider that the idea of a training audit should be broadened out to include issues and considerations not only at the event level, but also at the levels of the organization and the function (i.e. Training Department). Figure 10.1 illustrates this tripartite focus and the direction of the interrelationship between the three levels.

Because of the nature of what has been covered in previous chapters the intention here is to concentrate on the training audit at the event/programme level. However, in addition, a series of key questions will also be raised that would inform and direct an audit exercise conducted at the organizational and/or functional levels.

AUDITING THE TRAINING SYSTEM AT THE EVENT LEVEL

It has been seen that a systematic approach to training involves the application of a number of processes, skills and techniques to a sequence of wide-ranging activities. It is possible that a number of trainers will have been involved at different stages. For example, some may have investigated the training needs

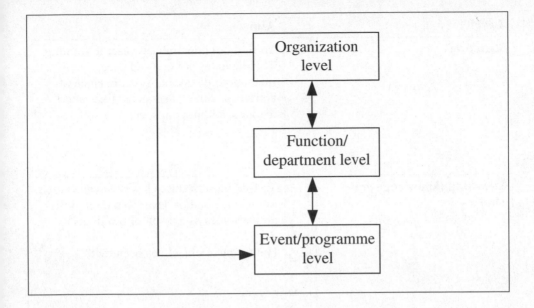

Figure 10.1 Levels of the training audit

and designed the training, others may have delivered the training and yet another group may have conducted the validation and evaluation exercises.

Diagrams of a systematic approach to training show through its many feedback loops that the system should be self-maintaining. However, that will not just happen because a set of arrows on a diagram indicate that this is the case. There needs to be some form of superordinate control function which monitors the system to ensure that it works properly. The training audit fulfils this function. This function is quite separate from, and should not be confused with, any of the levels of validation and evaluation discussed earlier. Figure 10.2 shows how the training audit relates to the other forms of assessment or evaluation.

The process of auditing the training system involves a detailed examination of a particular training programme to see if every stage of its design, implementation and validation has been carried out properly. This kind of audit can be divided into seven stages (Figure 10.3). As they are described here, they relate to a course but with appropriate adjustments they are equally applicable to other training strategies.

Stage one: Familiarization

In order to put the current training into perspective the training auditor should ascertain, at the outset, how it was conceived. Naturally, the questions which will have to be raised about the programme will depend on whether it had

Level			Aim
Reaction			To find out how trainees react to training. This includes volume and pace, methodology, tutorial style, balance of activities, value of sessions, likes and dislikes, admin points, etc.
Learning (knowledge and skills)	I N T E R N A L	V A L I D A T I O N	To find out if trainees have increased their knowledge and/or developed their skills and attitudes as a result of training. Have course objectives been met?
Behaviour and performance (application of knowledge and skills)	E X T E R N A L	V A L I D A T I O N	To find out how far former trainees have applied their learning to improve their job performance. To find out how well training has met their needs/needs of the line supervisor.
Organizational outcome		E V A L U A T I O N	To find out the extent to which training has improved or influenced organization performance, e.g. reduced costs, improved quality/quantity increased profits, etc. To assess the cost and value of training.
Training audit-event level			To find out if a Systematic Approach to Training is being applied, in particular internal and external validation. Where it is not, undertake or establish procedures.

Figure 10.2 The relationship between training audit and levels of evaluation

When done and by whom	Method	Action
During training and/or completion of training. (Trainer)	Daily reviews, questionnaire completed during or at end of training. Open Forum/Course Wash Up Class monitoring	'First Aid' treatment to training programme and content.
During training and/or at end of training. (Trainer)	Tests, exercises, case studies, oral questioning, etc.	Remedial treatment for individuals, re-training, reinforcement. Change/review methods.
After an interval which allows learning to be put into practice (on average 2–3 months after training). (Trainer/Training Manager)	Postal-questionnaires and/or interviews with former trainees and their managers/supervisors.	Continuous development and updating of training content in response to changing needs, etc.
Periodically. After sufficient time has passed for training outcomes to have had an effect on the function of the organization. (Training Manager/Head of Training)	Postal-questionnaires, interviews with former trainees, departmental managers and other departments who may monitor results, e.g. Standards of Service. Study of company results	Provide feedback on effectiveness and value of training to the organization. Recommend future pattern of training.
At any time. (Internal/External Training Auditor or audit team)	Audit the Training Manager's procedure for review of objectives, course content, instruments for internal and external validation and use of feedback.	Provide feedback on effectiveness of procedures. Recommend procedures to be adopted.

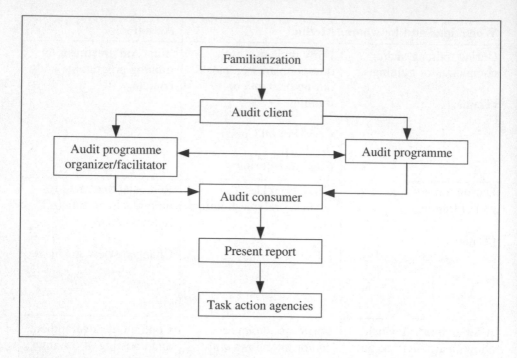

Figure 10.3 The training audit model

proactive or reactive beginnings. In the case of proactive training, information will need to be sought from departments such as manpower planning, management development, etc. With reactive training the auditor may have to establish whether the training programme derives from a traditional or a consultative approach. The traditional approach involves management defining the problem and dictating the solution, i.e. training. The trainer in this situation is in a weak position in terms of organizational power and hence usually complies with management dictats and all that this implies. On the other hand, the trainer operating within a consultative framework is involved with management in problem diagnosis and causal analysis. He uses powers of persuasion to get management to accept its responsibility for ownership of the problem and resists attempts to have solutions imposed on him.

Whatever the origins of the training, at the familiarization stage the training auditor undoubtedly will have to try to establish what are the aims and specific objectives of the training, what is the current target population and demand for training, what changes or developments in procedures, etc, if any, have taken place over time.

Surprisingly the sources of information pertaining to these questions may be many and varied. For example, with regard to a training course, besides the training programme and training manual the training auditor may need to refer to past and present members of the training department, scrutinize training records/documents, examine reports concerning the course, etc. Some of the key questions to be raised in this stage are set out below.

Stage one: Familiarization

Title and aims

- What is the current course title? Has it changed and if so why?
- What are the broad aims of the training?

Objectives

- Have behavioural objectives been established? If so what level – terminal, enabling, learning points, etc?
- Have there been any amendments to the objectives? If so when were the amendments made?

Target population and demand

- What is the current target population? Has it changed over time and are there any proposals for change?
- What is the current demand? Is there any over or under subscription?

Changes and developments

- What changes, if any, have there been to the training programme over time? If any, what are the reasons for such changes?
- Has a previous audit and/or project investigation been undertaken in connection with the training? If so, is the report available? What were the recommendations/observations in this report?
- What additional feedback is held by the Training Department?

Tasking

- Has there been any specific tasking from the Training Manager for this audit?
- Have there been any specific requests from training manager/clients for this audit?

Stage two: Auditing the client

The second stage of the process is to audit the client. Sometimes during the familiarization stage, it is difficult to identify who the client is. In a large organization the client could be the head of a sizeable department who has a direct responsibility for the area in which the need for training has been established, or he could be representing sections of his department without being completely familiar with their needs. It is important to ensure that discussions are at the appropriate level of client involvement and that those who most directly represent client needs are involved in the audit.

Channels of communication available to clients are likely to be determined, and possibly limited, by their respective positions in the organizational structure. One of the objectives of the audit is to confirm that lines of communication between trainers and clients exist, but at times the audit can serve to provide a means of communication when other channels are limited.

It is only through effective communication that training can respond to change. Changes in target population and in procedural or other aspects of the job are likely to alter the need for training and unless this is reflected in the training which is provided it follows that there could be a deficit in the end product.

The outcomes of training and its effectiveness can be gauged by monitoring the performance of students and their reactions, but it needs to be confirmed that this process of monitoring exists. Most training is designed against a background of influences and constraints and these need to be re-examined if training is to develop to best meet the needs of the client. The key questions are set out below.

Stage two: Auditing the client

Commencement

- When did the training commence and why?

Training needs

- What changes, if any, have taken place in the target population? If any, how has this affected the training need?
- What degree of precision is there regarding training needs?

Changes in procedure

- What changes, if any, have taken place in procedures and working practices since the last audit or since the training was established? Have these been reflected in the current objectives?
- Are there any future changes in procedure and working practice planned or anticipated? When are they going to be implemented?
- Have the changes been communicated to the training course manager?

Monitoring and feedback

- Are there any arrangements for monitoring how well the training meets the needs of the target population? If so, what are they, who is responsible, and what communication, if any, is there with the course manager or organizer?
- Is there a feedback system designed to obtain information from ex-course members? If so, what kinds of information are sought and how is the information used?

Constraints and influence

- What are the constraints in meeting the training needs? Are these financial, course member availability, nature of the target population, etc?
- What external/future influences bear on the course content and structure?

Stage three: Auditing the programme

When these preliminary stages of the audit have been completed it is possible to examine the actual training in greater detail and in relation to the training needs. Unless the training needs, as they have been confirmed by the client, are those from which the training has been derived, its effectiveness must be held in question.

It follows that the auditor must confirm that those responsible for the delivery of the training are familiar with the training needs and that these needs are the prime source of reference when training and learning strategies are developed. Most designers of training, whatever the method of delivery, like to improve on and develop their work. It should be confirmed that innovation and revision have remained within the framework of the training needs.

It is the training objectives which serve to translate needs into operational statements of the outcomes of training. Not only should objectives be presented in a style which conforms with the criteria for writing objectives, but there should be a system for regular reviews with the client of both objectives and needs.

As the audit moves into the area of examining the structure of training, the methods, media, tests and assessments which make up the internal validation, etc, it might appear that the auditor takes on the role of inspector. While it is acknowledged that elements of inspection are involved, this is not the prime function of the auditor.

The role of the auditor, together with the associated interpersonal skills which are needed, will be reviewed later when consideration is given to who should conduct the audit.

During this phase the auditor and the trainer need to review together the training programme, precis, exercises, tests, training aids, questionnaires, etc to see if they are appropriate, up-to-date and conform with relevant and acknowledged design principles and conventions. It is important also to identify what use is made of any form of feedback from students either as answers to tests or responses to validation questionnaires. Equally important is what feedback is given to students.

It is likely that from the outset the training will have been designed within a framework of constraints. Few training activities enjoy freedom from constraints in manpower, money, materials or time. It is possible through the medium of the audit to review these constraints together with those which may have been imposed subsequently and to present the case for the trainer to try to initiate change.

However, this does not mean that the developmental needs of trainers should be considered only when an audit is being carried out. Training managers, like any other line manager, should see this as a continuous process. In many instances this means observing and monitoring how trainers deliver their training sessions. It does not necessarily mean that the training manager has to devote a large amount of time to sitting in on sessions. Trainers can support each other in this role and often it has been found valuable for trainers to video record some of their sessions and to review their performance against a checklist. Such support, analysis and feedback is especially useful when the trainer finds a particular session difficult to teach or feels that it could be improved.

It is almost impossible to provide a general checklist that would embrace skilled trainer performance in all contexts. Such a document would be too cumbersome for any observer to handle. Appendix 5 is an example which focuses on basic teaching skills. As with the assessment of interpersonal skills, the checklist is made up of statements which are presented as indicators of high and low performance on a number of features relating to teaching a group. The checklist can be adapted or used as the basis of design for assessing specific teaching skills or for teaching specialized subject matter which demands the use of particular techniques or strategies. For example, the skills used by the trainer during role-playing exercises could be looked at in much greater detail. Also, there could be a need to include factors that relate to safety, economy in the use of materials, professional ethics, etc.

It might be appropriate at this stage to consider how trainers assess their own performance. The checklist below is an example of how trainers could review their performance at the end of training sessions or training events to help to identify their strengths and any areas where they feel that they could improve. Most of the questions that the trainers have to ask themselves relate to what they did rather than whether or not they did it. This makes the exercise more focused, more objective and of greater value for developmental purposes.

How well did I prepare?
How did I motivate the trainee(s)?
How did I put the session into the context of the job?
Did I state my objectives?
How did I explain the structure of the session?
Did I check the previous experience of the trainee(s)?
Was the training delivered in a logical sequence and broken down into digestible
    chunks?
How did I make the session interesting?
How did I get the trainee(s) to participate?
How did I monitor the progress of the trainee(s)?
What, if any, areas of weakness did I identify?
What use did I make of questions?
Did I highlight the key learning points?
How did I assess the overall performance of the trainee(s)?
Did I show confidence and enthusiasm?
What use did I make of my notes?
Overall was the session a success?

It would be wrong to proceed without giving consideration to the main participants in the training activity – those responsible for the delivery and those who receive the training. The trainers should be considered in terms of their own training and development to meet the needs of the tasks which they have to carry out at present and those which they will be called upon to undertake in future.

The trainees should be considered in terms of the training needs and the stated target population. The knowledge and skills expected of entrants to the training can change considerably over time and it has not been unknown for trainees to have gained nothing from their training because they knew it all before they joined the course. This emphasizes the need for channels of communication between tutors/training designers and technical line staff not only to be available but to be open and to be used. Some of the key questions that must be considered at this stage are set out below.

Stage three: Auditing the programme

Training needs analysis

- Has the training needs analysis been undertaken? If so, when?
- Have the tutorial staff familiarized themselves with the report?

Objectives

- Have the tutorial staff/courses manager access to or a copy of the current objectives?
- Have there been any amendments to the objectives since the last audit?
- If the objectives have been updated, what was the nature of, and reasons for, the changes?
- Do the objectives conform with the criteria for the writing of good objectives?

Course structure

- Is there a satisfactory balance between different methods of training, e.g. exercise, case study, etc?
- How does the balance of the course reflect the different degrees of importance attached to the objectives?

Methods and media

- Are the methods and media relevant to the objectives in the light of target population characteristics?
- What is the quality of handouts, exercise material and other training aids?

Tutor training

- How are tutors selected (criteria and methods)?
- What is the training and development programme (internal and external) for tutors in respect of:
  - (i) tutorial skills?
  - (ii) professional and technical skills?

Course member details

- What numbers have attended the courses over the last two years?
- Have there been any changes in the target population profile?
- How far does the student profile match that of the stated target population?

Internal validation

- At what points during the course are tests and exercises used?
- What is the purpose of the tests and exercises, e.g. pre/post, confirmation, practice, assessment, end of course, etc?
- How are the tests and exercises designed, e.g. objective test formats, in-tray, self-assessment, etc? Are they reliable and valid?
- What action is taken relevant to student needs identified in tests and exercises, e.g. remedial work?
- How are test and exercise results/scores recorded and what use is made of them, e.g. comparison of courses, review of tests, etc?
- Is an end-of-course questionnaire administered? Is it designed properly?
- Is there an end-of-course 'wash up' with students?
- Is there an end-of-course 'wash up' with tutors?
- How frequently are reports written on courses? (If not covered above)
- To whom are they sent? What use is made of them?

External validation

- Is there a system of external validation? How does it work? Is it effective?

Formal links between training staff/technical – line staff

- What links exist to receive information about technical/procedural changes/updates?

Constraints on training

- Has training been affected by any constraints? What are they? Are they acceptable?

Stage four: Auditing the programme organizer/facilitator

The key person in co-ordinating the communication and the work of trainers is the programme organizer/facilitator. The way the role is played will be a major influence bearing on the success or otherwise of the training programme/experience. As with the origins of the training, the facilitator's actions may be seen as basically reactive or proactive. In the former mode the organizer may be little more than an administrator of the programme, taking little initiative for its development. The facilitator may view his function in this situation as essentially that of maintenance. Others are seen as responsible for suggesting changes and modifications to the programme and the organizer simply responds or reacts to their requests. The personal and organizational power of the facilitator is usually low in these circumstances.

If, on the other hand, a more proactive stance is adopted by the facilitator, potentially he could become crucial to the training programme's development and in ensuring its relevance. He will see it as his responsibility to open up and strengthen lines of communication with the client and the consumers and take an active part in extending the professional competence of any subordinates intimately involved with the programme. By being proactive and dynamic in approach, the facilitator can have a major influence over the direction and quality of the training programme.

The training auditor will need to bear in mind the above reactive/ proactive distinction when addressing the facilitator in the course of the audit as it will determine the depth and nature of the questioning.

In this respect, apart from the specific questions highlighted in the previous section, the auditor would need to gauge the facilitator's general impressions of the programme's effectiveness, the reactions of the consumers and the degree of satisfaction felt by him and the staff. The problems and constraints that the programme organizer has experienced or anticipates would also need to be examined. Finally, the training auditor must give the facilitator the opportunity to express views and opinions on how the programme could be improved. Some of the key questions are below.

Stage four: Auditing the programme organizer/facilitator

Impressions

- What is your overall impression of the effectiveness of the training?
- How far do you feel that students committed themselves to the training?
- How did students react to methodology, tests, exercises, etc?
- How far do the training materials meet the needs of trainers?

- How far do methods and media (AVA) meet the needs of the trainers?
- Is the training programme well balanced with appropriate time allocations?
- What do you find satisfying/dissatisfying about the training?

Managers only

- How far do you feel that trainers were prepared for the training?
- How competent do you feel that the trainers are?
- Are there any deficiencies in training which need to be made good?
- Any development activity you would personally like to undertake in relation to this training?

Problems and constraints

- What problems have you encountered with the training?
- Can you anticipate problems which might arise in the future?
- Are there any constraints which have made your work difficult, e.g. time, individuals on the course, target population?

Suggestions

- What suggestions can you offer to improve:
  - The training as a whole?
  - Specific exercises, precis, visual aids, etc?
  - Administration?
  - Problem areas identified earlier in discussion?

Stage five: Auditing the consumer

Like validation, the audit must take into consideration 'consumers'. These are the graduates of the training and their line managers.

The first area of concern is the external validation. There is a requirement to confirm that it has been carried out and that both graduates and line managers had the opportunity to contribute as fully as they wished. There is a danger that the auditor may, in fact, conduct a second external validation which is not the main object of the exercise. But should it be found that it has not been done, it would be difficult not to follow that line and it is likely to be valuable to do so.

The main part of the discussion with graduates is to examine their needs. This should identify career patterns, how the training was relevant to careers and how well the timing of the training fitted into that pattern. The trainees' expectation of the training should relate to the pre-course and post-course briefings given by the line manager.

The expectations of, and need for, training as perceived by trainees hinge on line managers. The auditor should try to identify how far line managers are able to be proactive and how far they have to be reactive in terms of career planning. While managers may begin the process of planning ahead and nominating staff for training, it could happen that non-availability of courses, etc, results in the training coming too late.

Hence, proactive managers appear to be reactive as a result of constraints which are beyond their control. The nature of these and other constraints are all of interest to the auditor in taking his global view of the training under review. Some of the questions to be asked are listed below.

Stage five: Auditing the consumer

Graduate

- What was the overall impression of the effectiveness of the course?
- How well has the course met training needs?
- Was a course briefing and/or a course debriefing received?
- Was post-course feedback requested by the course organizer/manager? If so, what form of feedback was asked for?

Line manager

- What is the overall impression of the value of the course to subordinate?
- How has subordinate's on-the-job performance/behaviour changed since returning from the course?
- What does the course nomination procedure consist of?
- What constraints, if any, have been placed on subordinate's ability to put into effect what was learned on the course?
- Was any post-course feedback on the subordinate asked for by the course organizer/manager? If so, what form did the feedback take?

Stage six: Presenting the report

During the course of the audit, the auditor will have collected a considerable amount of data, observations and comments. The manner in which the findings are presented, i.e. style and method, will depend very much on how the auditor has been tasked and the report writing conventions of the organization concerned.

However, before reaching this stage there is a need for a period of consolidation. During this time the auditor should be evaluating findings, clarifying any areas of ambiguity and drawing conclusions.

In the presentation of the report, the auditor should ensure that the document will be readable, understandable and usable by all of those who may have to react to the conclusions and any recommendations which are made. This means that the technical language of the auditor's own specialist field may need to be modified for the sake of simplicity and comprehension.

Stage seven: Tasking action agencies

It is expected that the originator of the audit would act on the conclusions and recommendations of the report by initiating some reactive or proactive tasks. Those tasked could include personnel specialists, the operational unit for whom the course was designed, course managers or tutors, training specialists to investigate or research specific areas, etc.

AUDITING THE TRAINING SYSTEM AT THE FUNCTIONAL LEVEL

Auditing at this level is designed to assess the professional competence of the training department/function to deliver structured learning efficiently and to ensure it is effective. The prime focus of the audit is on how the training function manages the people, systems and routines associated with the systematic approach to training. Some of the key questions that would need to be raised at the functional level are below.

Audit at functional level

- How conversant is the training department with the organization's policies, corporate objectives and strategies and resources?
- Is the training function operating in a reactive/maintenance role or in a proactive/change mode?
- What kinds of training does the training function develop and carry out?
- What methods does the training department employ to ascertain training needs?

- What degree of liaison and co-operation is there with line managers in identifying individual and departmental needs?
- Does the training function develop a training plan for every department? If so, how is it developed and what form does it take?
- What statistical and evaluative information is collected by the training function on the current state of training in the organization?
- What encouragement, if any, is given by the training function to the transfer of learning?
- What forms of validation and evaluation are carried by the training department? How is such information used to reassess needs and redesign training strategies, tactics and solutions?
- What forms of training and planned experience are received by training personnel?

AUDITING THE TRAINING SYSTEM AT THE ORGANIZATIONAL LEVEL

The training function should not work in glorious isolation. It is not enough for it to simply operate efficiently. In order to be effective the training function's activities must be planned in a co-ordinated way, linked closely to the organization's overall objectives, plans and strategies rather than being tacked on as an after-thought. Top management involvement is required in setting the training function's agenda and assessing and managing its performance and contribution. Furthermore, as pointed out in Chapter 1, the training function must not work as a closed system insulated from its internal and external environment. An open systems philosophy within the organization will help to ensure the function is responsive to, and influences, organizational changes and demands. Answers to the following questions should help to ascertain whether this is the case.

Audit at organizational level

- What involvement does the training department have in helping top management to formulate clear manpower objectives and strategies?
- Are training plans formulated in relation to the organization's corporate objectives and plans?
- What are the critical criteria of organizational effectiveness? To what degree do the activities of the training function focus on these critical areas?

- Is the training department represented at board level? If so, what role does the training representative play both in relation to manpower development and other issues?
- What is the image of the training function within the organization? How is its present image assessed?
- What contribution does the training function make to the creation of a 'learning organization'?
- How is the interface between training and the rest of the organization managed?
- Does the training function consciously market its services to the rest of the organization? If so, what form does the promotion take?

THE TRAINING AUDITOR

Consideration must now be given to what kind of auditor is needed and what skills need to be exercised in order to elicit the information described within the context of the audit model.

The training auditor would certainly have to be very well versed in the technology of training and possess a number of technical skills associated with designing data collection instruments, problem diagnosis and causal analysis, appraising training methods and techniques and in written communication.

In addition, the auditor should have interpersonal skills in such areas as interviewing, acting as a 'sounding board', counselling, giving feedback and one-to-one training.

Training, in an organizational context is, however, more than just concern with subject matter. This is clear from the types of judgement that the auditor may need to make in response to the answers that the questioning elicits.

Ideally the auditor should be very familiar with the organization and the potentials of the training function. An understanding of aspects of organization theory, especially communication, also would be of value.

Furthermore, the auditor would need to give careful consideration to the role that should be played in relation to the client or programme co-ordinator. There are several possibilities which include:

Helper

'Let me deal with this.' 'I'll deal with that bit for you.'

Monitor

'Have you done this?' 'When will it happen?' 'Let's see how you're getting on.'

Inspector

'Where is. . .?' 'Why?' 'Show me.' 'If you don't. . .'

Specialist/expert

'I'll show you how to do. . .' 'This means that. . .'

Motivator

'That's very good. . .' 'You've met the standards. . .' 'We can now go on to. . .'

Consultant

'Tell me where you feel the problem lies.' 'What alternatives do you have?' 'How do you see it developing?'

The most appropriate role or roles for the auditor to adopt would be partly contingent on circumstances and conditions. These would include management climate, future organization changes, maturity of training personnel, established relationships, proactive/reactive training initiatives, etc.

This suggests that the auditor should have acquired a superordinate skill, over and above the technical and interpersonal skills already mentioned, namely that of role diagnosis and appropriate role selection. The role or roles adopted will, in part, depend on the organization's current 'state of health', its developing needs and the nature of its product.

This audit function is a demanding task and not all organizations may be large enough to sustain an audit section or even an individual auditor. When this is the case, it might be that the training manager takes on the additional role of auditor. Alternatively, an outside consultant could be taken on in the same way that external financial auditors act for organizations.

In both of these circumstances some caution needs to be exercised. The training manager/auditor has to take care that the audit function remains a distinctly separate activity and does not become lost within the general managerial role. When an outside consultant is used as auditor, care should be taken to ensure that the concept of the training audit is understood and that the auditor has the capacity and expertise to undertake the task. Time is well spent when an outside auditor has the opportunity to spend some time building up a rapport with the organization and getting to read the way in which it works.

11

The Role of the Trainer

THE TRAINER IN CONTEXT

Towards the end of the 20th century, it was recognized that change was becoming, and would continue to become, more frequent and more rapid. Since the early 1990s organizations have found the need to diversify, to change their structure, to develop a new culture, to introduce a new work ethic and to accept change as a feature of their development and survival in the face of national and worldwide competition.

In managing these changes, most organizations have experienced some or all initiatives such as devolution of central functions, empowerment, flattened organizational structures, downsizing/rightsizing, objective setting and performance management.

The emerging relationship between employee and the organization has been described by McCrimmon (1994):

> One of the most profound changes sweeping through organizations is contracting out: yesterday you were an employee, today you are an external supplier. In theory at least, you can now supply your services to other 'clients'. Your 'employer' no longer has the same obligations to you, no promise to retain you, look after your career, train you or provide you with a pension. Your relationship to your client is transformed as it would be if you suddenly became a privatized industry.

Whilst there is evidence of this happening in some organizations the change has not been as dramatic as McCrimmon portrays. However, there have been a number of initiatives which give some credibility to what he has described.

In the context of training, many trainers in both the public and private sectors have found that they have had to compete directly with 'outside' providers and other providers within their own organization. When responsibility for training has been devolved and smaller units empowered to make their own arrangements there have been mixed outcomes. The sharpening of the business skills of trainers has in many cases enhanced the quality of training, but the downside has often been inadequate training delivered at low cost.

This means that trainers must become more business orientated and develop their knowledge and skill to make a measurable contribution. This will involve establishing the position of training in the organization, identifying the changing roles of the trainer, deciding what kind of trainers are needed to meet these roles, marketing the training function and measuring its effectiveness in business terms.

WHO ARE THE TRAINERS?

Everyone within the organization should have a degree of responsibility for training and development. At board level there should be sufficient expertise and knowledge to be able to create a realistic training policy to link corporate strategy with its achievement through those who have to implement it. At the other end of the spectrum is the individual who is learning rapidly that he or she must take responsibility for his or her own career development, and pursue the concept of Lifelong Learning and the practice of Continuing Professional Development. At all points, whatever the organizational structure is, there are others who can be regarded in some way as 'trainers'.

It has always been considered that line managers and supervisors, or their equivalents (team leaders, charge hands etc) have a responsibility for training. This aspect of their work has not always been discharged effectively. Reasons for this have included (with some justification) that they have been too busy performing other managerial tasks and that training is the responsibility of the training department. Their argument is understandable in a number of respects, especially when there are many staff who need the same kind of training. However, there are aspects of all jobs where specialist training or specific job training is needed, and only the manager or team leader can provide that training. In most instances this is carried out, but it is regarded as 'showing' someone what to do rather than training.

The line manager's function also includes discussing training and development needs with individuals, arranging appropriate training and assessing its effectiveness in the workplace. Again, this is not always seen as being involved in training.

In the same way, individuals are trained on a one-to-one basis by members of their peer group who do not see themselves as trainers. Those working on open-learning programmes are often helped by 'supporters' who may know little about the subject matter, but who make an important contribution to learning by providing encouragement and general support.

From this scenario it can be seen that there are many who could be described, to varying degrees, as 'trainers'. Whilst accepting that a variety of people have a hand in training, and that their roles cannot be ignored, it is usually those whose full-time role is training who are described as 'trainers' and who regard themselves as 'professionals'.

However, it is not always clear what is meant by the term 'professional trainer'. In fact, there are at least three possible meanings which readily come to mind. It could mean the training specialist who has been brought into the organization from outside, it could mean the career specialist within the organization who has decided to make his or her future in training or it could refer to those who, as part of their career plan, spend some time in training during which they develop considerable expertise in, and commitment to, training. There is no reason why all three categories shouldn't exist side by side and be regarded as 'professionals'. The most important factor is that training staff should be of a high calibre so that they can contribute to making the training departments the centres for excellence that they should be.

The career specialists in training are vital to the training function because of its scope and the need for expertise. This book has indicated the demands which are made on trainers generally and there is scope for further specialization within training as new technology offers alternative methods of delivery which need to be researched and subsequently employed through the application of specific skills.

Developing the general and the specific skills cannot be achieved by a short-term training and development programme. It takes a considerable time to build up a competence and confidence level to take on the role of a training specialist. Many who have reached this level have done so just at the time when, in the normal course of events, they are moved back to their main career discipline. It is at such a point when potential is just about to be realized that the organization loses one of its most useful assets. Organizations which allow and encourage their personnel to make their careers in training will get a valuable return from their contribution.

From this it might be suggested that it is a waste to take into the training department those who are only likely to stay for perhaps two years before pursuing their careers in other directions. This is not strictly true and it is believed that training departments need staff who fall into this category. It is true that the gifted amateur approach is no longer appropriate and that a thorough training is needed. The short-stay trainer is not only able to bring recent practical experience to the training department but subsequently takes a knowledge of, and hopefully a commitment to, training back to the main operational functions of the organization. The professionalism of the trainers who are in this category is reflected partly in the expertise which they develop and also in the attitude that they display towards training and their own need to be trained.

A deficit in this area is often found in the training manager who may believe that the training function can be managed with very little knowledge of training or, even worse, the manager who may believe that the little knowledge that he or she has represents the sum total of what training is all about. Training managers must be credible in the eyes of their staff and be given thorough training rather than the overview which they feel is all that they need.

Apart from adopting a sensible selection policy and devising proper training, meaningful career paths, development programmes and reward systems should be developed for both career and short-stay trainers. In the case of career trainers working in large training departments it may be feasible to draw up coherent promotion structures. However, if the training section is relatively small, but part of an integrated personnel department then it may be sensible on occasions to create personnel specialists rather than career trainers. These individuals would spend several periods in training as their career and promotions take them through the various specialisms within the personnel function, e.g. industrial relations, job evaluation, recruitment and selection, etc, thus combining the advantages of being pure career trainers with those of the short-stay trainer. It could ensure that they 'keep in touch' with training whilst at the same time broaden their perspectives by operating elsewhere. In addition their 'pick-up' on re-entering the training sphere should be relatively smooth.

It is essential that the true short-stay trainer, going back to his or her main operational area after a spell in training, does not perceive this period as a sentence in the organizational 'gulag'. The secondment must be linked clearly to the individual's past and future experiences and must be seen to contribute to the development of knowledge and skills of value to their careers. Above all, the period in training must not adversely affect an individual's promotion prospects by apparently taking them out of their mainstream activity and forcing them to mark time.

TRAINER SKILLS

When the strategies and tactics for training programmes are selected, the skills demanded of the trainers are often overlooked. The assumptions are made that those who are full-time trainers are omnicompetent and that those who could be described as occasional trainers need only to have technical competence to be able to train others. Trainers who are involved in the delivery of training are likely to have to call upon a variety of skills which is not always appreciated by some training managers nor by many of the direct trainers themselves. There is a range of specific skills that are needed to undertake one-to-one coaching, training groups, facilitating, counselling and supporting distance learning, and writing distance learning materials. However appropriate the strategy or tactic may be when measured against the constraints, target population, budget and the principles of learning, unless the trainers have been selected and trained to meet high standards, the training will not be effective.

When selecting tactics for training, the perceived advantages of on-job training or 'sitting by Nellie' as it is sometimes described, has meant that in many circumstances the training has been introduced and conducted in a less than professional manner. This has come about because of two fundamental and interrelated assumptions about 'Nellie' training.

The first of these assumptions is that 'Nellie' training is a natural and familiar process. This assumption has origins in the earliest form of training and learning given by parent to child. There are also historical precedents for 'Nellie' training to be found in craft apprenticeships. Many master craftsmen were highly motivated trainers, as they were an integral part of the process of ensuring continuity within their trade. These kinds of relationship are found between personal tutors and pupils in private and higher institutes of learning. However, despite our familiarity with some of these forms of learning and teaching, it is neither logically nor factually correct to conclude that being an effective one-to-one trainer will come naturally to everyone.

The second assumption is that having expertise or skill in a subject or discipline is intimately associated and causally linked with the ability to teach or educate others in that field. This is an entrenched assumption within parts of the British education system and was personified by the comparative lack of training in teaching techniques that was once experienced by most university lecturers and student teachers. In addition, the attitudes engendered by the traditions of the well-rounded and motivated amateur still have not been removed. Unfortunately, there has been a carry-over of some of these attitudes to training where it is often believed that if the technical expertise is available within a particular area, any associated training problem will be solved automatically.

From this, it can be seen that there are numerous precedents and prejudices to persuade people into accepting the view that the ability to be an effective 'Nellie' is a natural and widely dispersed phenomenon. It seems that 'sitting by Nellie' training is regarded by many as simply a matter of observing an expert and that learning will occur by some process of psychological osmosis. Furthermore, there is a tendency to be complacent about, or even antagonistic towards, the notion of, and the need for, the training of 'Nellies'.

With these attitudes prevailing, it is hardly surprising that training by 'sitting by Nellie' is often a hit-and-miss affair leading to inconsistent results. Such unpredictable outcomes have, no doubt, helped 'Nellie' training to acquire unprofessional connotations.

Given this situation, there is an obvious requirement for the basic assumptions about 'Nellie' training to be examined critically. In many circumstances it will be necessary to replace 'sitting by Nellie' with systematically designed training and properly trained one-to-one trainers.

The training of one-to-one trainers is an area of considerable neglect. When one of the aims of 'sitting by Nellie' has been to reduce the costs of training, it seems unreasonable to managers that they should have to invest time, effort and money into training the trainer. However, assuming that management does take the appropriate steps to select the right person, it would be remiss of them to ignore the need for adequate training.

Normally more attention is given to the training of those trainers who teach groups of trainees on courses although there are many examples to be found of the 'instant trainer'. This happens when trainers are selected for their technical expertise with little or no regard for the skills they have to use as trainers. This is not to say that technical expertise is not important; the credibility of the trainer hinges on technical expertise. However, that expertise is almost totally wasted if the trainer cannot 'put it over' efficiently. In some cases the trainers are found to be inadequate even after having been trained in instructional techniques and therefore it is worth the investment to give close consideration to the selection of trainers.

In order to decide what criteria should be used for their selection and also what their training needs are, it is important to identify the positive and negative qualities found in trainers.

The characteristics which have been observed in poor trainers include:

- Adopting a highly directive style of teaching which does not allow participation nor confirmation that learning has taken place.
- Making unrealistic assumptions about the trainees' level of knowledge or failing to establish their level of knowledge in the first place.
- Displaying impatience or intolerance when trainees fail to understand or are slow to learn.
- Lacking commitment to the subject being taught or to training as an important function in the organization.
- Lacking in verbal/oral skills.
- Trying to teach too much too quickly.
- Refusing to accept criticism or advice on teaching methods.
- Lacking in sociability and interest in the trainees.
- Having an untidy appearance.

No doubt, readers will be able to think of other poor qualities that they have experienced or observed. Similarly, the list of examples which follows is not intended to be exhaustive but to illustrate the qualities good trainers have. Apart from the opposites to those shown above, one might add:

- Demonstrating technical competence in the area being taught.
- Showing a 'natural' ability to teach and gain satisfaction from it.
- Possessing a high level of interpersonal skills.
- Being good listeners and questioners.
- Having a genuine interest in people.
- Being flexible in the use of training strategies and tactics.
- Valuing the need for thorough planning and preparation.
- Accepting a share of accountability for the trainees' future performance.

Selecting competent trainers

In describing the CTAT course model (Chapter 8), Anderson suggests that each of the stages require the use of a range of training methods and the application of a complex mix of skills that tutors would need to possess and exercise if all four stages of the learning process are to be realized successfully. Figure 11.1 illustrates the breadth of this range of methods and skills.

It might be that sophisticated selection and assessment instruments need to be developed in order to find the best trainers. The training centres of some organizations have potential tutor courses which provide the opportunity for candidates to observe current training in progress, to talk with tutors and to present a period of instruction so that their potential can be judged. When this is not possible or when it is not cost-effective to employ a selection strategy, which might be the case with one-to-one trainers, a simple matching system can be used which compares the qualities of the potential trainer with those of a good trainer.

Areas in which these qualities could be reflected include:

- Outside interests, particularly those which are people-orientated and exercise interpersonal skills or which may involve teaching others.
- Simulated exercises which resemble training situations.
- Informal judgements based on relationships within the work situation.
- Formal judgements based on performance appraisal, group meetings, developmental training.

Above all, the people selected should actually want to be trainers. In the past it has been thought that the subject 'expert' has been the ideal trainer. Undoubtedly, in most circumstances there is a requirement for subject competence. However, it may be more profitable in the long term to improve the technical competence of someone with potentially good trainer qualities rather than try to develop the interpersonal skills, etc of the subject 'expert' who is unsuited or unwilling to be a trainer.

To begin with there is the need to systematize and to organize the training for potential trainers. This can be examined in terms of the knowledge, skills and attitudes required to be an effective trainer.

It is important for trainers to appreciate that people learn in different ways and have preferred learning styles which may be influenced by individual differences of personality, age, experience, etc. Knowledge of some of the interrelated principles of human learning and motivation help the trainer to arrange the appropriate learning conditions for the trainee. In connection with these principles it would be useful to have in mind a profile of the nature of trainees in one-to-one situations.

While it is accepted that on occasions the trainer may have to deal with the over-confident and the unwilling, the majority of students who undertake

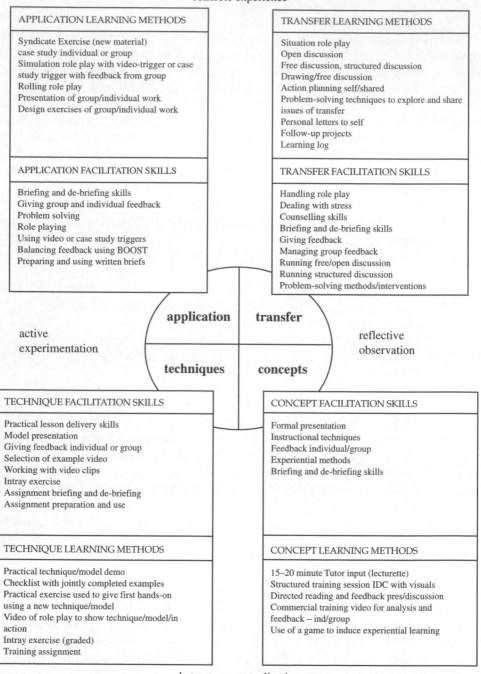

Figure 11.1 The CTAT model and facilitation and learning methods

training programmes are usually well motivated. They may feel apprehension about the experience and about the possible consequences of failing to learn. However, they place trust in their trainer and have a desire to do well. There is often a failure to appreciate this and to take it into consideration in both the preparation for, and the conduct of, training.

In order to structure a training session the trainer needs to have diagnostic skills and a range of technical, interpersonal and judgemental skills. The technical skills would include preparing and planning a period of instruction, deciding the style and methods of presentation, organizing the logistics of syndicate, role-playing and other activities, making visual aids and using them correctly.

There is a need to develop questioning skills, to design tests or test sample pieces. These are closely associated with the judgemental skills required to make an appraisal and gain an impression of the nature of the trainee, to set realistic goals during training and to recognize when the trainee is sufficiently competent to apply what has been learned.

The interpersonal skills which the one-to-one trainer has to exercise are described by Megginson and Boydell (1979) as being similar to those required by the skilful counsellor. This includes attending, observing, remaining silent, drawing out, giving and receiving feedback and suspending judgement. The importance of these skills become clear when it is remembered that coaching is undertaken at all levels in the organization where individuals are being developed to undertake greater responsibilities.

The same, and additional skills, have to be exercised by the trainer who is involved with groups of trainees. Without a thorough appreciation of, and training in, the appropriate skills, then activities such as syndicate exercises, discussions, role plays, etc can deteriorate into time fillers or rest periods for the trainer. These activities or tactics should be used to achieve objectives and demand a range of skills from the trainer which, in addition to those listed above, include listening, analysing, correcting, guiding, prompting, controlling and summarizing. In exercising these skills the trainer acts as a facilitator which is quite different from the role which many trainers usually adopt. One of the reasons that tactics such as role play and discussion may not be effective is because the trainer, or those who have designed the training, do not understand the demands that facilitating makes on the trainer.

In discussing one-to-one and group training, it has been seen that control over the direction and content of the training has been exercised by the trainer. Facilitating places the trainer in a position where he or she becomes an enabler for students to learn by themselves. The trainer and the trainees become interdependent and draw upon one another's knowledge and skills to achieve the learning objective. In effect, control over the learning process passes in varying degrees, depending on the tactic, to the trainee. Figure 11.2 illustrates the difference in tutor roles.

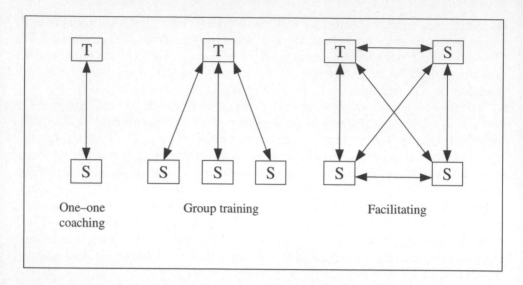

Figure 11.2 Traditional tutor roles compared with facilitating

In the facilitating mode the trainees contribute knowledge, skills and experience which have been acquired over a number of years which they can share with others. Also they are likely to bring with them their own learning style, self-confidence, esteem, motives for learning, prejudices and expectations. Facilitators have to adapt their approach to meet the needs of the trainees and individuals within the group which could involve a change in, or development of, the trainer's attitudes. There must be an acceptance of openness within the group so that it can establish its own ground rules to work together as a cohesive unit and that the facilitator is a resource for the group to draw upon to direct activity and contribute to their learning. In performing this function, the facilitator will need to exercise a variety of skills. There is a need to be aware of, and to monitor, the individual learning and emotional needs of members of the group, to create a secure climate to structure the learning experiences and activities of the group and to control the learning experiences so that they remain relevant and that the objectives are achieved.

The role of facilitator is demanding and not all trainers may be able to adapt to it. Training departments that plan to use their trainers as facilitators could overcome potential problems by being more rigorous in the assessment of attitudes and skills of potential trainers. Rogers (1969) identifies a range of qualities of facilitative trainers which can be used to build a profile for selection:

● Less protective of their own constructs and beliefs than other trainers.
● More able to listen to students, especially to their feelings.
● Able to accept the ideas of students even if they are seen to be troublesome, provoking, etc.

- Able to devote as much time to developing relationships with individuals and the group as to training content.
- Able to accept positive and negative feedback and use it in their own development.

Clarke (1986) describes the tutor's role in open learning programmes as that of a facilitator and lists the following personal qualities which may need to be considered when selecting tutors:

- Patient, tolerant and able to cope with frustration.
- Perceptive (ability to put themselves in student's shoes), understanding, sympathetic.
- Friendly, approachable and trustworthy.
- Prepared to tolerate disruption in private life.
- Able to change quickly from one task or subject to another.
- Prepared to accept interruptions to non-open tutor activity, e.g. lecturing.

It is not likely that all of the qualities presented by Rogers and by Clarke will be required of all facilitators in every learning situation. However, an assessment of the demands of the programme will help to identify which qualities are relevant.

In addition to the selection and development of trainers as facilitators, some consideration must be given to the logistics of a training programme which includes facilitative methods. More time may be required to allow for a number of the tactics, e.g. role-playing and discussions, to be exploited fully and for individual counselling. The size of the group may have to be reduced or more than one tutor may be needed so that syndicates can be formed. Experience has shown that when numbers are larger than eight, smaller syndicate groups are needed. More space is likely to be needed to cater for group and individual activity and possibly a resource bank of information and equipment.

The functions and skills of the trainer or tutor which have been examined so far are those which involve direct contact with trainees. The skills and competencies of those who are involved in the design and presentation of open learning are of equal importance. Bhugra (1986) has identified the value of the use of 'creative teams'.

In the context of computer-based training, the creative team relies upon the trainer to ensure that the analysis of behaviour, the identification of training needs and the writing of terminal objectives, enabling objectives and learning points are carried out properly. Then the creative team of wordsmiths, a graphic artist and a coder can design the training. The role of the wordsmiths is to apply their skills in the use of the English language to ensure that the 'scripted' message is presented economically, accurately and simply. The graphic artist contributes the skills of layout, presentation, colour, illustration and typeface, and the coder programmes the material. The team roles are not seen as discrete:

the wordsmiths edit material and graphic artists code their own graphics. The concept of a creative team is equally applicable to those trainers who are involved in the production of learning packages, training kits and job aids. They are all involved in the process of helping people to learn and must use appropriate skills and techniques which will substitute for those used by the face-to-face trainer.

A considerable emphasis has been placed on the skills needed by trainers operating in different modes; however, theirs is not the only contribution which influences effective learning. Murray (1987) described how 'supporters' helped trainees in the glass industry to overcome problems with study techniques, the feeling of being abandoned and the difficulty of approaching tutors when they had problems. Supporters do not necessarily have to be subject experts; they make their contribution by taking an interest, checking progress, acting as a sounding board and giving encouragement. Murray indicated that those who gained most from open learning were those who received formal and informal follow-up from senior managers in their parent organizations.

The responsibility of line managers must not be neglected when consideration is given to trainer skills. Apart from the fact that they have a managerial responsibility to ensure that their staff are trained and involved in developmental programmes, they may be involved in coaching activities and they should ensure that trainees are properly briefed before embarking on training programmes and that they are debriefed on its conclusion. Trainers who ensure that line managers appreciate the value of thorough briefing and who provide briefing guides for their use are often rewarded with better prepared and better motivated trainees entering the training programme.

CHANGING ROLES OF THE TRAINER

The economic, technological, social and political context within which organizations are now required to operate is in a state of continual flux. It is imperative for them to adapt and adjust to or capitalize on these changes in order to flourish and survive. But to do so they must become, in Garrett's (1987) phrase, 'The Learning Organization'. If trainers are going to make a significant contribution to bringing this about and to effecting what, for many organizations, will be a major cultural shift in this respect, then they will have to adopt a different attitude to the nature and level of their own involvement in their organizations. Many of them will have to change:

- from being passive to being more active in communicating the benefits of training
- from merely adopting a reactive response to taking on a more proactive stance in dealing with performance problems

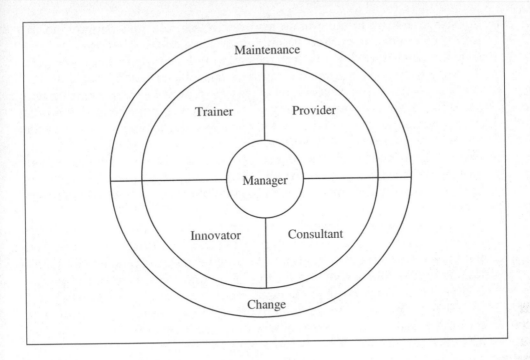

Figure 11.3   General trainer roles (Bennett, 1988)

- from seeing themselves as peripheral, to perceiving themselves and the training function as central to and a key influence on the organization reaching its objectives
- from simply being technologists, to developing a more strategic role; giving direction to the learning function and formulating training policy.

In other words the roles trainers perform will have to expand to enable them to take their rightful place in human resource development. Bennett (1988) maintains that five key roles emerge from the various classifications he surveyed. Figure 11.3 shows the links and interrelationships between these classifications.

- *Trainer* is mainly concerned with actually carrying out training, i.e. directly assisting the trainee to learn, supplying feedback, etc. This role may involve a variety of different training methods ranging from one-to-one instruction to project work.
- *Provider* – designing, up-dating, maintaining and delivering training programmes are the key functions of this role. More specifically the trainer would be involved in undertaking training needs analysis(es), establishing training objectives and possibly training or coaching trainers to deliver training.

- *Consultant* – there are two main features to this role, analysing organizational problems and then recommending solutions, that may require training. The more detailed activities include liaison with line managers, advising training managers on training aims, objectives and policies, etc.
- *Innovator* – the primary concerns in this training role are supporting and assisting organizations to bring about effective change and to solve performance problems. These would involve the trainer in some of the following: working closely with middle and senior managers on change issues, identifying where learning and educational events, such as seminars and workshops, can help managers to understand and facilitate change, advising the training function as to its possible contribution to the change process.
- *Manager* – in this role there is concern fundamentally with planning, organizing, controlling and developing the training function. In particular the manager sets training goals and formulates training policies and plans, liaises with other departments to show them the ways training can contribute to improving their employees' performance, ensuring and overseeing the development, delivery and evaluation of appropriate training activities, recruiting and developing training personnel, controlling activities against an overall training plan and budget.

In reality, the actual job of any trainer is probably going to contain elements from more than one of the above and, by virtue of its make-up, the manager's role is likely to be the common denominator. However, in the past and in a large number of organizations in the present, the emphasis has been or is on the trainer and provider roles. To be more influential, to command a higher profile in organizations and realize their full potential, trainers must move into the innovator and consultant modes.

MANAGING THE TRANSFER OF TRAINING

Vast sums of money are invested annually, directly and indirectly, in training and other developmental activities. Of critical concern to organizations and to the training profession is the wastage of a large part of this investment. In a survey of over 2,500 end users, Rogers and Woodford (1999) found that only a third of respondents claimed that training had made any significant difference to their performance in the workplace and a quarter felt that the training they had received was not sufficiently tailored to meet their needs. Perhaps more significantly, less than half thought that their line manager had given them any guidance on how they should apply in the workplace what they had learned during training.

This finding supports the view of Broad and Newstrom (1992) who, if anything, strike an even more pessimistic note. They suggest that, according to some estimates, 80 per cent of the investment in training is wasted, and that this can be mainly attributed to the fact that knowledge and skills acquired through a training event are not fully applied when trainees return to their place of work. They see the lack of involvement on the behalf of line managers and the lack of reinforcement on the job as major barriers to the transfer of training.

All of this suggests that it is imperative that the training transfer process is managed effectively before, during and after the training has taken place. To this end, line managers and trainees would certainly need to take a more active role in all three phases than they seem to have done to date. The trainer's role would also have to expand to encompass the management of the transfer of training.

Broad and Newstrom emphasize that decisions about performance improvement through training should be the result of consultation involving the line manager, the trainee and the trainer rather than being solely the prerogative or responsibility of one of the parties. Furthermore, they recommend that a transfer partnership should be established between the line manager, the trainee and the trainer prior to the implementation of the training programme. A compilation of transfer strategies that might potentially be employed by the three parties involved in the transfer process is set out below.

Manager

Pre-training	Incorporate into management and supervisory performance standards and responsibility for staff development and training transfer
	Send two or more fellow workers to attend the same course to create a 'critical mass' on their return to work
During training	Ensure the trainee is not interrupted during the course of the training
	Allocate the trainee's workload to other employees for the duration of the programme so that he or she does not return to face a large amount of work that is outstanding. Anticipating such a prospect could be extremely depressing
Post-training	Provide the trainee with an early opportunity to put into practice the skills and knowledge learnt on the training programme
	Allow the trainee to brief others about the training programme; moving from trainee to trainer can often deepen an individual's understanding of what has been learnt

Trainee

Pre-training	Have an input into the planning processes, e.g. training needs analysis, event design, which will help to ensure that training is relevant
	Review any pre-course material and raise questions with the manager and the trainer
During training	Keep an ideas and applications logbook for the duration of the training programme
	Draw up an action plan consisting of specific and assessable objectives to be worked towards after the completion of the programme
Post-training	Develop a 'buddy' or mentoring relationship to help to critically evaluate the application of knowledge and skills acquired during training
	Undertake an early post-course review of the training material to aid retention

Trainer

Pre-training	Design the programme by following a systematic approach
	Develop a peer-coaching component for post-course application of knowledge and skills
During training	Encourage trainees to visualize how they would look and feel if they carried out their job or tasks employing the knowledge and skills learnt during training
	Provide trainees with job aids, e.g. algorithms, checklists etc, during the instructional phases of the training which can then act as memory joggers or reminders in the workplace
Post-training	Visit former trainees and act as facilitators in their efforts to apply their new knowledge and skills
	Set up and run group-refresher or problem-solving sessions to reinforce learning

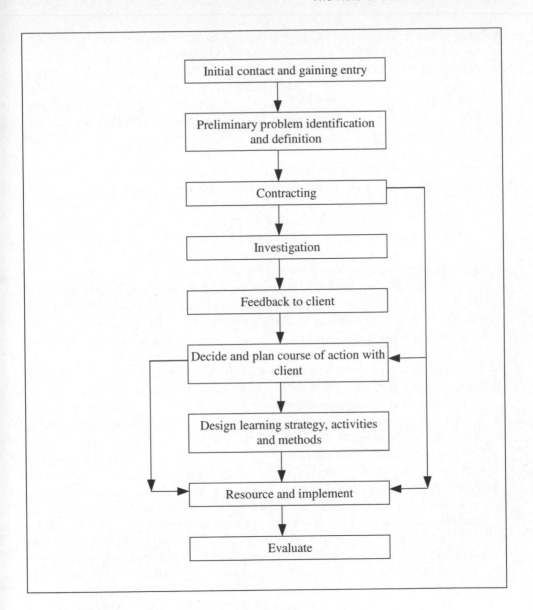

Figure 11.4   A model of training consultancy

THE CONSULTANCY ROLE OF THE TRAINER

The transition into the consultancy mode is of particular interest when considering the development of trainers. To be effective as a consultant the trainer must understand the main phases of the consulting model and acquire the appropriate knowledge, skills, attitudes and perspectives associated with each phase. Figure 11.4 is a model of training consultancy. It has nine main stages:

- *Initial contact and gaining entry* – in organizations where training consultants or training consultancy services are well established, potential clients will often make the first contact. However, where trainers are developing their consultancy role they may want to take the initiative. There are a number of ways in which they may be able to gain access to managers including training course follow-up visits, mounting special marketing events, etc. Establishing rapport and credibility will be a major requirement of the consultant at this stage.

- *Preliminary problem identification and definition* – the training consultant should assist the client to articulate clearly his or her version of the nature of the problem or how the problem is perceived. In addition, the client should be helped to separate out symptoms from possible causes. The training consultant may need to persuade the client to allow him or her to undertake some preliminary enquiry in order to obtain a more secure database on which to take forward the discussion.

- *Contracting* – this involves the training consultant and client agreeing upon the terms of reference for the project or assignment that they feel is necessary bearing in mind what emerged at the previous stage. Constraints, resources, time scales, expectations and client involvement are issues to be considered and, if necessary, negotiated when drawing up a contract.

- *Investigation* – this entails designing and implementing the methodology for gathering further information about the problem. An attempt is made to pin down the cause or causes of the problem. In addition, possible solutions are generated and evaluated, ideally by both consultant and client.

- *Feedback to client* – findings, conclusions, interpretations and recommendations are presented to the client orally or in writing. Although the consultant should be persuasive, overselling must be avoided. The consultant must maintain the involvement of the client, which should have been nurtured from the outset. If it has not been then there is a danger that the client will not feel a sense of ownership or commitment to proposals for future action.

- *Decide and plan course of action with client* – the consultant will need to analyse what contribution of training or learning initiative will be needed to resolve the problem. This may involve him or her in undertaking a new project or assignment for which a fresh contract will need to be agreed with the client. Agreement will also have to be reached at this stage about the criteria against which to evaluate the learning strategy that may be developed and implemented.

- *Design learning strategy activities and methods* – the trainer consultant should consider learning strategies that go beyond, or even exclude, traditional training activities. Such strategies might include projects, self-directed workshops, team development and self-development groups.

- *Resource and implement* – with the client the consultant considers the resourcing implications of the agreed learning strategy. This may result in the training consultant helping the user organization, department or section to develop its own training resources. To cover this possibility further contracting may need to be undertaken at this point. In particular, if the learning activities are work-based the trainer consultant will have to be more flexible in the implementation of the learning strategy.

- *Evaluate* – this should be both in terms of learning and in organizational terms. The client and the 'trainees' must be intimately involved in this process. In addition the trainer consultant may also want to evaluate his or her own performance as a consultant, so that lessons can be carried forward to the next project (although feedback from the client should be sought throughout the consultancy process).

Adopting this model means that the trainer, as Holdaway and Saunders (1992) suggest, becomes less of a course provider and more of a diagnostician and problem resolver. As a training consultant, the trainer is likely to have to:

- work with the client manager, as an equal partner, in a collaborative way
- provide training that is more tailored to the client's specific needs rather than simply presenting a set menu of courses or programmes
- help trainees to acquire the skills of learning so that they become more responsible for, and more in control of, their own learning and development
- operate, in many instances, at the workplace or 'in' the organization
- train and develop line managers to become trainers and developers of others.

All of these features indicate that the trainer could potentially develop beyond the pure training consultancy role, which tends to emphasize training as the main learning medium, towards becoming, as Phillips and Shaw (1989) suggest, a learning consultant. Training consultants must not become rigidly wedded to nor too firmly locked into traditional training technology, as otherwise they may not be able to understand and translate an organization's needs into relevant learning objectives for individuals. Furthermore, they must appreciate their contribution in terms of helping people to learn rather than simply in terms of training. This will require them to recognize that a formal training context is just one of the appropriate learning environments for the development of knowledge, skills and attitudes.

There has been a rise in the use of self-directed and self-managed learning, as opposed to trainer-controlled learning, and on people learning from 'out there' activities and from the jobs they do. Bearing all this in mind the training consultant must show flexibility and experiment with methods and activities which they build into their learning/training strategy and design. Examples of less traditional, 'on-the-job' learning strategies, methods and activities, that could be part of the training consultant's brief, include:

- *Action planning and implementing* – back-at-work action follow-up tutorials and clinics planned with training course delegates, which might also involve 'bosses'
- *Action learning groups or sets* – groups of managers getting together with the training consultant to work on problems facing each member
- *Self-development groups* – these are less task-oriented than action learning groups, where group members consider their own development needs
- *Coaching, counselling or mentoring* – the training consultant carries out these activities at the workplace or trains managers in the requisite skills, possibly combining on-course and on-the-job settings
- *Project work* – identifying, designing, supervising and evaluating projects is a strategy that will supplement formal training and help to ensure current and future transfer of training
- *Family groups* – working with intact work groups to encourage more effective team work and team development is another activity that is within the scope of some training consultants
- *Role clarification* – as the role an individual performs is a major determinant of his or her knowledge and skills acquisition it is legitimate for the training consultant to be involved in assisting managers and their subordinates in role clarification, maybe as part of some 'follow-up' activities
- *Secondments* – advising on these kinds of activity could be part of a training consultant's role

In considering the above tactics, as part of a learning strategy, the training consultant should ensure the involvement of the clients and recipients in the development of objectives and the managers, in particular, in the on-going activities, evaluation and review. This involvement is very necessary if the strategy and tactics used are going to be 'owned' by the participants and their managers.

It is not always possible for trainers to undertake the consultancy role in full. There can be a number of reasons for this. Some consultancy projects could be time-consuming, trainers may have an existing heavy workload, the work may be of a sensitive nature or involve internal politics, or the subject matter could require specialist knowledge or techniques that the trainer does not have. Another reason which cannot always be justified is that the organization feels work undertaken by outside consultants has more credibility than that of an internal consultant. Sometimes this belief has proved to be costly.

There is no doubt that using outside consultants has many advantages, but before such decisions are made it is worth considering the relative advantages and disadvantages of using internal and external consultancy.

Advantages of internal consultants
- The organizational structure and personalities are known.
- The culture, language and politics of the organization are familiar.

- Gaining entry may be easier because of existing work relationships.
- There may be an existing network of contacts from which information and support can be sought.
- An amount of information about the problem may be held already.
- They can work unobtrusively and take opportunities to observe by being in situ.
- They can monitor progress closely.
- They are well placed to support implementation of outcomes.
- They are in a position to implement strategies to evaluate the project.
- They may be more cost-effective.
- They can identify appropriate and inappropriate reasons for bringing in external consultants.

Disadvantages of internal consultants
- They may be regarded as too much a part of the organization.
- They could face difficulties establishing credibility with senior management.
- There is a danger of making assumptions or being biased by being too close to the problem or the organization.
- Could they possibly be part of the problem?
- Their status could make it difficult to challenge people, policies and practices.
- It could be difficult to gain access to some key players, especially those in senior positions.
- They could have political or hierarchical pressures applied to favour specific outcomes.
- The project could be treated superficially through lack of time or specialist knowledge.

Advantages of external consultants
- They are seen as impartial and independent of influences of the organization.
- They are regarded as having credibility through being independent.
- Their involvement may highlight the problem and promote greater involvement of key players.
- They can have wide access within the organization.
- They can be more challenging and direct and cut through entrenched views and practices
- People are more likely to be open in their contributions and trust that they are given in confidence.
- They can open communication channels across the organization.
- They can introduce new ideas and draw upon a wide experience of different organizations.
- They can provide networking and benchmarking with other organizations.
- There is often a greater acceptance of recommendations from outside.

Disadvantages of external consultants
- They may need more time than can be afforded to learn about the organization.
- They may have only sufficient time to identify and explore part of the problem.
- Recommendations may be accepted too readily.
- Recommendations may be rejected if they are considered to be too radical for the organization.
- Contracted time may expire before the recommendations are implemented fully.
- They may encourage the client to become dependent on outside consultancy services.
- The costs of external consultancy are high and visible.

The roles of internal and external consultants should not be seen as mutually exclusive, although it is accepted that they may see one another as competitors. Very often they can work closely together with benefits all round. Key factors in achieving successful outcomes with external consultants are careful selection and clear contracting.

When selecting an external consultant there are a number of checks that can be made. The organization may have an approved list of consultants who have been used before, some of whom may be appropriate to use again. Otherwise a little probing is a valuable use of time. A starting point is to look at their experience in the field and the occupational sector of the study, their track record with other organizations and their experience and qualifications. Most consultants will be pleased to give the names of other organizations for whom they have worked and who can be approached for a reference. Many will list current or previous clients in their publicity material. Taking such a list at face value could prove to be a mistake. The authors approached one such listed organization only to receive a damning report on the consultants concerned. Thankfully, such situations are rare but it illustrates the importance of a thorough check. When these factors have been considered, more practical issues can be addressed such as their costs.

The next stage is to agree a contract for the work. There are likely to be a number of clauses that are specific to the project in mind, but one would expect the following to be included as standard: the general terms of the agreement; a consultancy proposal or plan which includes objectives, time scales, reporting process and documentation; fees, warranties and penalty clauses; indemnity details; a statement of confidentiality, and details of contacts and roles.

MARKETING THE TRAINING FUNCTION

It cannot be ignored that, in some organizations, training does not appear to be held in such high esteem as other functions. There are historical precedents which have made this understandable up to a point. However, as the role of the trainer has changed and trainers have developed their skills and expertise to meet these changes, the training department has become a more potent resource, and one which has the potential to make significant contributions to the success of an organization.

Although this has been recognized in most organizations, there remains a need for trainers to maintain a high profile, highlight their successes and encourage those who ignore or merely pay lip service to the training function to make better use of what is on offer. There have been many instances of the expertise of the training department being overlooked as a result of initiatives such as empowerment, which has given line managers the opportunity to make their own decisions about training needs and how they can be met. However, not all line managers have the necessary skills or experience to identify needs accurately, nor the necessary knowledge to be able to select the most appropriate form of training or the most appropriate provider.

It is against this kind of background that trainers have to market their expertise and the services they have to offer. Very often it is the reactions of former trainees that influence line managers' decisions about the value and effectiveness of training, and their perception of the training function. Image is the key factor in marketing, and the training function needs to be proactive in promoting that image and not leave it to chance.

This proactivity includes being involved whenever there is a change to the organizational structure, when business plans are written or reviewed, and when there are changes to the staff and the skills and knowledge that they require. In order to achieve this it is important to identify the key players, the decision makers and those who hold the 'purse strings' within the organization, and to become their advisor on all matters relating to training and development. In developing this relationship manager role, a large proportion of time needs to be given to listening. That involves listening not only to those in the power positions but to line managers and to staff, and showing them that the training function is able to meet the need, and that the training can be structured and delivered in a way that suits them. In some cases the training function may not be able to meet the need from its own resources but it should be able to offer outside providers or recommend alternative forms of learning. By offering such a service, it helps to develop a system by which all training and development issues are channelled through the training function.

However, this only works if the training function and those in it have the respect and confidence of line managers. This is down to image. First impressions really do count, and trainers need to give careful and deliberate consideration to how they want to be seen by all of those who become involved with them. One might expect such words as 'professional', 'well organized' and 'responsive' to be included. It is easy to make a list but it is more demanding to limit that list to four or five key descriptors, and then to develop and implement strategies and guidelines to ensure that the desired image is created and maintained.

The majority of effective trainers apply such image-creating practices as a matter of course. The pride that they have in their professionalism makes it common sense to them, but it is worth giving some consideration to these practices from the marketing perspective. They include:

- *Appearance.* All members of the team should look smart and be alert. They should be responsive, welcoming and supportive. The manner in which telephone calls are dealt with, the way in which visitors are treated, the way in which training is delivered and the way in which participation in meetings is exercised have a great impact on image.
- *Punctuality.* Training sessions should begin on time and as far as is practical the timings for sessions should be adhered to. Even though some trainees may be late, the trainer should always be in attendance. Being on time for meetings and appointments is equally important, and a prompt follow-up letter or memorandum to summarize what has been discussed or decided underlines the efficiency of the trainer.
- *Administrative procedures.* Standard administrative procedures should be drawn up in such a way that all of the training team are familiar with them and are in a position to advise or initiate them when needed. These include receipt and confirmation of nominations for courses, booking rooms and catering.
- *Correspondence.* A standard format for letters, memoranda, e-mail, joining instructions etc should be used by the whole team.
- *Training facilities.* The appearance of the training facilities is as important as personal appearance. It is accepted that in many cases the training function is not allocated the best of accommodation. However, a clean environment which is free of broken and unwanted furniture, together with appropriate seating arrangements and an uncluttered well laid-out training room, goes a long way to compensate.
- *Training materials.* As with correspondence, items such as handouts, exercises, pre-course material, OHP/PowerPoint slides, and questionnaires should conform to a house style which identifies the material with the training function. They should be neat, well designed and up-to-date.
- *Packaging.* Ring binders or files for course material should be of an appropriate size for what they have to contain. An attractive and well-designed cover or front sheet, particularly one that indicates the material has been designed to meet the needs of a specific group, shows that special attention has been given to them.

- *Learning strategies.* Activities such as role play, discussion, case study and syndicate work need to be supported with clear and specific guidelines. The management of these activities demands close monitoring, intervention when direction is lost, and realistic allocation of time so that the exercises are actually completed and debriefed.
- *Language level.* In addition to an appropriate level of language being used in written materials and in the delivery of training, it is important to ensure that in meetings everyone understands what the trainer is talking about. Senior managers are not impressed by the use of technical terms they do not understand.
- *Advertising.* Keeping training 'in the public eye' should be an on-going activity. It has been suggested already that trainers should become involved in meetings and events at organizational level. In addition, trainers can make use of house journals to promote training by submitting articles, success stories and course reviews by former students, photographs, details of forthcoming training events etc. The training function may be able to produce its own newsletter or make use of an intranet to promote its role. Offering to speak at meetings to update senior staff on trends, achievements and the results of evaluation exercises may also be of value.
- *Staffing.* In order to maintain the image the training function wants, staff should be selected who will help to uphold that image. It is to be expected that they are sufficiently qualified for the role to have credibility, and that provision is made for them to receive further training and to develop their skills and knowledge.

This list is not intended to be exhaustive, and experienced trainers will be able to add to it. Its intention is to focus on a few critical areas so that those damaging nightmare scenarios do not occur.

It is a reasonable guess that most trainers have themselves experienced some if not all of the following.

> The trainees arrive at different times clutching badly duplicated maps and joining instructions which show different times for the start of the course. They are set to work by the trainer to arrange the seating and stack unwanted furniture at the back of the room. The trainer leaves to find out what has happened to the coffee and to collect his notes and the handouts which hadn't come back from photocopying when he arrived. The course eventually gets under way. The trainer writes the objectives on a flip chart using different coloured pens because some of them had dried up. The coffee arrives. . . There is no need to continue. The implications of the image that has been created are clear.

However more needs to be done than creating the desired image. Stuart and Long (1985) suggest that trainers look at their activities from a *marketing* perspective. Marketing may be defined here as 'promoting the right product at the right price in the right place at the right time'.

From this viewpoint the activities of the trainer should focus clearly on the real needs of its internal clients. The trainer's marketing efforts should be attempting to provide a match between the resources of the training function and their needs. In order to fulfil this requirement the trainer must be quite definitely customer/client orientated. This might involve the training function in:

- initiating reactive investigations
- persuading other functions to look at the manpower implications of their future plans and initiatives
- helping other functions to anticipate their training and development needs by the training function itself carrying out forms of market research into the training requirements of new technology, systems, etc
- working within the 'art of the possible' – attempting to match its abilities and resources with the needs of its clients and if there is any shortfall advising how this may be satisfied by internal or external means
- being prepared to implement the 'quick and clean' approach while still having an overriding concern with the quality of the product
- carrying out pre-delivery and after-sales services including pre-course questionnaires, briefing and debriefing sessions
- presenting training through various strategies and tactics, as an opportunity for clients and not as a threat or as a bureaucratically and centrally organized hindrance.

Stuart and Long believe that this marketing orientation is, in some areas of training, preferable to the production, sales, finance and people orientations which they describe in fairly critical terms. A summary of what these orientations involve is set out below:

- *Production orientation* There is in this orientation an over-emphasis on the absolute quality of the service being offered. Obsessive concerns with detail, high development and design costs, inflexibility of programmes, and trainer rather than learner centredness characterize this approach.
- *Sales orientation* Not surprisingly selling the product, without necessarily emphasizing the quality, is at the root of this approach. 'Bottoms on seats' is the overriding consideration with learning outcomes and appropriateness taking very much a 'back seat'.
- *Finance orientation* Cost is the major factor influencing the training decision in this approach and not effectiveness of learning. Although cutting back on costs is often the main concern of a trainer working within this orientation, ironically on some occasions the converse may be true. There are trainers who think good training must be expensive or seen to be expensive. 'Never mind the quality look at the width' or 'An ounce of image is worth a pound of performance' are sentiments which often motivate both the finance and sales-orientated training function.

- *People orientation* This orientation might be retitled self-orientation. The trainers produce programmes more in line with their own interests than those of their potential clients. Such interests may be rather esoteric and 'progressive' and consequently divorced from matters of particular everyday relevance.

It requires little imagination to predict what can happen eventually to the image of the training function if one of the above orientations comes to dominate the thinking and attitudes of training personnel.

A FINAL WORD

From reading this book the impression may be gained that training is a complex business which is beset by constraints and frustrations. There are many trainers who would agree with this viewpoint. However, in those organizations which understand training and have used it as a principal instrument in the pursuit of their corporate objectives, the trainers have gained considerable job satisfaction and the organization has seen a valuable return on its investment in the training function.

Appendix 1

Methods for Obtaining Information about Performance Problems and Job/Task Content

STRUCTURED INTERVIEW

Description

A face-to-face conversation structured around a checklist of prepared questions (usually a mixture of open-ended, problem-solving and closed questions, i.e. Yes/No or rated answer questions) that can take place in or away from the workplace. The interview can be conducted with any individual or a small group who may have relevant information. These might include job holders, supervisors, higher management or, in some cases, the customer.

Purpose

To investigate reasons why certain units or individuals in the organization are not performing satisfactorily or to gather information about jobs and tasks. The views, opinions, attitudes, perceptions and observations are obtained from key personnel connected with the job or task under review. More senior personnel may need to be included when behavioural problems are being investigated to see how they perceive the nature of the problem and why it is believed to be important.

Recording information

The information can be recorded on prepared interview schedules (these may include pre-coded answers) while the interview is taking place or written up later from notes taken at the time. Sometimes it may be possible to tape-record the interview and then categorize and analyse the content later.

Level – time/response

Normally, the interview is an appropriate instrument to use at the occupational and individual levels of investigating training needs for both present/reactive and future/proactive studies. It may be employed also in a supplementary or back-up role in organizational studies.

Advantages

- Permits responses to be probed in detail to reveal facts, fictions and feelings.
- Useful for long- and short-cycle jobs.
- Flexible in terms of time allowed for each interviewee.
- Useful for jobs with high psychological content.
- Has face validity.

Disadvantages

- Expensive in use of time. Some interviews could take up to two or three hours.
- Could be the slowest way to obtain information. Setting up and arranging the interview can be a protracted process in itself.
- The interviewee can distort the facts, not answer candidly or may have difficulty in verbalizing what he or she does or feels.
- The interviewer needs to be skilful and therefore thorough and possibly expensive training has to be undertaken.
- In group interviews, some individuals may feel inhibited by more senior or dominant personalities and may not contribute reliable information.

OBSERVATION

Description

A period of time dedicated to watching a job holder performing the various tasks which make up the job. The observer can watch an individual or a number of people doing the same job or task. It can be used in conjunction with the interview in the workplace.

Purpose

To gain a clear picture and an understanding of a job or a task within its environmental, social and psychological context. The observer can compare and contrast the styles and skills of an individual with others doing the same work and with existing job descriptions, standard operating procedures, etc. When used with the interview in the workplace it provides cues and prompts for the interviewer to probe.

Recording information

Information can be recorded at the time on prepared grids or checklists or noted on a prepared grid after the event to match the observations that have been made.

Level – time/response

Observation is best used at the individual and occupational levels of investigating training needs for present/reactive and future/proactive studies.

Advantages

- Clear picture gained of total job conditions.
- When observation is used by itself, it does not interrupt work process.
- Flexible in use of time.
- Useful for short-cycle jobs.
- When used with the interview it enhances the quality of information gathered.
- Has credibility.

Disadvantages

- Can be time-consuming for long-cycle jobs.
- Not all of the job may be observed depending on frequency of tasks.
- Job holder may feel inhibited, may resent close scrutiny or may behave in an uncharacteristic way.
- Difficulty in recording observations in a usable format.
- May require skilled observer with some knowledge of the job or task in order to 'make sense' of the observations.

QUESTIONNAIRE

Description

A document which contains questions that may be set down in a variety of formats: closed, open-ended, forced choice, priority listing.

Purpose

To gather data about jobs and tasks and the job holders' attitudes towards various aspects of work. Job holders may be asked to indicate how they view the levels of difficulty and importance of the tasks they carry out and how frequently they perform them. Questions could focus on areas of distaste or dislike and seek information relating to experience, training and motivation of job holders.

Recording information

The questionnaire format itself provides the outline format for recording information. However, provision may need to be made to record answers to questions from which comparisons can be made (e.g. different categories/grades of staff and how they respond). Answers to open questions need to be scanned for common themes and then recorded in the same ways as other items.

Level – time/response

An appropriate instrument to use at the organizational and occupational level of investigating training needs for both present/reactive and future/proactive studies.

Advantages

- Comparatively inexpensive to produce and administer.
- Can be used with large numbers if adequate facility for collating data is available.
- Can be used with job holders over widely dispersed geographical area.
- Design should enable job holder to respond easily and quickly.
- Can provide basis for an interview or series of interviews.
- Easy to distribute.
- Data is collected in standardized format.

Disadvantages

- Generally, response rate to questionnaires is not high.
- Assumes that the questions cover all aspects of the job being investigated.
- Questions may be ambiguous or misunderstood by respondent.
- Inflexible as an instrument.
- Answers to open questions are difficult to standardize and to quantify.
- Analysing information can be time-consuming.
- Design skills are needed to produce a questionnaire which will give reliable data.
- Response rates for questionnaires may be low which in time may bias the database and conclusions.

PARTICIPATION

Description

A period of time during which the investigator undertakes the tasks and responsibilities of the job holder.

Purpose

To gain a closer understanding of the work involved particularly in respect of those tasks which the job holder finds it difficult to explain and when new procedures, new equipment, etc are being introduced and there is no one who has any expertise or experience in the job to whom the investigator can refer.

Recording information

The circumstances of using participation as a technique often make it difficult to prepare any specific method for recording information in advance. However, some form of checklist could be produced when it is a job that exists already. For new tasks and procedures, etc, the analysis and recording may have to be developed concurrently or post hoc.

Level – time/response

Participation is used mainly at individual and occupational levels of investigating needs and both in present/reactive and future/proactive studies.

Advantages

- Gives a feeling for the physical, social and psychological working conditions.
- Gives an experience of the difficulties and distasteful aspects of the job.
- Enables the investigator to work at own speed to help understanding.
- Useful for short-cycle jobs which are easy to pick up.
- Can be used to sample tasks within the job.

Disadvantages

- Experiences and feelings of job holder not necessarily the same as those experienced by investigator.
- Information collected could be incorrect.
- With long-cycle jobs investigator cannot do everything.
- With complex tasks and those which require lengthy training often involving development of a 'knack', the investigator cannot get involved.
- May have an effect on job holders which makes them behave in an uncharacteristic way.

SELF-WRITTEN JOB DESCRIPTION

Description

A job description which is the product of analysis carried out and written up by the job holder.

Purpose

To produce a comprehensive description of a job which draws upon the perspective and experience of the job holder to distinguish between the levels of importance and difficulty of the main tasks and duties which make up the job.

Recording information

The job holders can record all relevant information on a pre-formatted job description form which can be collated by the investigator.

Level – time/response

The self-written job description best lends itself to use at the individual and occupational levels. Its main use is for the reactive approach and in particular for those jobs that have been in existence for a long time and for which no formal training exists.

Advantages

- Presents the job from the job holder's perspective.
- Can be quick and inexpensive.
- Information provided in job description format.
- Different viewpoints reflected if more than one job holder used.

Disadvantages

- Job holders may find it difficult to analyse their duties and tasks.
- Job holders may find it difficult to write the job description.
- The information may be incomplete and would need to be checked.
- Difficult to standardize – investigator would need to design format and give detailed instructions on how to draw up the description.
- Job holders could overestimate or underestimate the importance and difficulty of their jobs and the tasks within it.

WORK DIARY

Description

A structured log which is filled in by the job holder on a continuous or a periodic basis to record the activities which make up a job.

Purpose

To record information about jobs which can indicate the tasks undertaken by the job holder, the frequency with which they are performed and the length of time spent on each task, or to sample activities performed by the job holder.

Recording information

Job holders record details of their activities on pre-formatted log sheets which can be collated by the investigator.

Level – time/response

The diary or log best lends itself to use at the individual and occupational levels.

Advantages

- Useful for long-cycle jobs.
- Comparatively inexpensive.
- Can be used with job holders over widely dispersed geographical area.

Disadvantages

- May take a long time to collect data.
- Job holders need instructions on how to complete the diary.
- Can be time-consuming.
- Can be a nuisance for job holder to carry around.
- Could be an interruption to the working activities of the job holder.

FILM-VIDEO-PHOTOGRAPHY

Description

A pictorial record of the activities and skills of a particular job or task.

Purpose

To investigate those activities and skills which are complex, speedily performed or which contain a high level of interpersonal skill. Using the media of film and video, the investigator is able to view repeatedly the information which has been recorded to ensure accurate analysis.

Recording information

The film or video is in itself a record but is not in a usable form for analysis. The investigator would record the information in the same way as for observation using prepared grids and checklists.

Level – time/response

This technique is best used at the individual level and on occasions at occupational levels when investigating present/reactive studies.

Advantages

- Provides permanent record of the job as it exists at the time of recording.
- It can be viewed many times over without further interruption to the job holder.
- A team of investigators can analyse and discuss the performance without interruption to the job holder.
- Fine detail and precise movements can be examined using slow motion and freeze-frame facilities.
- The camera can be less obtrusive than an observer.

Disadvantages

- Can be time-consuming and expensive to set up equipment.
- Time has to be given to analysis.
- Not practicable for long-cycle jobs.
- May affect behaviour of job holder.
- Ethical considerations may make it limited for use in application of interpersonal skills.

STUDY OF EXISTING PERSONNEL RECORDS

Description

A detailed analysis or an outline review of personnel documents such as job descriptions, appraisal forms, training records, memoranda of interviews, job evaluation documents, employee records concerned with grievances, turnover, accidents, etc, which relate to the job/task being studied.

Purpose

To gain an insight into a particular job before a detailed study begins, to assist in providing a framework for asking questions and recording data and to confirm or otherwise data collected already.

Recording information

Documents such as job descriptions may already have information recorded in a set format in which the investigator has an interest.

Level – time/response

A study of documents is appropriate at the occupational and individual levels of needs and applies to the reactive approach when job changes are envisaged.

Advantages

- Provides investigator with an overview before the study begins.
- Could provide useful framework for the study.

- Can provide attitudinal information such as reasons for leaving, difficulty and failure.
- Doesn't interrupt work of job holder.
- Provides clues and hints to areas of difficulty.

Disadvantages

- Personnel records may not be accessible or cannot be released for reasons of confidentiality.
- The information may be out-of-date.
- It could take a long time to collate the information.

TECHNICAL CONFERENCE/GROUP DISCUSSION

Description

A discussion centred around a job to which a number of people who are connected with that job contribute to the study. Those present could include the job holder(s), supervisors, managers, technical experts, etc.

Purpose

To gather relevant information about every aspect or specific aspects of a job when direct access to the job is difficult, when there are differing views on how the job should be carried out and when jobs are likely to change significantly in the content or operating methods.

Recording information

It is difficult to record information during the discussion because in many cases information available in advance is limited and not always sufficient to prepare grids and checklists. A tape recorder is useful in these circumstances.

Level – time/response

The technical conference can be used best for investigating training needs at the occupational and organizational level and has a particular value in the proactive approach when perhaps a new job is being introduced.

Advantages

- Provides opportunities for different perspectives on the same job.
- Group contribution can see problem areas and aspects of the job that the job holder might miss.
- Potential for all aspects of the job to be covered.

Disadvantages

- Could be expensive and time-consuming.
- May not produce the kind of information the investigator wants.
- Needs skilful control of the group.
- Participants of junior status could be inhibited by senior-status staff or influenced by peers of strong personality.
- Analysis could be time-consuming and difficult to structure.
- In proactive situations there could be a battle of wills.

Appendix 2

Sampling

In the context of investigating the performance of job holders, sampling is a technique which enables the investigator to draw conclusions about all holders of a particular job by studying the performance of a selected group or sample. The technique can be used in many other contexts where large numbers are involved and is accepted as a reliable instrument when applied properly.

Advantages of sampling

- Cost-effective in terms of fewer interviews or questionnaires, fewer staff needed and less time required to collect and analyse data.
- Fewer subjects in the investigation mean that more time can be dedicated to in-depth study and to analysis of data.

Disadvantages of sampling

- If the sample isn't chosen carefully the findings could be inaccurate or misleading.
- Jobs which sub-divide into a variety of activities may not be represented fully if the sample is not large enough.
- There is always the chance that some information will be missed especially tasks which are either performed infrequently or by only a few of the job holders.

METHODS OF SAMPLING

There are two main methods of sampling:

- Random sampling
- Stratified sampling (proportional and disproportional)

Random sampling

This form of sampling assumes that each individual has an equal chance of being selected as a member of the sample. This means that they would be selected by such random methods as drawing names out of a hat, selecting names at regular intervals from a list, using a table of random numbers, etc.

It is best used in investigating job performance when little or nothing is known about the job or those who do it. The randomness of the selection of the sample should reveal a clear picture of the variability of the group as a whole (i.e. the total population). However, many trainers would not be in the position of knowing so little about the job and would be unlikely to rely upon the chance of the method of selection to provide a reliable sample.

Stratified sampling

This method of sampling is usually regarded as the most proficient method for obtaining a sample which is representative of the population.

Proportional stratified sampling

This is the description given to a sample which is taken from each sub-group or part of the organization (e.g. job holders, supervisors, trainers, etc). The proportion or percentage taken depends on the size of the total population but is the same for each sub-group.

The main advantage of proportional stratified sampling is that it ensures that there is a balanced representation within the sample of the features of the group as a whole.

Disproportional stratified sampling

This is the description given to a sample which is made up of an equal number of individuals from each sub-group irrespective of the numbers in each sub-group. It is a useful method when sub-groups are being compared but the results must be weighted according to the numbers in the sub-groups. For example when ten members of each sub-group are selected to make up the sample, this figure should represent all members of one group but perhaps only a small proportion of another.

Main advantages of stratified sampling

- It ensures that all essential sub-groups and activities are included in the investigation.
- It saves time because it usually requires fewer people to study.
- It can be directed towards geographical location and availability of individuals.

Main disadvantages of stratified sampling

- The trainer or investigator must have a detailed knowledge of the activities and grouping of the total population.
- It could become complicated, especially if weighting is involved.

SAMPLE SIZE

There is no easy answer to the question of what the size of a sample should be. It is conceivable that a sample of one would be sufficient to represent a large population whose work is strictly procedural and not subject to local variation. When this is not the case it is just within the bounds of possibility that a total population study may have to be carried out.

The sample should be small enough to make the study efficient but large enough to ensure that useful information is not lost. It is good practice to err on the large size rather than to take too small a sample.

Factors which influence the size of the sample include:

- Size of the total population.
- Number and nature of sub-groups within the total population.
- Geographical distribution of total population.
- Level of accuracy required.
- Constraints affecting the investigation such as time, staff available, resources, budget, administrative support, etc.

Appendix 3

Example of a Learning Journal

Name   *Karen Farthing*

Department   *Training*

Date of Commencement   *14 March 20XX*

This journal serves a number of purposes:

- It helps to reflect on what has been learned and the ways in which benefit has been gained from different learning events.
- It provides a record of personal development which can be used for course debriefs, updates with training and development advisers and appraisal with line managers.
- It can be included as part of a Portfolio of evidence for those working for Vocational Qualifications.

NAME   *Karen Farthing*

COURSE/WORKSHOP TITLE *Train the Trainer*   DATE *14–18 March 20XX*

EXPECTATIONS.   Write a brief outline of what you expect to gain from the course/workshop. Include any points discussed during your briefing.

How to plan and organize my training sessions and to allocate time properly.

Way to get trainees involved.

Mostly, I want to develop my confidence and identify ways in which I can improve. I hope that the practice sessions will help me in this respect.

EVALUATION.   Consider your expectations and comment on what you have gained from the course/workshop as a whole. Include details of any further training or developmental needs that have to be met.

Most of my expectations have been met together with a number of needs that I didn't realize that I had until I came on the course e.g. using visual aids properly, personal skills and questioning techniques.

I now feel more confident and have confidence in my planning. I am still not very good at self-appraisal and need someone to give me feedback on my sessions over the next few weeks.

NAME *Karen Farthing*

LEARNING EVENT *Train the Trainer Course*   DATE *15 March 20XX*

<u>What I did/What happened</u>

Watched video of my first practice training session and given feedback by course tutor.

<u>What I learned</u>

I didn't look as nervous as I felt and the places where I hesitated were not as long as I thought. I need to learn the Introduction to my sessions so that I can have more eye contact with the group and I must avoid talking to the flipchart. I was pleased with the way I related to the group and the time spent on preparation showed me how much easier it makes the session.

LEARNING EVENT *Train the Trainer Course*   DATE *16 March 20XX*

<u>What I did/What happened</u>

Tried to begin session by telling a joke to get the attention of the group. Somebody shouted out the punchline and the joke fell flat. I lost confidence and it took me a long time to recover.

<u>What I learned</u>

Not to tell jokes unless I am very sure of my ground. Tutor advised me that amusing anecdotes are better, however, I shall try them out on colleagues first.

LEARNING EVENT *Train the Trainer Course* DATE *17 March 20XX*

What I did/What happened

Filled in Questionnaire on Learning Styles and compared results with the rest of the group.

What I learned

I scored highly as an Activist, (16) the other scores were 8 or 9. There was quite a variance within the group. From the discussion with the tutor I learned that I should make sure that I don't try to impose my preferred learning style on others. It has also helped me to understand why people react in different ways to learning strategies.

LEARNING EVENT *Meeting*   DATE *27 March 20XX*

What I did/What happened

Attended meeting of local trainer support group for presentation and discussion on Continuing Development.

What I learned

By attending the meeting I learnt that it was a useful way of networking.

The presentation reinforced the message that it is not only professionals who need to participate in Continuing Development Schemes. Everyone in the organization should be involved in development programmes of some sort if the organization is to cope with change and have a team that has developed a readiness and the skills to learn.

Appendix 4

Illustration of a Tutor's Review of a Course

TUTOR'S REVIEW
Instructional Techniques Course No 4
European Operations Division
5–17 May 20XX

BACKGROUND	Action

1. This was the fourth of six special courses for European Operations Division. There had been a break of 10 months since the last course because there was a restructuring within the Division, and it took over six months to identify precisely how trainers would function.
2. The TNA indicated that trainers needed the additional skills of role-playing, case study and in-tray exercise design, and feedback skills. This resulted in the course being extended from one week to two weeks.

INTRODUCTION

3. The course was held in the new annex of the Marketing Unit because all Training Unit rooms were in use and the course was needed urgently.

4. Eleven delegates attended the course (list attached), one having dropped out at the last moment due to illness. Alison assisted with teaching practices on Thursday and Friday of Week 1.

MP – 'Thank You' letter to Tim in Marketing Unit

COURSE PROGRAMME

Action

5. The restructured course included three changes to the old programme which were made as a result of feedback from students and because of tutors' dissatisfaction with teaching practices:

- The session on qualities of a good trainer was reduced from 45 mins to 20 mins and changed from a syndicate exercise to a group discussion.
- The visiting speaker was dropped because his experience had proved to be out-of-date and no longer relevant.
- A new session of micro-teaching was included to practise 'Introductions' and 'Conclusions' to lessons.

6. Week 2 contained all the new material which included role-playing, case study and in-tray exercise design, and feedback skills (new programme attached).

COURSE REVIEW

7. Generally a good hardworking group. Only six had been briefed by their line managers but everyone was highly motivated.

8. Overall the programme fitted the allocated timings well. Small adjustments will need to be made in Week 2 (see annotated programme).

9. The session on qualities of a good trainer worked well as a group discussion but the session went over time by 10 minutes. However, this was made up before the end of the day.

10. The session on 'Introductions' and 'Conclusions' made a noticeable difference to the teaching practices. Everyone said that they felt more confident and it helped them to appreciate the importance of a well-structured lesson plan.	
11. Overall the teaching practices were far better than have been seen before and Helen Taylor should be recommended to her line manager as outstanding.	Trg Mgr
12. The new session in Week 2 fitted into the timings as planned. However, it is recommended that role-playing should be approached differently. The scenarios were not appropriate to the group's needs, i.e. interviewing was not demanding enough.	Tutors discuss with Trg Manager
13. A new visual is needed for 'Tutor Skills – Discussion Leading'.	Liz
14. All student handouts need 'topping up' – 30 of each.	Liz

STUDENT REACTION

15. Everyone said that they had enjoyed the course and felt more confident as a result of attending.	
16. There was a general feeling that they thought they knew about training until they came on the course, but now had a different attitude. In particular they appreciated the need for preparation and planning.	
17. It was felt that the joining letter could have been more helpful if it had listed some of the topics which had been taught in teaching practices on earlier courses.	Liz review letter
18. There was total agreement that the role-play exercises should be much more demanding and include 'tricky' personnel situations. They also wanted more time on this.	Tutors discuss with Trg Mgr

ADMINISTRATION

19. There were complaints throughout the week about poor service in the hotel.	MP take up with Admin Mgr
20. Two students had to ring up to ask for joining instructions.	

21. There was some difficulty in finding the annex to Marketing Unit. If we use it again we need to send out maps with joining instructions.

M Plumb
Course Tutor

Note: The attachments referred to in the text have not been included.

Appendix 5

Example of a Checklist to Assess Trainer Performance

Trainer: .... Observer: ....

Course: .... Dates: ....

Session: ....

Action points (if any) from previous observed session:

Assessment

Listed in the columns below are indicators of low (Score 1) and high (Score 6) levels of tutor performance. Indicate the level of performance observed by entering a score on the scale of 1–6 in the box provided. When a behaviour has not been observed or is not relevant to the session being observed enter X.

Preparation		
High Score Indicators	Score	Low Score Indicators
Had a complete set of up-to-date course objectives, enabling objectives and critical learning points.		Did not have a set of course objectives OR objectives were out-of-date and incomplete.
Personal notes were clearly written, well organized and covered thoroughly the content reflected in the objectives.		Did not have personal notes OR personal notes were badly written, badly organized and incomplete.
Visual aids (including handouts) were up-to-date, well designed, in pristine condition, totally relevant/appropriate for the subject being taught.		Visual aids (including hand-outs) contained out-of-date information, were badly designed or dirty and totally irrelevant/inappropriate for the subject being taught.
Training room was arranged in the most appropriate way for the session being taught. All equipment had been set up and checked in advance.		Training room was in disorder, equipment had not been set up or did not work.
Trainer well turned out. Looked confident and at ease. Reflected enthusiasm for, and commitment to, the session to be taught.		Personal appearance was untidy. Was late, flustered and in a hurry/not bothered. Showed little enthusiasm for, or commitment to, the session to be taught.

Structure		
High Score Indicators	Score	Low Score Indicators
The Introduction included a clear statement of objectives and explained clearly the context and structure of the session.		There was no Introduction OR Introduction was poor in that objective(s), structure and context of session were omitted.
Every effort was made to motivate trainees and to explain why they needed to learn the subject matter.		No attempt was made to motivate trainees or explain why they needed to learn the subject matter.
The session was presented in a logical order and divided into appropriate and manageable 'chunks' of learning.		The session was presented in a disjointed order without a logical progression or was delivered as one long unbroken 'tell' session.
The material taught was technically accurate, relevant and complete.		The material taught contained many inaccuracies, lacked relevance and omitted important facts.
Every opportunity taken by use of questions, exercises or discussion to confirm that trainees had learned and understood the session.		Failed to confirm, in any way, that trainees had learned or understood the session.
The Conclusion included accurate feedback on the achievement of objectives and overall performance. Gave clear summary and link with next session.		There was no Conclusion OR Conclusion was poor in that no feedback or totally inaccurate feedback was given on achievement of objectives and overall performance. No summary or link with next session.

Tutor Skills		
High Score Indicators	Score	Low Score Indicators
Posture, body language and expression gave an impression of enthusiasm and commitment to the session. Alert in movement and when seated.		Posture, body language and expression gave an impression of total lack of enthusiasm and commitment to the session. Paced aimlessly or flopped on desk/in chair.
Established/maintained a good rapport with the group demonstrated by relaxed atmosphere, good eye contact and easy two-way communication.		Failed to establish/maintain rapport with group demonstrated by tense or aggressive atmosphere, lack of eye contact and uneasy or little two-way communication.
Good use made of voice in terms of range, pitch, tone, emphasis and interest supported by effective use of gesture.		No range, variation of pitch and tone, emphasis or interest in voice. Total lack of gesture.
Notes were used easily and naturally as a prompt. Trainer was clearly familiar with material to be taught.		Notes were relied on heavily – to the point of reading them aloud. Trainer was clearly unfamiliar with material to be taught.
Consistently encouraged trainees to participate and contribute to sessions when appropriate. Listened to and used or built on contributions.		Discouraged or did not allow trainees to participate and contribute to sessions. Ignored trainees' attempts to contribute.
Answered questions from trainees accurately and with interest.		Failed to respond to questions from trainees or answered inaccurately or incompletely.
Dealt with 'difficult' trainees (e.g. those with limited aptitude or slow to learn) with patience, tolerance and tact in a detached unemotional manner.		Showed no patience, tolerance or tact in dealing with 'difficult' trainees. Became emotionally involved and drawn into confrontation.

Tutor Skills (*Continued*)

High Score Indicators	Score	Low Score Indicators
Dealt with 'difficult' situations (e.g. involving complex/boring/conceptual material) with empathy and in a logical and appropriately paced manner.		Failed to identify difficulties created by complex, boring and conceptually difficult material. 'Bulldozed' through with no concern for trainees.
Dealt with 'difficult' situations (involving organizational/departmental policy and politics) tactfully without attacking the 'party' line.		With or without prompting voiced personal and tactless views in 'difficult' situations involving organizational and departmental policy and politics.
Managed time to ensure that all learning points were covered adequately within the time allocated OR made sensible decisions on time allocation to meet needs of trainees.		Had no concept of time. Complete imbalance of time allocated to different learning points. Overran/stopped short.
In *discussion* sessions had complete control over time, range of topics and participants. Remained detached and impartial; involved everyone and achieved objective(s).		In *discussion* sessions lost control to the point that it became a free-for-all or dominated by one or two personalities, involved self too much. Failed to achieve objective(s).
In *syndicate* exercises briefed group clearly, monitored work closely and prompted and guided their efforts when needed. Conducted a well-structured and accurate plenary session.		In *syndicate* exercises briefed the group badly, left them to their own devices or interfered to the point of imposing solutions upon them. Omitted or conducted badly structured and inaccurate plenary session.
In *role-play* situations had total control over flow and activity. Identified situations needing intervention before they developed and intervened without causing conflict.		In *role-play* situations lost control of events and allowed participants to go their own way, develop confrontation situations resulting in anger and bad feelings.

Tutor Skills *(Continued)*		
High Score Indicators	Score	Low Score Indicators
In giving *feedback* on inter-personal skills was completely objective, sensitive to trainees' problem areas, constructive and tactful in discussing remedial action.		In giving *feedback* on inter-personal skills was rude, offensive, biased and inaccurate. Didn't allow participants to contribute. Caused offence and confrontation.

Use of Visual Aids		
High Score Indicators	Score	Low Score Indicators
Had no difficulty in operating equipment. Did not leave switched on unnecessarily, did not mask view of trainees or talk to screen.		Had greatest of difficulty in operating equipment. Left switched on unnecessarily for long periods, continually masked view of trainees and talked to screen.
Used flip chart without masking view of trainees or talking to the chart. Writing was very clear, neat and accurate with good use of colour.		Continually masked flip chart from view of trainees and talked to chart. Writing was almost unreadable, thoroughly untidy and contained many misspellings.
Operated video easily, making adjustments for sound and vision as needed and without detracting from viewing for trainees.		Couldn't get video to work. Needed help from trainees or another trainer. Paid no regard to volume, colour etc.
Used camera and recorder with ease and produced good quality videos which provided relevant and valuable feedback.		Made frequent basic errors in operating the equipment. Failed to make recording or made one of such poor quality that it was not usable.

Trainer's comments on session

Observer's comments on session with particular reference to action points from previous observed session

Action points for next session

References

Adams, J.A., (1987). Historical review and appraisal of research on the learning retention and transfer of human skill, *Psychological Bulletin*, 101 (1), 41–74.

Adamson, P. and Caple, J., (1996). The Training Audit evolves: Is your training and development budget wasted?, *Journal of European Industrial Training*, 20 (5), 3–13.

Anderson, J.R., (1987). Skill acquisition – compilation of weak method problem solution, *Psychological Review*, 94, 192–210.

Annett, J. and Duncan, K.D., (1967). Task analysis and training design, *Occupational Psychology*, 41, 211–21.

Annett, J. and Sparrow, J., (1985). Transfer of training: A review of research and practical implications, *Programmed Learning and Educational Technology*, 22, 116–24.

Applegarth, M., (1991). *How to Take a Training Audit*, Kogan Page, London.

Argyle, M., (1969). *Social Interaction*, Methuen, London.

Arkin, A., (1999). Return to the centre, *People Management*, 5 (9).

Armstrong, M. and Baron, A., (1998). *Performance Management: The new realities*, IPD, London.

Atkins, B., (1983). To what extent is a systems model appropriate to the diagnosis of training needs and the conduct of training in organizations?, *Programmed Learning and Educational Technology*, 20, 243–52.

Baldwin, T.T. and Ford, J.K., (1988). Transfer of training: A review and directions for future research, *Personnel Psychology*, 41, 63–105.

Bass, B.M. and Vaughan, J.A., (1966). Training in industry, *The Management of Learning*, Tavistock Publications, London.

Beckhard, R., (1969). *Organization Development: Strategies and models*, Addison-Wesley, California.

Bennett, R., (1988). The right role, in R. Bennett (ed), *Improving Trainer Effectiveness*, Gower Publishing Company, Aldershot.

Bhugra, A., (1986). Computer-based training: A case for creative skills within development teams, *Programmed Learning and Educational Technology*, 23 (3).

Bloom, B.S. (ed), (1956). *Taxonomy of Educational Objectives, Handbook 1: Cognitive domain*, Longman, New York.

Blum, M.L. and Naylor, J.C., (1968). *Industrial Psychology: Its theoretical and social foundations*, Harper & Row, New York.

Boot, R. and Boxer, P., (1980). Reflective learning, in, J. Beck and C. Cox (eds), *Advances in Management Education*, John Wiley and Sons, Chichester.

Boud, D., Keogh, R. and Walker, D., (1985). What is reflection in learning? in, D. Boud, R. Keogh and D. Walker (eds), *Turning Experience into Learning*, Kogan Page, London.

Boyatzis, R., (1982). *The Competent Manager: A model for effective performance*, Wiley, New York.

Boydell, T. and Leary, M., (1996). *Identifying Training Needs*, IPD, London.

Boydell, T.H., (1976). *A Guide to the Identification of Training Needs* (2nd edition), British Association for Commercial and Industrial Education, London.

Bramham, J., (1982). *Practical Manpower Planning* (3rd Edition), Institute of Personnel Management, London.

Bramley, P., (1986). *Evaluation Training: A practical guide*, British Association for Commercial and Industrial Training, London.

Bramley, P. and Hullah, H., (1987). Auditing training, *Journal of European Industrial Training*, 11, 6.

Bramley, P. and Newby, A.C., (1984). The evaluation of training Part 1: Clarifying the concept, *Journal of European Industrial Training*, 8 (6), 10–16.

Broad, M.L. and Newstrom, J.W., (1992). *Transfer of Training*, Addison-Wesley Publishing Company.

Brown, G.F. and Read, A.R., (1984). Personnel and training policies: Some lessons for Western companies, *Long Range Planning*, 17 (2), 48–57.

Buckley, W., (1968). *Modern Systems Research for Behavioural Objectives*, Aldine, Chicago.

Burgoyne, T., (1999). Feature article: The learning organization, *People Management*, June.

Cameron, K., (1980). Critical questions in assessing organizational effectiveness, *Organizational Dynamics*, Autumn 1980, 66–80.

Campbell, C.P., (1987). *Instructional Systems Development: A methodology for vocational–technical training*, MCB University Press Ltd, Bradford, UK.

Campbell, J.P., Dunnette, M.D., Lawler, E.E. III and Weick, K.E., (1970). *Managerial Behaviour: Performance and effectiveness*, McGraw-Hill, New York.

Caple, J. and Martin, P., (1994). Reflections of two pragmatists, *Journal of Industrial and Commercial Training*, 26 (1), 16–20.

Chadwick, E.S.M., (1983). Manpower planning, in, D. Lock and N. Farrow (eds), *The Gower Book of Management*, Gower-Aldershot, UK.

Chalmers, A.F., (1982). *What is This Thing Called Science?* (2nd edition), University of Queensland Press, Open University, Milton Keynes.

Cheese, J., (1986). Cascading the training, *Programmed Learning and Educational Technology*, 23, 248–52.

Clarke, A., (1986). *Tutor Competencies for Open Learning*, Manpower Services Commission, UK.

Coopers and Lybrand Associates (1985). *A Challenge to Complacency*, Manpower Services Commission and National Economic Development Office, UK.

Davies, I.K., (1971). *The Management of Learning*, McGraw-Hill, New York.

Decker, P.J., (1982). The enhancement of behaviour modelling training of supervisory skills by the inclusion of retention processes, *Personnel Psychology*, 32 (2), 323–32.

Department of Employment, (1978). *Glossary of Training Terms*, The Stationery Office, Norwich.

Department for Education and Employment, (1999). *Skills and Enterprise Network Briefing Document, issue 6/99*.

Dixon, M., (1982). Incorporating learning style into training design, *Training and Development*, July.

Downs, S., (1985). *Testing Trainability*, NFER-Nelson, Windsor, UK.

Downs, S. and Perry, P., (1982). Research report: How do I learn?, *Journal of European Industrial Training*, 6 (6), 27–32.

Downs, S. and Perry, P., (1984). Developing learning skills, *Journal of European Industrial Training*, 8 (1), 21–26.

Fitts, P.M., (1962). Factors in complex skill training, in, Glaser (ed), *Training Research and Education*.

Flanagan, J.C., (1954). The critical incident technique, *Psychological Bulletin*, 51, 327–58.

Fleishman, E.A. and Hempel, W.E., (1955). The relationship between abilities and improvement with practice in a visual discrimination task, *Journal of Experimental Psychology*, 49.

Folkard, S., (1987). Circadian rhythms and hours of work, in, P.D. Warr (ed), *Psychology at Work*, Penguin, London.

Frank, E. and Margerison, C., (1978). Training methods and organization development, *Journal of European Industrial Training*, 2 (4), 1–32.

Franks, Lord, (1963). *British Business Schools*, British Institute of Management, London.

French, W.L. and Bell, H., (1984). *Organization Development: Behavioural science interventions for organization improvement* (3rd edition), Prentice-Hall, New Jersey, USA.

Gagné, R.M., (1965). *Conditions of Learning*, Holt, Rinehart & Winston, London.

Gagné, R.M., (1977). *The Conditions of Learning* (3rd edition), Holt, Rinehart & Winston, London.

Gagné, R.M. and Briggs, L.J., (1979). *Principles of Instructional Design*, Holt, Rinehart & Winston, New York.

Garavan, T.N., (1997). Training, development, education and learning: Different or the same? *Journal of European Industrial Training*, 21 (2), 39–50.

Garrett, R., (1987). *The Learning Organization*, Collins, London.

Gilbert, T.F., (1982). A question of performance, Part 1: The PROBE model, *Training and Development Journal*, September 21–30.

Glaser, R., (1962). *Training Research and Education*, University of Pittsburg Press, USA.

Goldstein, I.L., (1986). *Training in Organizations: Needs assessment, development and evaluation*, Brooks/Cole, Monterey, USA.

Goldstein, I.L. and Ford, J.K., (2002). *Training in Organizations* (4th edition), Wadsworth Group, Belmont, USA.

Hall, D.T., (1986). Dilemmas in linking succession planning to individual executive learning, *Human Resource Management*, 25 (2), 235–65.

Hamblin, A.C., (1974). *Evaluation and Control of Training*, McGraw-Hill, Maidenhead, UK.

Harbridge Consulting Group, (1991). *Management Training in Large UK Business Organisations*, Harbridge, London.

Holdaway, K. and Saunders, M., (1992). *The In-house Trainer As Consultant*, Kogan Page, London.

Holding, D.H., (1965). *Principles of Training*, Pergamon Press, London.

Honey, P., (1984). Reflections of Two Pragmatists, *Training and Development Journal*, January.

Honey, P. and Mumford, A., (1986). *Using Your Learning Styles* (2nd edition), Peter Honey, UK.

Hussey, D.E., (1985). Implementing corporate strategy using management education and training, *Long Range Planning*, 18 (5), 28–37.

Jinks, M., (1979). *Training*, Blandford Press, Poole, UK.

Kenny, J. and Reid, M., (1986). *Training Interventions*, Institute of Personnel Management, London.

Kepner, C.H. and Tregoe, B.B., (1981). *The New Rational Manager*, KepnerTregoe Inc., published in UK by John Martin, London.

Kirkpatrick, D.L., (1967). Evaluation of training, in Craig and Bittel (eds), *Training and Development Handbook*, McGraw-Hill, New York.

Knowles, M.S., Holton, E.F. and Swanson, R.A., (1998). *The Adult Learner* (5th edition), Gulf Publishing Company, Houston, Texas.

Kolb, D.A., (1984). *Experiential Learning: Experience as a source of learning and development*, Prentice-Hall, New Jersey.

Kolb, D.A., Rubin, I.M. and McIntyre, J.M., (1974). *Organizational Psychology: An experimental approach*, Prentice-Hall, New Jersey.

Krathwohl, D.R., Bloom, B.S. and Masia, B.B., (1964). *Taxonomy of Educational Objectives, Handbook 2: Affective domain*, Longman, New York.

Latham, G.P. and Wexley, K.N., (1981). *Increasing Productivity Through Performance Appraisal*, Addison-Wesley, California.

Leigh, D., (1996). *Designing and Delivering Training for Groups* (2nd edition), Kogan Page, London.

Lloyd, C. and Cook, A., (1993). *Implementing Standards of Competence: Practical strategies for industry*, Kogan Page, London.

Locke, E.A. and Latham, P., (1984). *Goal Setting: A motivational technique that works!*, Prentice-Hall, New Jersey.

Lynch, J.J., (1968). *Making Manpower Effective Part 1*, Pan Books, London.

McCormick, E.J. and Ilgen, D., (1985). *Industrial and Organizational Psychology*, Allen & Unwin, London.

McCrimmon, M., (1994). Assessing and selecting employees as suppliers, *Selection and Development Review*, 10 (3), British Psychological Society.

Mager, R.F., (1973). *Measuring Instructional Intent*, Fearon, California.

Mager, R.F., (1975). *Preparing Instructional Objectives* (2nd edition), Fearon, California.

Mager, R.F. and Pipe, P., (1970). *Analysing Performance Problems: Or, you really oughta wanna*, Fearon, California.

Mangham, I. and Silver, M., (1986). *Management Training: Context and practice*, School of Management, University of Bath, England.

Mawhinney, T.C., (1979). Intrinsic v extrinsic work motivation: Perspectives from behaviourism, *Organizational Behaviour and Human Performance*, 24, 379–422.

Megginson, D. and Boydell, T., (1979). *A Manager's Guide to Coaching*, British Association for Commercial and Industrial Education, London.

Mills, H.R., (1967). *Teaching and Training*, Macmillan, London.

Mumford, A., (1983). Learning effectiveness through learning styles, *Training and Development*, 4, 15–16.

Mumford, A., (1986). Learning to learn for managers, *Journal of European Industrial Training*, 10 (2), 1–28.

Murphy, B.P. and Swanson, R.A., (1988). Auditing training and development, *Journal of European Industry Training*, 12, 2.

Murray, A., (1987). *The Trainer as a Catalyst*, British Association for Commercial and Industrial Training Workshop.

National Research Council, (1991). *In the Mind's Eye: Enhancing human performance*, National Academy Press, Washington, D.C.

Naylor, J.C., (1962). *Parameters Affecting the Relative Effectiveness of Part and Whole Training Methods: A review of the literature*, US Naval Training Devices Center, Rep. No. 950–1. 85.

Nemeroff, W.F. and Cosentino, J., (1979). Utilizing feedback and goal setting to increase performance appraisal interviewer skills of managers, *Academy of Management Journal*, 22, 566–76.

Newby, A.C., (1985). *Training Evaluation Audit Method*, Newby Research and Training, Harrow, UK.

Newsham, D.B., (1969). *The Challenge of Change to the Adult Trainee*, Training Information, Paper 3, 109–112, The Stationery Office, Norwich.

Patrick, J., (1992). *Training: Research and practice*, Academic Press, London.

Pearn, M. and Kandola, R., (1988). *Job Analysis: A practical guide for managers*, Institute of Personnel Management, London.

Pedler, M., Boydell, J. and Burgoyne, T., (1991). *The Learning Company: A strategy for sustainable development*, McGraw-Hill, London.

Perry, P. and Downs, S., (1985). Skills, strategies and ways of learning: Can we help people learn how to learn?, *Programmed Learning and Educational Technology*, 22, 177–81.

Phillips, K. and Shaw, P., (1989). *A Consultancy Approach for Trainers*, Gower, Aldershot.

Rackham, N. and Carlisle, J., (1978). The effective negotiator Part 1: The behaviour of successful negotiators, *Journal of European Industrial Training*, 2 (6), 6–11.

Rackham, N. and Morgan, T., (1977). *Behaviour Analysis in Training*, McGraw-Hill, Maidenhead, UK.

Rogers, A. and Woodford, J., (1999). 'Training' supplement in *Personnel Today*, November.

Rogers, C.R., (1969). *Freedom to Learn*, Columbus.

Romiszowski, A.J., (1981). *Designing Instructional Systems*, Kogan Page, London.

Russell, T., (1994). *Effective Feedback Skills*, Kogan Page, London.

Salmon, G., (2000) *E-Moderating: The key to teaching*, Kogan Page, London.

Senge, P., (1990). *The Fifth Discipline*, Doubleday, New York.

Simpson, E.J., (1966). *The Classification of Educational Objectives: The Psychomotor Domain* (unpublished project report), University of Illinois, Chicago.

Spencer, L.M., McClelland, D.C. and Spence, S.M., (1992). *Competency Assessment Methods: History and state of the art*, Hay/Mcber Research Press.

Stammers, R. and Patrick, J., (1975). *The Psychology of Training*, Methuen, London.

Stewart, J. (1996). *Managing Change Through Training and Development* (2nd edition), Kogan Page, London.

Stuart, R. and Holmes, L., (1982). Successful trainer styles, *Journal of European Industrial Training*, 6 (4), 17–23.

Stuart, R. and Long, G., (1985). Towards marketing the training function, Part 1: Adopting a marketing perspective, *Personnel Review*, 14 (2), 32–38.

Talbot, R., (1985). Situational Influences on Learning Styles, *ICT*, Nov/Dec, 19–28.

Ungerson, B., (1983). *How to Write a Job Description*, Institute of Personnel Management, London.

Warr, P., (2002). Learning and training, in P. Warr (ed), *Psychology at Work* (5th edition), Penguin, London.

Wexley, K.M. and Nemeroff, W.F., (1975). Effectiveness of positive reinforcement and goal setting as methods of management development, *Journal of Applied Psychology*, 60, 446–50.

Whiddett, S. and Hollyforde, S., (1999). *The Competencies Handbook*, IPD, London.

Woodcock, C., (1991). Management discovers long-term training, *The Guardian*, Sept 2.

Woodruffe, C., (1991). Competent by any other name, *Personnel Management*, Sept 1991.

Woodruffe, C., (1993). Assessment Centres, Institute of Personnel Management.

Zemke, R. and Kramlinger, T., (1982). *Figuring Things Out: A trainer's guide to needs and task analysis*, Addison-Wesley, California.

Index